Cohabitation

COHABITATION

Division of Property on Relationship Breakdown

Stephen Parker

The Law Society

ISBN-13: 978-1-78446-172-0

Published in 2021 by the Law Society
113 Chancery Lane, London WC2A 1PL

Typeset by Columns Design XML Ltd, Reading
Printed by Hobbs the Printers Ltd, Totton, Hants

FSC
www.fsc.org
MIX
Paper from responsible sources
FSC® C020438

The paper used for the text pages of this book is FSC® certified. FSC (the Forest Stewardship Council®) is an international network to promote responsible management of the world's forests.

For my sons Matthew and William Parker, Grace Gacula and in loving memory of Catherine

Contents

Preface

Dealing with the separation of couples in cases where they are not married is an area of law that often falls outside the comfort zone of many family solicitors encompassing, as it does, alien concepts such as trust law and the Civil Procedure Rules and statutes which are often not as well known as others in the family practitioner's library.

This book aims to provide an invaluable resource and 'comfort blanket' to those who are required to act, advise, negotiate and litigate these disputes.

The book is structured in such a way as to be easily navigable:

- **Chapter 1** provides a basic introduction as to what is meant when we talk of 'cohabitation' and provides some statistics as to its exponential growth.
- **Chapter 2** deals with the ownership of land covering subjects such as joint tenancies and tenancies in common; express, constructive and resulting trusts; and the equitable remedy of proprietary estoppel.
- **Chapters 3** and **4** focus on the case law including the seminal cases of *Stack* v. *Dowden* and *Jones* v. *Kernott* and their subsequent development.
- **Chapter 5** deals with equitable accounting.
- **Chapter 6** addresses the key sections of the Trusts of Land and Appointment of Trustees Act 1996.
- **Chapter 7** focuses on practice and procedure to include taking instructions and initial actions followed by a detailed analysis of the procedure in initiating a claim from start to finish and focusing on key aspects of the Civil Procedure Rules 1998 that practitioners are most likely to encounter such as costs budgeting and Part 36 offers. It also includes a myriad of good practice points to avoid procedural 'tripwires' for the unwary.
- **Chapter 8** deal with tenancies.
- **Chapter 9** deals with applications made pursuant to the Children Act 1989, Sched.1, both law and procedure.
- **Chapter 10** focuses on personal property such as chattels and bank accounts.
- **Chapter 11** deals with additional discrete remedies where a couple were previously engaged.
- **Chapter 12** explores the benefits of cohabitation/living together agreements and their enforceability.
- Finally, **Chapter 13** deals with potential future reforms in this area of law.

The appendices include a checklist of matters to consider when advising clients in this area of law and a case planner to assist with costs budgeting.

I hope that this publication serves the purpose that it sets out to do and that you find it both useful and informative.

The law is stated as at 31 December 2020.

Stephen Parker
December 2020

Table of cases

Table of statutes

Table of statutory instruments

Table of international legislation

Abbreviations

ADR	alternative dispute resolution
AQ	allocations questionnaire
CCMC	case/costs management conference
CMC	costs management conference
CPR	Civil Procedure Rules 1998
CSA 1991	Child Support Act 1991
DQ	directions questionnaire
ECHR	European Convention on Human Rights
ENE	early neutral evaluation
FDA	first directions appointment
FDR	financial dispute resolution
FLA 1996	Family Law Act 1996
FPR	Family Procedure Rules 2010
LPA 1925	Law of Property Act 1925
LQ	listing questionnaire
LRA 2002	Land Registration Act 2002
MCA 1973	Matrimonial Causes Act 1973
ONS	Office for National Statistics
PTR	pre-trial review
SJE	single joint expert
TOLATA 1996	Trusts of Land and Appointment of Trustees Act 1996

CHAPTER 1

Introduction

1.1 COHABITATION: A DEFINITION

Before we enter the arena of advising couples in relation to the repercussions of the breakdown of a non-marital union, it is important to achieve consensus as to whether it is accepted that the parties were indeed living together as a couple, akin to a husband-and-wife relationship.

In many cases this is often a key factor in any subsequent advice given, particularly in cases where there is no joint ownership of property or children as a result of that union, and in relation to whether other statutes – such as the Family Law Act 1996, Part IV – are relevant.

So what do we mean when we refer to 'cohabitation'?

In the Family Law Act 1996, s.62(1)(a) (definition of 'cohabitants' for the purposes of Part IV of that Act) 'cohabitants' are defined as:

> two persons who are neither married to each other nor civil partners of each other but are living together as if they were a married couple or civil partners...

As for case law:

> ... a couple are said to be cohabiting if they are living together outside the state of marriage.
>
> (*Kimber* v. *Kimber* [2000] 1 FLR 383)

However, as with many aspects of the law there is no agreed formal definition of cohabitation, so more often than not we are left with deriving an answer to the question by examining the particular circumstances of each case based on a factual analysis of the presenting evidence.

Firstly, there is the objective analysis:

> There is no exhaustive definition of 'cohabitation'. The judicial task is to stand back, to look at the totality of the evidence and to come to a common sense decision ... In the final analysis, making a finding that cohabitation is taking place is a matter of impression based on an assessment of all of the available evidence ...
>
> (*X* v. *Y (Maintenance Arrears: Cohabitation)* [2012] EWCC 1 (Fam) at [84])

Secondly, there is the subjective analysis based on what are perceived to be the parties' intentions:

> ... setting up a matrimonial home together ... involves a bi-lateral intention on the part of both spouses so to do...
>
> (*Mummery* v. *Mummery* [1942] P 107, at 110)

> ... it is not sufficient, to establish that a man and woman are living together in the same household as husband and wife, to show that they are living in the same household. If there is the fact that they are living together in the same household, that may raise the question whether they are living together as man and wife, and, indeed, in many circumstances may be strong evidence to show that they are living together as man and wife; but in each case it is necessary to go on and ascertain, in so far as this is possible, the manner in which and why they are living together in the same household ...
>
> (*Crake* v. *Supplementary Benefits Commission* [1981] 2 FLR 264)

In the joined case of *Butterworth* v. *Supplementary Benefits Commission* [1981] 2 FLR 264 the couple were held not to be living together as husband and wife because it was not their intention to do so.

Perhaps the best approach, drawing both the objective and subjective analyses together, is to look at the various signposts put forward within the context of welfare benefits law, namely the Social Security Contributions and Benefits Act 1992, ss. 80(7) and 137(1) ('"unmarried couple" means a man and a woman who are not married to each other but are living together as husband and wife' and 'couple' means 'two people who are not married to, or civil partners of, each other but are living together as if they were a married couple or civil partners') and the resulting case law (see above) which resulted in the following exposition in *Kimber* (see above):

- Membership of the same household and the sharing of daily tasks and duties. Generally this means that the parties live under the same roof with a degree of mutuality.
- Stability and degree of permanence. That is, not a temporary infatuation or passing relationship.
- Financial support
- Sexual relationship
- Children
- Intention and motivation
- Public acknowledgment. Cohabitation existing in the opinion of a reasonable person with normal perceptions.

1.2 STATISTICS

Although married or civil partner couples remain the most common family type representing two-thirds of families in the UK (12.8 million) (Office for National

Statistics (ONS), *Families and Households in the UK: 2019*) since 1979 the proportion of people getting married in the UK has been falling.

The number of marriages registered in England and Wales in 2009 was 231,490, which was the lowest number of marriages since 1895 (ONS, *Marriages in England and Wales: 2009* (March 2011)).

Correspondingly, the number of couples divorcing has also fallen in successive years.

In 2009, the number of divorces (113,949) was at its lowest rate since 1977 (ONS, *Divorces in England and Wales: 2009* (February 2011)).

In the UK over the last 10 years, the proportion of families containing a married or civil partnered couple decreased from 68.6 per cent in 2009 to 66.8 per cent in 2019 (ONS, *Families and Households: 2019*).

Moreover, the proportion of the adult population of England and Wales who are married is projected to fall over the next 25 years (from 2008 to 2033) from 49 per cent to 42 per cent.

Cohabitation, however, has increased as the incidence of marriage has declined. Cohabiting couple families are the second-largest family type in the UK (3.5 million) (ONS, *Families and Households: 2019*).

They are currently the fastest growing family type in the UK (ONS, *Families and Households: 2017*).

Since 2009, the proportion of families containing a cohabiting couple has increased from 15.3 per cent to 18.4 per cent, reflecting the declining trend seen in the proportion of the population who are married and an increasing trend in the proportion cohabiting (ONS, *Families and Households: 2019*).

In 2016 there were 3.3 million cohabiting couple families in the UK (ONS, *Families and Households: 2016*), an increase from 2.1 million in 2001 (ONS, *Families and Households: 2001 to 2011*) and 1.5 million in 1996.

In 1996, around 10 per cent of all opposite-sex couple families were cohabiting (rather than married) compared with 20 per cent in 2015.

As for same-sex cohabiting couples these remain the most common type of same-sex couple family, accounting for just over half of same-sex families in 2019 (ONS, *Families and Households: 2019*).

Together, cohabiting couple families (including both opposite-sex and same-sex) now account for approximately 17 per cent of all families in the UK.

Currently, one in five couples cohabit. This is more common with younger people with over two-thirds of people aged between 16 and 29 cohabiting (ONS, *Population Estimates by Marital Status and Living Arrangements, England and Wales* (2019)).

The number of children being born to cohabiting couples is also increasing. Between 2009 and 2019 the number of cohabiting couple families with dependent children increased by more than a quarter (ONS, *Families and Households*: *2019*).

A survey conducted in 2017 by the organisation Resolution found that one in five families cohabit outside a marital union, 50 per cent of whom have dependent children.

The Marriage Foundation in its research note of May 2020 found the following:

- The longer couples live together the lower their chances of getting married.
- 40 per cent of couples are likely to split up within 10 years irrespective of how long they have already lived together.
- When compared to couples who marry only a minority of couples who never married stayed together.

Thus, living together for a longer time makes almost no difference whatsoever to the chances of staying together but substantially reduces the likelihood of getting married.

It is, therefore, inexorable logic that in family departments within the private practice of solicitors, one is increasingly likely to be faced with problems concerning people who live together but who remain unmarried.

Indeed, cases regarding the beneficial ownership of land on breakdown of cohabitation now constitute 50 per cent of all cases that appear before the adjudicator at HM Land Registry.

Cohabiting adults are also predicted to become older, with the number aged 45 to 64 set to more than double between 2008 and 2033, from 0.9 million to 2.2 million, while the number aged 65 or more is projected to quadruple from 130,000 to almost 600,000. Whereas in 2008 only 23 per cent of male cohabitants and 19 per cent of female cohabitants were aged 45 or more, by 2033, these proportions are projected to rise to 37 per cent for males and 33 per cent for females.

It is thus now more likely than not that cohabitants are going to have more sizeable and significant property and assets, which may necessitate the need for legal assistance on a subsequent breakdown in that relationship.

Of further note is that the incidence of cohabitation among couples who have been through a prior divorce is also high, given the fact that that particular group of people tend to prefer cohabitation second time around as opposed to remarriage.

These couples will often bring with them into their new relationship property acquired during the breakdown of their first marriage and indeed children of that prior relationship, which in itself may pose some interesting problems should that new relationship subsequently falter and break down.

In a 2008 *British Social Attitudes Survey* (carried out by the National Centre for Social Research) entitled 'Cohabitation and the law: myths, money and the media', key findings included the following:

- Cohabitation is a popular partnering and parenting choice.
- Cohabitation is lasting longer particularly where there are children of that relationship.
- The 'common law marriage' myth still persists (51 per cent of those polled). A poll by Resolution in 2017 found that two-thirds of cohabiting couples are unaware that there is no such thing as a 'common law marriage' in England and Wales.

- Cohabitants who make legal agreements regulating their relationship remain a very small minority. It is estimated that only 15 per cent of cohabiting couples have a written agreement in place regulating their shares in property.

The 2019 *British Social Attitudes Survey* found that 46 per cent of people surveyed were under the impression that cohabiting couples form a common law marriage.

As can be seen, this figure has remained largely unchanged over the last 14 years (47 per cent in 2005, 51 per cent in 2008) despite a significant increase in the number of cohabiting couples.

Clearly, for solicitors' practices within the field of family law, this not only provides a golden opportunity for educating the public at large but also provides a captive audience for the purposes of a clear marketing opportunity.

Furthermore, responses to the question on common law marriage, commissioned by the University of Exeter and funded by the Economic and Social Research Council, show that people are significantly more likely to believe in common law marriage when children come into the equation.

Finally, K Kiernan, 'Cohabitation and divorce across nations and generations' (LSE Case Paper 65, 2003) and J Ermisch, 'Births outside marriage: the real story' (in *In Praise of Panel Surveys*, ISER, 2008) reported:

- The median duration of a cohabitative relationship is two years (a similar survey in 2011 showed that 35 per cent of cohabitants separate within five years).
- 65 per cent of all cohabitative relationships where there are children dissolve, half of which do so before the child is five. Only 35 per cent of children of cohabitants will find themselves with both parents at the age of 16 as opposed to 70 per cent of children where their parents are married.

CHAPTER 2

Real property

2.1 INTRODUCTION

Many people who decide to live together often discover to their horror, and indeed their cost, that the mere fact of living together does not in itself found an automatic interest in any shared property (consider the fate of Mrs Burns in *Burns* v. *Burns* [1984] Ch 317).

When a cohabitative relationship breaks down, unlike with married couples where the court has discretionary powers vested in it by the Matrimonial Causes Act 1973 to adjust property rights, cohabitants are entirely reliant upon the principles of land and trust law to determine any dispute, which has merely declaratory powers as to determining what those rights are as opposed to adjusting them to achieve overall fairness to the parties.

2.1.1 Law of Property Act 1925: a quick summary

> The purchase of residential accommodation is perhaps the single most important financial transaction which any individual transacts in a lifetime. It is therefore of the utmost importance ... that those who engage in these transactions, and those who advise them, should take the greatest care over such transactions, and must – particularly if they are unmarried ... address their minds to the size and fate of the respective beneficial interests on acquisition, separation and thereafter. It is simply impossible for a court to analyse personal transactions over years between cohabitants, and the costs of so doing are likely to be disproportionate in any event. Cohabiting partners must, it seems to me, contemplate and address the unthinkable, namely that their relationship will break down and that they will fall out over what they do and do not own.
>
> (*Kernott* v. *Jones* [2010] EWCA Civ 578 at [61])

In light of the above it is therefore worth noting the following conveyancing points when it comes to creating interests in real property:

- Law of Property Act (LPA) 1925, s.52 provides that a deed is necessary to create or convey any legal estate in land.
- Section 53(1) provides that:

  (a) no interest in land can be created orally; and

(b) no declaration of trust in respect of land can have effect if made orally.

- Section 53(2), however, excludes from the ambit of s.53(1) 'the creation or operation of resulting, implied or constructive trusts'.

Thus, if you wish to create specific rights in relation to an interest in real property those rights need to be committed to written format, otherwise you are solely reliant upon the law relating to the creation of trusts.

There are, of course, two ways a couple can own property jointly, namely as:

- beneficial joint tenants; or
- tenants in common.

As joint tenants:

- Co-owners have equal rights to the whole property.
- The property automatically goes to the other joint owner on the death of the other (rights of survivorship).
- Co-owners cannot pass on their ownership of the property in a will as it is excluded property for the purposes of their estate.

As tenants in common:

- Co-owners can own different shares in the property.
- The property does not automatically pass to the surviving co-owner on the death of the other co-owner (there are no rights of survivorship).
- Co-owners can pass on their share of the property through a will.

A joint tenancy, however, can be changed to that of a tenancy in common by severance, and a tenancy in common can be changed to that of a joint tenancy by a subsequent deed.

Severance of a joint tenancy can be effected by:

1. Written notice
2. Mutual agreement
3. A course of dealing between the parties.

The case of *Bedson* v. *Bedson* [1965] 2 QB 666 established the principle that, where there are two beneficial joint tenants, severance produces a beneficial tenancy in common 'in two equal shares'.

Similarly, in *Nielson-Jones* v. *Fedden* [1975] Ch 222 Walton J stated that, in the typical case of two joint tenants, the interests of such tenants are 'necessarily equal ... [and] cannot possibly be unequal'.

Goodman v. *Gallant* [1986] 1 FLR 513 further reiterated that severance of a beneficial joint tenancy results in a beneficial tenancy in common in equal shares:

> ... it seems to us that it is of the very nature of a joint tenancy that, upon a severance, each takes an equal aliquot share according to the number of joint tenants. (at [118])

In *Wallbank* v. *Price* [2007] EWHC 3001 (Ch) it was observed that:

> the creation of a 'half share' is the inevitable consequence of the severance of a joint tenancy in equity where there are two joint tenants.

However, although these cases suggest that severance will normally separate off an equal aliquot share, there is no reason – at least in principle – why severance should not operate so as to separate the beneficial ownership to unequal shares if that reflects the parties' altered intentions (see *Barton* v. *Morris* [1985] 1 WLR 1257).

As for severance by mutual agreement, in *Hunter* v. *Babbage* [1994] 2 FLR 806 it was observed that severance by mutual conduct could include:

> cases where what is to be inferred is that the parties have mutually treated their interests as a tenancy in common in ignorance that they were really joint tenants. (at [49])

As a course of dealing, severance may be effected by 'any course of dealing sufficient to intimate that the interests of all were mutually treated as constituting a tenancy in common' (*Williams* v. *Hensman* (1861) 1 J & H 546; see also *Davis* v. *Smith* [2011] EWCA Civ 1603).

Upon separation, consideration will need to be given as to whether or not the joint tenancy should be severed. Such severance is, however, a double-edged sword: if the tenancy is severed and the other co-owner dies the party whom you represent will have lost automatic entitlement to the whole of the property; however, if severance is not effected, if your client were to predecease the other party then – by the rules of survivorship – your client's interest would pass automatically to that other party.

Needless to say, advice will need to be given as to the effects of severance and whether to effect a severance will be dependent upon the specific facts of each individual case, taking into account the respective parties' state of health and age. A detailed risk analysis should be undertaken and documented. Either way, no notice should be served without express authority to that effect.

Furthermore, at the very outset of a conveyancing transaction practitioners who are instructed in the purchase of a property by an unmarried couple should deal thoroughly and effectively with the following:

- The differences between holding the property as beneficial joint tenants as opposed to tenants in common with an explanation of the disadvantages and advantages of both (rights of survivorship versus ability to quantify defined shares and estate planning).
- If clients are holding the property as tenants in common, to assist them in reaching a decision as to how to deal with their respective beneficial interests and if necessary to advise one or other party to obtain independent legal advice.
- That where a property is held as joint tenants it will be assumed that the beneficial ownership mirrors the legal ownership unless there is evidence of a contrary intention (*Stack* v. *Dowden* [2007] UKHL 17).

Considering the above points is particularly prudent in situations where the purchase price for the property is funded in unequal proportions.

Regrettably, it is my experience that such basic investigation is more observed in the breach despite repeated warnings from the courts and the clear prospects of a subsequent negligence claim.

In the unreported case of *Taylor and Herman* v. *Warners* (21 July 1987) Mr Justice Warner stated that it was not sufficient simply to explain the difference between the two ways that property might be held, as merely to inform prospective purchasers of the survivorship right in a beneficial joint tenancy was, in his words, 'perfunctory'. (In that case the solicitor was found guilty of negligence in not fully explaining the effects of a joint tenancy and specifically the right of survivorship.)

Of more direct warning is the statement of Lord Justice Ward in *Carlton* v. *Goodman* [2002] 2 FLR 259:

> I ask in despair how often this Court has to remind conveyancers that they would save their clients a great deal of later difficulty if only they would sit the purchasers down, explain the difference between a joint tenancy and tenancy in common, ascertain what they want and then expressly declare in the Conveyance or Transfer how the beneficial interest is to be held because that will be conclusive and save all arguments. When are conveyancers going to do this as a matter of invariable standard practice? This Court has urged that time after time. Perhaps conveyancers do not read the Law Reports? I will try one more time. ALWAYS TRY TO AGREE ON AND THEN RECORD HOW THE BENEFICIAL INTEREST IS TO BE HELD. It is not very difficult to do.

Note the repeated reference to 'conveyancers'.

It is, therefore, crucial to have a clear statement of the parties' intentions with regard to the ownership of the property set out and recorded at the time of the initial purchase rather than have to rely upon the court attempting to determine the position at a later date in the event of a dispute.

See also the Law Society Practice Note on Joint Ownership issued on 10 June 2020:

> Case law has clearly demonstrated the benefits of joint owners of property declaring their beneficial interests. Declaring interests at the outset of a transaction provides clarity about the parties' intentions and may help to avoid disputes in the future.

2.1.2 Terminology: a quick summary

The Law Commission's paper *Sharing Homes* [2002] EWLC 278(2) (1 November 2002) contains the following useful definitions:

(1) An **express trust** is created where a person either expressly declares that he or she holds property on trust for another or transfers the property to another expressly subject to a trust. While no particular words are required to create a trust, it is usually very clear that a trust has been created.

(2) An **implied trust** is not expressly created, but arises by means of implication from particular circumstances. It can take one of two forms, a resulting trust or a constructive trust:

   (a) A **resulting trust** is implied (or 'presumed') where a person purchases property in the name of another, or where a person makes a direct financial contribution to the acquisition of property in the name of another.

(b) A **constructive trust** is implied to give effect to the 'common intention' of persons, typically where there is an agreement, arrangement or understanding between them that a property should be shared beneficially on which agreement one person relies to his or her detriment.

(3) **Proprietary estoppel** is a doctrine applicable where a person has been encouraged or allowed to believe by an owner of land that he or she has certain rights in or over it. That person then acts to his or her detriment in reliance on this belief. If it is unconscionable for the owner to deny the claimant the rights in question, the court may grant relief to give effect to the expectation which has been engendered. The relief may or may not comprise the grant of an interest in property.

So let us take each of these in turn.

2.2 EXPRESS DECLARATION OF TRUST

Ownership of real property consists of two elements:

- Legal ownership – whose name appears on the legal title; and
- Beneficial ownership – what are the parties' respective shares in that property.

What is clear from case law is that the one does not necessarily equate with the other.

Therefore, as we have seen previously, the importance of committing to paper the intentions of parties when purchasing property as a joint enterprise cannot be overstated.

LPA 1925, s.53(1)(b) provides that:

> a declaration of trust respecting any land or any interest therein must be manifested and proved by some writing signed by some person who is able to declare such trust ...

To emphasise the importance of this, as long ago as *Pettitt* v. *Pettitt* [1970] AC 777 it was said as follows:

> ... the beneficial ownership of the property in question must depend upon the agreement of the parties determined at the time of its acquisition. If the property in question is land there must be some lease or conveyance which shows how it was acquired. If that document declares not merely in whom the legal title is to vest, but in whom the beneficial title is to vest, that necessarily concludes the question of title as between the spouses for all time, and in the absence of fraud or mistake at the time of the transaction the parties cannot go behind it at any time thereafter... (at [813])

Again, in *Gissing* v. *Gissing* [1971] AC 886:

> Where the trust is expressly declared in the instrument by which the legal estate is transferred to the trustee or by a written declaration of trust by the trustee, the court must give effect to it. (at [905])

Yet again, in *Goodman* v. *Gallant* [1986] 1 FLR 513:

> If … the relevant conveyance contains an express declaration of trust which comprehensively declares the beneficial interests in the property or its proceeds of sale, there is no room for the application of the doctrine of resulting implied or constructive trusts unless and until the conveyance is set aside or rectified; until that event the declaration contained in the document speaks for itself.
>
> … in the absence of any claim for rectification or rescission, the provision in the conveyance declaring that the plaintiff and the defendant were to hold the proceeds of sale of the property 'Upon Trust for themselves as joint tenants' concludes the question of the respective beneficial interests of the two parties in so far as that declaration of trust, on its true construction, exhaustively declares the beneficial interests.

And more recently in the seminal case of *Stack* v. *Dowden* [2007] UKHL 17 at [49]:

> No one now doubts that such an express declaration of trust is conclusive unless varied by subsequent agreement or affected by proprietary estoppel [as for this latter qualification see **2.5.7**].

Thus, where the conveyance contains such an express declaration of trust comprehensively declaring the beneficial interests, that is the beginning and the end of the issue, it is conclusive. There is no place to argue otherwise such as through the application of the doctrines of resulting or constructive trusts, unless there is a basis on which to subsequently set aside or rectify the transaction such as fraud or mistake or undue influence, or the terms are subsequently varied by deed by the parties who originally entered into it or by the equitable doctrine of proprietary estoppel (see for example *Arif* v. *Anwar and Rehan* [2015] EWHC 124 (Fam)).

The case of *Pankhania* v. *Chandegra* [2012] EWCA Civ 1438 adds further to the jurisprudence in this area:

> The effect of executing the declaration of trust was therefore to make the claimant an equitable tenant in common regardless of what the parties may have subjectively intended and to estop the defendant from denying his title. The sham principle has no application to a situation in which the highest that a party to the deed can put it is that the document does not accurately record what they intended to achieve. Unless the conditions exist for the court to rectify the document, the parties are bound by the legal consequences of what they have signed. (at [22]) … There is no room for inserting a constructive trust in substitution for the express trust. (at [26]) … In the absence of a vitiating factor, such as fraud or mistake, as a ground for setting aside the express trust or as a ground for rectification of it, the court must give legal effect to the express trust declared in the transfer. In the absence of such claims the court cannot go behind that trust. (at [27]) … reliance on *Stack* v. *Dowden* and *Jones* v. *Kernott* for inferring or imputing a different trust in this and other similar cases which have recently been before this court is misplaced where there is an express declaration of trust of the beneficial title and no valid legal grounds for going behind it. (at [28])

As far as the declaration itself is concerned this need not be contained in the actual conveyance or transfer but can be contained in a separate trust document executed at the time of completion (see *Chopra* v. *Bindra* [2009] EWCA Civ 203):

> The Declaration of Beneficial Trusts could perfectly well have been contained in a separate document altogether off the face of the title to the land, and many conveyancers would regard that as the more proper method of proceeding.
>
> (*Wilson* v. *Wilson* [1969] 3 All ER 945)

Moreover, such declaration need not be made at the time of its creation; a subsequent declaration will suffice provided it is in existence before any action is brought (*Rochefoucauld* v. *Boustead* [1897] 1 Ch 196).

One can clearly see, therefore, the importance of dealing with matters at the outset and there is a very good argument to say that if this is not done the conveyancing solicitors could well find themselves open to a claim in negligence.

The positive aspect of this, of course, is the potential benefits of cross-selling. Family and conveyancing departments in solicitors' practices need to work closely and have procedures/checklists in place in order to provide a holistic service to couples acquiring property when in a non-marital union so as to cover aspects such as trust deeds, living together agreements and mutual wills.

Should the parties subsequently decide to alter their shares on the basis of future events then such change should be reflected in a properly drawn variation to the declaration of trust or a new trust document should be drawn up.

The starting point, therefore, for ascertaining the parties' respective shares in any dispute over property will be from an examination of the title deeds and documents. Thus, access to the conveyance/transfer and office copy entries (if registered) of the title register and the solicitor's conveyancing file will be essential.

2.2.1 Challenging an express declaration

As expressed earlier and in the words of Buckley LJ in *Pink* v. *Lawrence* (1978) 36 PCR 98:

> Once a trust has been effectively declared, it can only be got rid of either by rescinding the document containing the declaration of trust on the ground of fraud or mistake, or rectifying it in the appropriate manner to vary to delete the declaration of trust.

In *Stack* v. *Dowden*, Baroness Hale gave two different formulations to the class of exceptions:

- 'No one thinks that such a declaration can be overturned, except in cases of fraud or mistake.'
- 'No one now doubts that such an express declaration of trust is conclusive unless varied by subsequent agreement or affected by proprietary estoppel.'

A claimant who seeks to go behind an express declaration of trust in relation to the former will need to plead either rescission or rectification (*Wilson* v. *Wilson* [1963] 1 WLR 601; *Singla* v. *Brown* [2007] EWHC 405 (Ch)).

2.2.1.1 Rectification

Rectification of a declaration of trust is covered by the Land Registration Act (LRA) 2002, Sched.4 and can only be sought by court order or through HM Land Registry.

It is defined as a correction of a mistake which prejudicially affects the title of a registered proprietor and cannot be undertaken without the proprietor's consent unless:

> (a) he has by fraud or lack of proper care caused or substantially contributed to the mistake; or
>
> (b) it would for any other reason be unjust for the alteration not to be made.
>
> (LRA 2002, Sched.4, para.3(2))

(See *Wilson* v. *Wilson* [1963] 1 WLR 601; *Singla* v. *Brown* [2008] 2 FLR 125; *Abbey National plc* v. *Stringer* [2006] EWCA Civ 338; *Smith* v. *Cooper* [2010] EWCA Civ 722 (undue influence).)

2.2.1.2 Undue influence/duress

In *Royal Bank of Scotland plc* v. *Etridge (No. 2)* [2001] 2 FLR 1364 it was said as follows (at [6]):

> ... Undue influence is one of the grounds of relief developed by the courts of equity as a court of conscience. The objective is to ensure that the influence of one person over another is not abused. In everyday life people constantly seek to influence the decisions of others. They seek to persuade those with whom they are dealing to enter into transactions, whether great or small. The law has set limits to the means properly employable for this purpose. To this end the common law developed a principle of duress. ...
>
> [7] ... The law will investigate the manner in which the intention to enter into a transaction was secured ... If the intention was produced by an unacceptable means, the law will not permit the transaction to stand. The means used is regarded as an exercise of improper or 'undue' influence, and hence unacceptable, whenever the consent thus procured ought not fairly to be treated as the expression of a person's free will. ...

In other words, one's free will has been overborne by duress or undue influence.

The judgment in *Etridge* went on to elaborate on these two sub-categories of behaviour:

> [8] Equity identified broadly two forms of unacceptable conduct. The first comprises overt acts of improper pressure or coercion such as unlawful threats. Today there is much overlap with the principle of duress as this principle has subsequently developed. The second form arises out of a relationship between two persons where one has acquired over another a measure of influence, or ascendancy, of which the ascendant person then takes unfair advantage ...
>
> [9] In cases of this latter nature the influence one person has over another provides scope for misuse without any specific overt acts of persuasion. The relationship between two individuals may be such that, without more, one of them is disposed to agree a course of action proposed by the other ... He abuses the influence he has acquired ...

> [11] … The principle is not confined to cases of abuse of trust and confidence … Several expressions have been used in an endeavour to encapsulate the essence: trust and confidence, reliance, dependence or vulnerability on the one hand and ascendancy, domination or control on the other. None of these descriptions is perfect. None is all embracing. Each has its proper place.

2.2.1.3 Misrepresentation

Misrepresentation is an untrue or misleading statement of fact made during negotiations by one party to another which then induces that other party into forming a contract.

Misrepresentation may be:

- fraudulent (i.e. where the person making the statement knows it is untrue, or makes it without believing it is true);
- negligent (i.e. where the person makes a statement carelessly or without reasonable grounds for believing its truth, or recklessly (i.e. they do not care about whether it is true or not)); or
- innocent (i.e. where the person making the statement has reasonable grounds for believing that the statement was true).

2.2.1.4 Fraud

Fraud is committed where a person wilfully makes a statement which the person knew to be false or did not believe to be true. The burden of proof rests on the person who asserts it on the civil standard of proof, namely, more likely than not. The nature of the fraud must change the nature of the case (*Kuwait Airways Corporation* v. *Iraq Airways Corporation* [2003] EWHC 31 (Comm)).

Within the field of the family jurisdiction it has been defined as:

> the intentional use of false or misleading information in an attempt illegally to deprive another person of money, property or legal rights.
>
> (*Neil* v. *Neil* [2019] EWHC 3330 (Fam) at [54])

2.2.1.5 Mistake

Rectification of a declaration is usually a remedy based on common or mutual mistake and involves a claimant proving:

- there was an agreement reached between the parties prior to the declaration of trust being executed;
- that the declaration of trust is executed in different terms from that agreement, but was not intended to replace or supersede that agreement;
- the agreement survives the declaration of trust and despite the terms of the declaration of trust the parties still, at its execution, regarded themselves bound by the terms of that agreement.

In essence, the declaration of trust incorrectly records the real agreement that the parties reached such that it should be amended or rectified to record the real agreement.

A mere unilateral mistake will not ordinarily suffice to bring a claim for either rescission or rectification:

> The commonest circumstance in which rectification is granted is where the written contract does not accurately record the parties' joint agreement. In other words, there is a mistake common to both parties. In the case of unilateral mistake, that is to say where only one party is mistaken as to the meaning of the contract, rectification is not ordinarily appropriate ... But the Court will intervene if there are 'additional circumstances that render unconscionable reliance on the document by the party who has intended that it should have effect according to its terms'.
>
> (*Commission for the New Towns* v. *Cooper (GB) Ltd* [1995] Ch 259 at [277])

This decision clearly opened the door for rectification in other circumstances, and in *Thomas Bates* v. *Windham's (Lingerie)* [1981] 1 WLR 505 it was held that rectification might be granted in the absence of mutual mistake where:

> ... first, that one party A erroneously believed that the document sought to be rectified contained a particular term or provision, or possibly did not contain a particular term or provision which, mistakenly, it did contain; secondly, that the other party B was aware of the omission or the inclusion and that it was due to a mistake on the part of A; thirdly, that B has omitted to draw the mistake to the notice of A ... fourth ... that the mistake must be one calculated to benefit B. If these requirements are satisfied, the court may regard it as inequitable to allow B to resist rectification to give effect to A's intention on the ground that the mistake was not, at the time of the execution of the document, a mutual mistake. (at [516])

In the case of *Commission for the New Towns* v. *Cooper (GB) Ltd* [1995] Ch 259 the judge was prepared to extend the principle:

> But were it necessary to do so in this case, I would hold that where A intends B to be mistaken as to the construction of the agreement, so conducts himself that he diverts B's attention from discovering the mistake by making false and misleading statements, and B in fact makes the very mistake that A intends, then notwithstanding that A does not actually know, but merely suspects, that B is mistaken, and it cannot be shown that the mistake was induced by any misrepresentation, rectification may be granted. (at [280])

In other words, it is mutual mistake, or one party spotting the mistake, not letting on and taking advantage of the other party not spotting the mistake which is tantamount to equity coming to the rescue.

From the Supreme Court decision of *Pitt* v. *Holt* [2013] UKSC 26 the following principles can be derived:

- There is an equitable jurisdiction to grant rescission of a voluntary disposition on the ground of mistake.

- A mistake must be distinguished from mere ignorance or inadvertence and also from what is called misprediction. These distinctions are reasonably clear in a general sort of way but they tend to get blurred when it comes to the facts of particular cases.
- Forgetfulness, inadvertence or ignorance is not, as such, a mistake but it can lead to a false belief or assumption which the law will recognise as a mistake. There are distinctions to be drawn between incorrect conscious beliefs, incorrect tacit assumptions and true cases of mere causative ignorance (i.e. but for a person's ignorance they would not have acted as they did).
- Mere ignorance, even if causative, is insufficient for relief, but the courts should not shrink when making findings of fact from drawing the inference of conscious belief or tacit assumption where there is evidence to support such an inference.
- Misprediction relates to some possible future event, whereas a legally significant mistake normally relates to some past or present matter of fact or law, although even this distinction is not always so clear.
- A careless mistake will be sufficient for relief, unless it can be shown that the person deliberately ran the risk, or must be taken to have run the risk, of being wrong. Normally the mistake will not be known to (still less induced by) the person or persons taking a benefit under the disposition.
- There is no requirement that the mistake must be as to the nature or effect of the disposition as opposed to its consequences or the advantages to be gained from entering into it.
- The true test is that there must be a causative mistake of sufficient gravity; and, as additional guidance to trial judges in their evaluation of the facts, the test will normally be satisfied only where there is a mistake either as to the legal character or nature of a transaction, or as to some matter of fact or law which is basic to the transaction.
- The mistake must be of so serious a character as to render it unjust on the part of the donee to retain the property given to them or unconscionable for the donees to insist upon their legal rights to continue enjoyment of the benefits given to them. The injustice, or unfairness or unconscionableness of leaving a mistaken disposition uncorrected must be evaluated correctly but with an intense focus on the facts of the particular case.

In short, the court should provide rectification for mistake where:

- there was a causative mistake; and
- that mistake was so great that it would be unconscionable to refuse relief.

This test will only normally be satisfied where there was a mistake either as to the legal character or nature of the transaction or as to some matter of fact or law which was basic to the transaction.

2.2.1.6 Sham transactions

Another example where a challenge might be appropriate and the transaction set aside would be where the trust itself is a 'sham'. In other words:

> acts done or documents executed by the parties to the 'sham' which are intended by them to give to third parties or to the court the appearance of creating between the parties legal rights and obligations different from the actual legal rights and obligations (if any) which the parties intend to create.
>
> (*Snook* v. *London and West Riding Investments Ltd* [1967] 2 QB 786 at [802])

> i) A sham means acts done or documents executed by the alleged shammers which are intended by them to give to third parties or to the court the appearance of creating between them legal rights and obligations different from the actual legal rights and obligations (if any) which they intend to create.
>
> ii) Subject to the next point, all the shammers must hold an expressed common intention that the acts or documents are not to create the legal rights and obligations which they give the appearance of creating. No unexpressed intentions of a shammer affect the rights of a party whom he deceived. The test of intention is subjective. The parties must have intended to create different rights and obligations from those appearing from the relevant document, and in addition they must have intended to give a false impression of those rights and obligations to third parties.
>
> iii) A sham transaction will still remain a sham transaction even if one of the parties to it merely went along with the shammer not either knowing or caring about what he or she was signing.
>
> iv) The court is not restricted to the four corners of the document. It may examine external evidence. This will include the parties' explanations and circumstantial evidence, such as evidence of the subsequent conduct of the parties.
>
> v) The fact that the act or document is uncommercial, or even artificial, does not mean that it is a sham. A distinction is to be drawn between the situation where parties make an agreement which is unfavourable to one of them, or artificial, and a situation where they intend some other arrangement to bind them.
>
> vi) The fact that parties subsequently depart from an agreement does not necessarily mean that they never intended the agreement to be effective and binding. The proper conclusion to draw may be that they agreed to vary their agreement and that they have become bound by the agreement as varied.
>
> vii) Because a degree of dishonesty is involved in a sham there is a very strong presumption that parties intend to be bound by the provisions of agreements into which they enter, and intend the agreements they enter into to take effect. However, this does not elevate the standard of proof, which is set at the balance of probability. Nonetheless the test is a stiff one and there is a requirement of very clear evidence given the seriousness of the allegation.
>
> (*Bhura* v. *Bhura* [2014] EWHC 727 (Fam))

ND v. *SD* [2017] EWHC 1507 (Fam) provides a helpful summary and clarification of the law regarding sham trusts. Roberts J began by considering the judgment in *National Westminster Bank plc* v. *Jones* [2000] All ER (D) 857 where it was held that where a contractual transaction is entered into for an 'artificial purpose' this 'does not by any means of itself render the transaction a sham' although she did add that it would 'require very unusual circumstances before the court held that a transaction which was not artificial was in fact a sham'.

An important further clarification was made in that case, which was that in:

> circumstances where the party relying on it was contending that it was not artificial, then that might be a further reason (although certainly not a conclusive reason) for deciding that the transaction was a sham, given that a sham transaction involves a degree of dishonesty on the part of the parties involved.

Therefore, if a party argues that an agreement or a trust is not artificial and it is found to be so, there is then the automatic conclusion that they have been dishonest in the court and therefore this can contribute as a factor in establishing whether that agreement or trust was actually a sham.

That case also considered Lord Justice Diplock's judgment in *Snook* v. *London and West Riding Investments Ltd* [1967] 2 QB 786 which made clear that:

> in legal principle, morality and the authorities ... that for acts or documents to be a 'sham', with whatever legal consequences follows from this, all the parties thereto must have a common intention that the acts or documents are not to create the legal rights and obligations which they give the appearance of creating.

Mrs Justice Roberts noted that *Snook* was cited with approval by the Court of Appeal in *Stone* v. *Hitch* [2011] EWCA Civ 63 in which Lady Justice Arden set out five fundamental principles in relation to the law on sham acts or documents:

> First, in the case of a document, the court is not restricted to examining the four corners of the document. It may examine external evidence. This will include the parties' explanations and circumstantial evidence, such as evidence of the subsequent conduct of the parties.
>
> Second, as the passage from *Snook* makes clear, the test of intention is subjective. The parties must have intended to create different rights and obligations from those appearing from (say) the relevant document, and in addition they must have intended to give a false impression of those rights and obligations to third parties.
>
> Third, the fact that the act or document is uncommercial, or even artificial, does not mean that it is a sham. A distinction is to be drawn between the situation where the parties make an agreement which is unfavourable to one of them, or artificial, and a situation where they intend some other arrangement to bind them. In the former situation, they intend the agreement to take effect according to its tenor. In the latter situation, the agreement is not to bind their relationship.
>
> Fourth, the fact that parties subsequently depart from an agreement does not necessarily mean that they never intended the agreement to be effective and binding. The proper conclusion to draw may be that they agreed to vary their agreement and that they have become bound by the agreement as varied...
>
> Fifth, the intention must be a common intention...

Having considered these authorities, Mrs Justice Roberts drew the conclusion that:

> ... two headline points emerge at the outset: (i) there must be a dishonest intent before the court will find an instrument to be a sham, and (ii) where instruments or agreements are properly and formally drawn (i.e. 'perfectly proper agreements on their face'), absent a dishonest intent, there is a strong presumption that the parties intend to honour their rights and obligations thereunder.

This makes it clear that dishonest intention is almost always required by all parties concerned in the agreement (whether that be a trust or contract) as without it there is a presumption that it is not a sham, making the already high standard of proof required to prove there is a sham trust even more difficult to meet.

It is important to note that Mrs Justice Roberts clarified that 'reckless indifference will be taken to constitute the necessary intention'.

Mrs Justice Roberts then went on to add that, in addition to the requirement of dishonest intention, *Stone* establishes that all the parties to the transactions or documents:

> must share a common intention that the documents themselves will not create the legal rights and obligations which they give the appearance of creating.

A final key authority analysed by Mrs Justice Roberts was the judgment in *A* v. *A* [2007] EWHC 99 (Fam) where it was held that a trust which is not initially a sham cannot subsequently become a sham.

Therefore, in order to establish a sham trust, there must have been a common dishonest intention from the creation of the trust:

> In this context it is important to distinguish between motive as distinct from intention ... It is sufficient for these purposes that the parties intended their agreements to be given effect in the form in which they are recorded, and the courts will not enquire into their motives for so intending. It is an established legal principle undisturbed by anything which has been said in the more modern authorities to which I have referred that 'if what is done is genuinely done, it does not remain undone merely because there was an ulterior purpose in doing it': see Megarry J (as he then was) in *Miles* v. *Bull* [1969]... (at [240])

Therefore, when considering whether or not a trust is a sham trust, Mrs Justice Roberts has made clear the following:

- the party looking to argue that there is a sham trust must prove that there is dishonest intent to deceive third parties which is common to all parties involved;
- if there is an intention to create a genuine trust, the motive is irrelevant and the trust cannot be a sham.

2.2.2 What wording constitutes a declaration of trust?

The old form of registered transfer (Form 19(JP)) for conveyancing transactions provided an optional tick box stating:

> The Survivor of them is entitled to give a valid receipt for capital money arising from a disposition of all or part of the property.

If the box is ticked the transfer provides for the rights of survivorship as set out in a joint tenancy, if not then the rights of survivorship do not apply. The question is, however, does it thereafter determine that the property is held on an express declaration of trust?

The answer was a resounding no. Such a declaration does not in itself constitute an express declaration of beneficial ownership as all it does is determine whether or not the rights of survivorship apply (see *Harwood* v. *Harwood* [1991] 2 FLR 274; *Huntingford* v. *Hobbs* [1993] 1 FLR 736; *Mortgage Corporation* v. *Shaire* [2001] Ch 743; *Stack* v. *Dowden* [2007] 1 FLR 1858).

Since 1 April 1998, in order to attempt to rectify potential problems, the new form of Transfer of Registered Land (Form TR1) contains a box for the transferee to declare whether they are to hold the property:

- on trust for themselves as joint tenants; or
- on trust for themselves as tenants in common in equal shares; or
- on such other trusts as the parties themselves may declare.

Thus, if properly completed, this will provide an express declaration of trust conclusively setting out the parties' legal and beneficial interests.

So over time, disputes concerning beneficial interests in jointly registered property should diminish due to the impact of the revised Form TR1.

However, there are clearly traps for the unwary.

The first thing to look out for is none of the tick boxes being completed. As Baroness Hale said in *Stack* v. *Dowden* [2007] 1 FLR 1858:

> The Land Registry form which has been prescribed since 1998 is to be applauded. If its completion and execution by or on behalf of all joint proprietors were mandatory, the problem we now face would disappear.

And therein lies the problem; its completion at present is not mandatory. Failure to complete it will lead to HM Land Registry entering a restriction in Form A upon the title by default recording the fact that HM Land Registry does not have clear evidence of a beneficial joint tenancy.

The other point to look out for is to ensure that Form TR1 is signed by the parties who wish to give effect to the declaration of trust, as to be effective as an express declaration of trust by deed conclusively declaring beneficial interests and enforceable as such (in the absence of mistake or fraud), it must not only be in writing but signed by the persons who are able to declare that trust (LPA 1925, s.53(1)(b)). (As a side note see *Silver Queen Maritime Ltd* v. *Persia Petroleum Ltd* [2010] EWHC 2867 (QB) as to the binding nature of deeds generally.)

Thus, check that Form TR1 (or JO – Trust form) is signed by the purchasers as well as the sellers.

For a case where Form TR1 was not signed see *Insol Funding Company Ltd* v. *Cowlam and Cowley* [2017] EWHC 1822 (Ch).

This was a case where joint buyers bought a property without signing Form TR1. The result in this case was held to be that there was no binding declaration of trust within LPA 1925, s.53. This allowed the court to approach the determination of the owners' equitable interests in accordance with the principles of constructive trusts.

It may be argued that of the three categories of ownership the 'joint tenants' box on Form TR1 in particular gives little clue as to the ownership of the beneficial interest that flows from it in much the same way as its predecessor Form 19(JP).

Indeed, the notes on the Land Registry website relating to the completion of Form TR1 currently state that:

> Joint ownership is a difficult area of the law. It can lead to disputes when ... the relationship between joint owners breaks down. Recording the joint owners' intentions in panel 10 of the transfer or in a separate form JO ... may help to avoid such disputes later on. However, this is only a starting point, as the joint owners' intentions may change over time ...

The new additional optional JO form which can be used to expand the position appears relatively little used; thus, there appears to be a suggestion that the ticking of any of the boxes may not be determinative, although *Stack* v. *Dowden* suggests otherwise.

While the starting point for determining who owns what in any dispute over property will be what the title deeds and documents have to say, what if the title deeds and documents do not contain an express declaration as to the beneficial interests?

In the absence of such an express declaration, anyone claiming a beneficial interest in the property will have to resort to the following doctrines of:

- resulting trusts;
- constructive trusts; and/or
- proprietary estoppel.

2.3 RESULTING TRUST

A resulting trust is based upon the rebuttable presumption that where a person has provided part of the purchase monies to buy a property which is then vested in the name of another, that property, by virtue of a trust, 'results' back to the person who paid the purchase price in accordance with the proportion of their financial contribution.

As Lord Browne-Wilkinson put it:

> where two parties have provided the purchase money to buy a property which is conveyed into the name of one of them alone, the latter is presumed to hold the property on a resulting trust for both parties in shares proportionate to the purchase price.
>
> (*Tinsley* v. *Milligan* [1994] 1 AC 340 at [371])

In other words, if you put in 30 per cent of the acquisition price you get a 30 per cent share.

The remedy, if established, is therefore purely an arithmetical one and is quantified in direct proportion to one's financial contribution.

This presumption, however, may be rebutted by evidence that the money provided was by way of a gift or a loan or even payment of rent or a family agreement or in anticipation of marriage with no intention to create legal relations (e.g. *Curley* v. *Parkes* [2004] EWCA Civ 1515; *Keondjian* v. *Kay* [2004] EWHC 2820 (Ch); *McHardy & Sons* v. *Warren* [1994] 2 FLR 338).

Historically, one could challenge the creation of a resulting trust using the presumption (albeit rebuttable) of advancement.

This is a 19th-century rule under which a man who gives property to his fiancée, wife or children is presumed to do so by way of a gift, unless a contrary intention can be found.

However, there is no rebuttable presumption of advancement (gift) as between cohabitants (*Lowson* v. *Coombes* [1999] Ch 373) and the rule is in any event now abolished by the Equality Act 2010, s.199.

Such an approach to establishing a beneficial interest can be distinguished from that of a constructive trust (see **2.4**) which, if established, enables the court to use a broader approach in order to ascertain the extent of a party's beneficial share as opposed to the purely arithmetical approach as propounded by the resulting trust model.

2.3.1 Quantifying: what type of contribution counts?

The financial contribution must be a direct contribution and relate to the acquisition of the property itself (e.g. deposit or part of the balance of the purchase monies) and, save as to mortgage instalments, subsequent payments will not suffice.

It has been held that ancillary expenses connected with the purchase, for example legal fees and stamp duty land tax, can be treated as part of the purchase price (see *Huntingford* v. *Hobbs* [1993] 1 FLR 736).

In contrast, fixtures, fittings and contents are not so regarded as relevant contributions (see *Pettitt* v. *Pettitt* [1970] AC 777) nor are payments of household expenses.

Springette v. *Defoe* [1992] 2 FLR 388 and *Evans* v. *Hayward* [1995] 2 FLR 511 held that the right to buy through the Council House Discount Scheme (Housing Act 1985) should be treated as an equivalent cash contribution to the purchase price from the person who was entitled to the discount in an amount equal to the discount to the purchase of the property.

Accordingly, the tenant whose occupation gives rise to the discount (even where exercised in favour of joint purchasers) is entitled to be credited with the discount when assessing the parties' shares in the beneficial interest by way of a presumed resulting trust in an amount proportionate to the value of the discount in comparison to the purchase price.

See *Marsh* v. *Von Sternberg* [1986] 1 FLR 526; *Ashe* v. *Mumford* [2001] 33 HLR 67; *Adekunle and Ben* v. *Ritchie* [2007] BPIR 1177; *Laskar* v. *Laskar* [2008] EWCA Civ 347.

Where a purchase is made, as is often the case, with the assistance of a mortgage advance, although this can complicate matters, as a general rule, monies raised by way of a loan and applied to the purchase price of a property will be regarded as a cash contribution from the person who obtained the loan.

As to the effect of taking the mortgage in joint names, it is usual to treat such joint and several liability as representing equal contributions:

> there was a very strong case for apportioning the mortgage equally between the parties when it comes to assessing their respective contributions to the purchase price.
>
> (*Laskar* v. *Laskar* [2008] EWCA Civ 347 at [29])

In *Stack* v. *Dowden* [2007] 1 FLR 1858 Lord Neuberger opined that there was a certain 'attraction' in the notion that liability under a mortgage should be treated as the equivalent of a cash contribution for the purpose of assessing the parties' beneficial shares – in other words, simplification.

However, any such conclusion may be displaced either by contrary agreement (see *Huntingford* v. *Hobbs* above) or by evidence that it was not intended that the claimant should acquire a beneficial share (*Carlton* v. *Goodman* [2002] 2 FLR 259, *Mckenzie* v. *Mckenzie* (unreported) 12 February 2003) and in the absence of an express declaration of trust regarding beneficial ownership purchased in joint names and financed by means of a mortgage, the fact that one of the parties has assumed liability for the mortgage payments does not of itself entitle them automatically to an interest in the property commensurate with the share of the purchase price financed by the mortgage.

This, of course, does not rule out the possibility that, in appropriate circumstances, the assumption of liability under a joint mortgage can be treated as a contribution to the payment of the purchase price capable of giving rise to a resulting trust; however, the appropriate enquiry is always to identify what was the intention of the parties when the property was purchased (*Re Gorman* [1990] 2 FLR 284).

The problem with the resulting trust model is its total reliance on proof of direct financial contributions (as opposed to non-financial contributions) at the time of purchase, which may create an imbalance particularly where a party's initial contribution is then followed by many years of cohabitation.

Some may also argue that the remedy itself is discriminatory as between breadwinner and home maker.

In contrast, in the case of a constructive trust the court looks at the conduct of the parties throughout their relationship. It is not restricted to examining the contributions made to the acquisition.

A common intention constructive trust is therefore more flexible. It is also more appropriate where the parties have incurred expenditure on the strength of their personal relationship and without expecting to have to account for every item, and therefore more reflective of quasi-marital relationships as home owners (see *Gallarotti* v. *Sebastianelli* [2012] EWCA Civ 865).

2.4 CONSTRUCTIVE TRUST

This effectively does what it says, namely, the court constructs a trust based upon either the express or the implied intention of the parties, at the time that the property was purchased, such that, despite the property being in one person's sole name, it was the parties' intention for it to be shared between them beneficially.

While a resulting trust, therefore, is generated in favour of the contributor proportionate to their cash contributions, a constructive trust is reliant upon there being an agreement between the parties, either express or implied, in reliance on which the non-owning party has acted to their detriment.

In order to establish a beneficial interest pursuant to a constructive trust, therefore, one has to find two things in favour of the non-owner:

1. A common intention to share the beneficial interest; and
2. An act by the non-owner to their detriment in reliance upon that common intention (*Gissing* v. *Gissing* [1971] AC 886).

There are two ways of establishing a common intention:

1. By way of direct evidence of an express agreement;
2. By indirect evidence by way of an inference drawn from conduct whereby common intention is deduced objectively from such conduct.

Thus, there is a distinction between direct evidence and indirect evidence, or alternatively between an express or implied agreement.

The classic definition in respect of an express declaration is given by Lord Bridge in the case of *Lloyds Bank* v. *Rosset* [1991] 1 AC 107 at [132]:

> The first and fundamental question which must always be resolved is whether, independently of any inference to be drawn from the conduct of the parties in the course of sharing the house as their home and managing their joint affairs, there has at any time prior to acquisition, or exceptionally at some later date, been any agreement, arrangement or understanding reached between them that the property is to be shared beneficially. The finding of an agreement or arrangement to share in this sense can only, I think, be based on evidence of *express discussions* between the partners, however imperfectly remembered and however imprecise their terms may have been. Once a finding to this effect is made, it will only be necessary for the partner asserting a claim to a beneficial interest against the partner entitled to the legal estate to show that he or she has *acted to his or her detriment or significantly altered his or her position in reliance on the agreement* in order to give rise to a constructive trust … [emphasis added].

The first port of call is therefore to see whether there is any evidence as to an express agreement, arrangement or understanding as between the parties as to the sharing of the beneficial ownership and thereafter detrimental reliance upon it.

However, there has to be a clear declaration of trust and that means there must be clear evidence from what was said or done of an intention to create a trust (*Paul* v. *Constance* [1977] 1 WLR 527; *Ong* v. *Ping* [2017] EWCA Civ 2069; *Hilton* v. *Cosnier* [2018] EWHC 3728 (Ch)).

This will, of course, require a finding based on the civil burden of proof as these cases inevitably turn on what one party maintains in deference to what is maintained by the other concerning what was or was not said.

As for detrimental reliance, for the purposes of an express common intention very little detriment is required and a wide range of conduct may qualify to support a constructive trust:

> ... once it has been shown that there was a common intention that the claimant should have an interest in the house, any act done by her to her detriment relating to the joint lives of the parties is, in my judgment, sufficient detriment to qualify. The acts do not have to be inherently referable to the house.
>
> (*Grant* v. *Edwards* [1986] 1 Ch 638 per Sir N Browne-Wilkinson)

However, a stricter approach was taken by Nourse LJ in the same case where he held that detrimental conduct must be such upon which the non-owning party could not reasonably have been expected to embark unless they were to have an interest in the house (*Grant* v. *Edwards* [1986] 1 Ch 638 – see also *Cox* v. *Jones* [2004] EWHC 1486 (Ch)).

If there is no such express agreement then one has to look at the conduct of the parties to see if an intention to share the beneficial ownership can be implied.

So, continues Lord Bridge in *Lloyds Bank* v. *Rosset* [1991] 1 AC 107:

> In sharp contrast with this situation is the very different one where there is no evidence to support a finding of an agreement or arrangement to share, however reasonable it might have been for the parties to reach such an arrangement if they had applied their minds to the question, and where the Court must rely entirely on the conduct of the parties, both as the basis from which to *infer* a common intention to share the property beneficially and as the conduct relied on to give rise to a constructive trust. (at [132]; emphasis added: note that there is no mention of *imputation* – see *Oxley* v. *Hiscock* [2004] EWCA 546 below, **3.4** and **4.2**)

In these circumstances the parties' conduct is relevant both as a basis from which to infer a common intention and as the detrimental conduct relied upon to give rise to a constructive trust.

Conduct thus serves a dual purpose when establishing a constructive trust in these circumstances, unlike in the case of an express oral declaration of trust where both an express intention and conduct to one's detriment in reliance on it need to be established.

Of course, if the oral expression were to be translated into a written expression we would have an express declaration of trust and all other forms of trust doctrine would not need to come into play (see LPA 1925, s.53).

Lord Bridge continues:

> In this situation, *direct contributions to the purchase price* by the partner who is not the legal owner, whether initially *or by payment of mortgage instalments*, will readily justify the inference necessary to the creation of a constructive trust. But, as I read the authorities, *it is at least extremely doubtful whether anything less will do* [emphasis added]. (at [133])

On this analysis the court looks for 'expenditure which is referable to the acquisition of the house' (*Grant* v. *Edwards*).

Accordingly, such agreement can be inferred from capital contributions but not contributions towards household expenses, contents, housework, decorating and gardening. However, such proposition sounds remarkably similar to that propounded by the resulting trust methodology.

To summarise the position following on from *Lloyds Bank plc* v. *Rosset* there are therefore two categories of case where a claim as to a beneficial entitlement for a non-owner can be found on the basis of a constructive trust:

1. An **express agreement**: where there is an arrangement or agreement (a common intention) and one party has acted to their detriment in reliance upon it or has significantly altered their position.
2. An **implied agreement**: where there is no evidence of an express agreement. In this case, the court has to rely upon the conduct of the parties from which to infer a common intention. Direct contributions to the purchase price will readily justify the inference necessary for the creation of a constructive trust although it was regarded as extremely doubtful as to whether anything less would do.

However, in the case of *Stack* v. *Dowden* (see **Chapter 3**) it was held that the bar set in point 2 above had been placed too high ('The law has indeed moved on in response to changing social and economic conditions').

Indeed, the case of *Le Foe* v. *Le Foe and Woolwich plc* [2001] 2 FLR 970 opened the door to a broader approach to the issue of beneficial entitlement where there was no express common intention but there were contributions which, although indirect, were directly referable to the purchase of the property.

In that case, Nicholas Mostyn QC considered that Lord Bridge in *Rosset* was not saying in absolute terms that there were no circumstances in which indirect contributions would suffice in cases where there is no express agreement to share the beneficial interest, but simply indicating that such cases would be the exception.

As we shall see below, the case law in this area has subsequently developed with the courts taking a broader, and in my view, far more sensible and modern approach, both as to the kinds of contributions from which a common intention may be inferred and to the corresponding quantification of those shares – much as the courts have done in the field of ancillary relief (e.g. *White* v. *White* [2000] UKHL 54).

A further development of the law came in the case of *Oxley* v. *Hiscock* [2004] EWCA 546 Civ (a sole name case) where Lord Justice Chadwick analysed the position by breaking down the issue into two succinct questions for determination:

(a) The **primary question** – was there a common intention that each should have a beneficial interest in the property? (The first hurdle) If the answer is no then that is the end of the enquiry (see *Walsh* v. *Singh* [2009] EWHC 3219 (Ch) for an example of where such a common intention was not established). If the answer is yes then we move to:

(b) The **secondary question** – what is the extent of that interest? (The second hurdle).

Lord Justice Chadwick found that Lord Bridge in his restrictive approach was addressing only the primary question in the two categories outlined above; thus, if a common intention could be inferred from conduct alone, the secondary question still had to be addressed.

Once the first hurdle of establishing a common intention was surmounted the court was no longer confined to the limited range of acts of financial contribution needed to support the constructive trust in the first place; it was now free to take into account all conduct which throws light on the question as to what shares were intended at the time of acquisition:

> in a case where there is no evidence of any discussion between them as to the amount of the share which each was to have – and even in a case where the evidence is that there was no discussion on that point – the question still requires an answer. It must now be accepted that (at least in this Court and below) the answer is that each is entitled to that share which the court considers *fair* having regard to the *whole course of dealing between them in relation to the property*. And, in that context, 'the whole course of dealing between them in relation to the property' includes the arrangements which they make from time to time in order to meet the outgoings (for example, mortgage contributions, council tax and utilities, repairs, insurance and housekeeping) which have to be met if they are to live in the property as their home [emphasis added]. (at [69])

Accordingly, rather than an arithmetical quantification of beneficial interest being determined pro rata in accordance with the parties' respective contributions to the purchase price (as with a resulting trust), a constructive trust, where there are no express discussions as to shares, is based upon ascertaining the parties' shared/common intention which the court considers fair having regard to the whole course of dealing between them in relation to the property, including the arrangements in respect of the outgoings, and therefore a broad-brush analysis should be undertaken by the court to produce a fair outcome:

> what the court is doing … is to *supply* or *impute* a common intention as to the parties' respective shares (in circumstances in which there was, in fact, no common intention) on the basis of that which, in the light of all the material circumstances (including the acts and conduct of the parties after the acquisition), is shown to be fair … [emphasis added]. (at [66])

It is important at this stage to highlight a number of concepts arising from this judgment that we will need to revisit later:

- Whole course of dealing in relation to the property.
- Imputation.
- Fairness.

But for now, as we can see, a constructive trust based upon an inferred common intention is more flexible in looking at the parties' conduct throughout their relationship as opposed to being restricted to direct contributions as to the property's acquisition.

For a slight twist in the tale, mention must be made of the judgment in *Archibald* v. *Alexander* [2020] EWHC 1621 (Ch) which held that:

> a constructive trust may arise in favour of beneficiaries in circumstances in which essential ingredients of a common intention constructive trust are absent, namely an agreement or understanding with the beneficiaries and detrimental reliance. The constructive trust in such circumstances depends on the agreed basis on which the transferee of property received it and on the fact that it would be unconscionable for them to treat the property as their own. (at [35])

In this case the High Court upheld an oral, informal agreement despite there being an alleged lack of detriment.

It confirmed that where a property is transferred gratuitously into the name of the owner on the basis of an express agreement to hold it on trust for another, detrimental reliance is not required. The trust arises from the terms of transfer, not from detrimental reliance on the agreement by the beneficiary.

However, this must be contrasted with cases where a party already owns a property; in such case any granting of a subsequent beneficial interest must meet the criteria of detrimental reliance.

In *Archibald* v. *Alexander* [2020] EWHC 1621 (Ch) the owner agreed to hold the property on trust and equity would not allow them to rely on the absence of a formal deed of trust and keep it for themselves. This was established in *Rochefoucauld* v. *Boustead* [1897] 1 Ch 196 and is a principle used in cases where it is difficult to prove detrimental reliance.

To support this, reference was made to the decision of *De Bruyne* v. *De Bruyne* where it was determined that a constructive trust may arise in favour of beneficiaries in circumstances in which the essential ingredients of a common intention constructive trust are absent. The constructive trust in such circumstances depends on the agreed basis on which the transferee of property received it and on the fact that it would be unconscionable for them to treat the property as their own:

> There are, however, a number of situations in which equity will hold the transferee of property to the terms upon which it was acquired by imposing a constructive trust to that effect. These cases do not depend on some form of detrimental reliance in order to re-balance the equities between competing claimants for the property. They concentrate instead on the circumstances in which the transferee came to acquire the property in order to provide the justification for the imposition of a trust. The most obvious examples are secret trusts and mutual wills in which property is transferred by will pursuant to an agreement that the transferee will hold the property on trust for a third party. In neither case does the intended beneficiary rely on any sense on the agreement (he may not even be aware of it) but, in both cases, equity will regard it as against conscience for the owner of the property to deny the terms upon which he received it. It is not necessary in such cases to show that the property was acquired by actual fraud (although the principle would

> apply equally in such cases). The concept of fraud in equity is much wider and can extend to unconscionable or inequitable conduct in the form of a denial or refusal to carry out the agreement to hold the property for the benefit of the third party which was the only basis upon which the property was transferred. This is sufficient in itself to create the fiduciary obligation and to require the imposition of a constructive trust. The principle is a broad one and applies as much to *inter vivos* transactions as it does to wills: see *Rochefoucauld* v. *Boustead* [1897] 1 Ch 196; *Bannister* v. *Bannister* [1948] 2 All ER 133.
>
> (*De Bruyne* v. *De Bruyne* [2010] EWCA Civ 519 at [51])

> … The different types of constructive trust are well summarised in paragraphs 10–018 to 10–024 of Megarry & Wade's *The Law of Real Property* (9th ed). These include, as three different subcategories: parties entering into a joint venture involving land; where it would be inequitable for a landowner to deny a claimant an interest in land; and where a person has acted to their detriment in reliance upon a common intention for that person to acquire an interest in a property.
>
> (*Archibald* v. *Alexander* [2020] EWHC 1621 at [38])

The reference to it being inequitable to deny a claimant an interest seems very much to morph constructive trust into that other creature of equity known as proprietary estoppel; however, as stated, this very much rests on the peculiar facts of that particular transaction, namely a party conveying a property to someone on the basis that they are to hold it on trust for another, as opposed to the situation where they had legal title already.

2.5 PROPRIETARY ESTOPPEL

2.5.1 Introduction

Proprietary estoppel differs from other forms of estoppel in that it can found a cause of action rather than simply being a defence (*Crabb* v. *Arun District Council* [1976] Ch 179).

In essence, this particular brand of estoppel arises where one party spends money on property belonging to another in the expectation or belief, which is encouraged by the other party, that by doing so they will acquire an interest in it.

Thus, it will arise in situations where the legal owner creates or encourages an expectation that the other party will have an interest in land in reliance on which the other party acts to their detriment:

> There are circumstances in which it is not possible to infer any agreement, arrangement or understanding that the property is to be shared beneficially but in which nevertheless equity has been prepared to hold that the conduct of an owner in allowing a claimant to expend money or act otherwise to his detriment will be precluded from denying that the claimant has a proprietary interest in the property … claims based on proprietary estoppel are more likely to arise where the claimant has acted after an informal promise has been made to him.
>
> (*Yaxley* v. *Gotts* [2000] Ch 162 at [192])

> An equity arises where – (a) the owner of land (O) induces, encourages or allows the claimant (C) to believe that he has or will enjoy some right or benefit over O's property; (b) in reliance upon this belief, C acts to his detriment to the knowledge of O; and (c) O then seeks to take unconscionable advantage of C by denying him the right or benefit which he expected to receive.
>
> (*The Law of Real Property* by Megarry & Wade, 8th ed., at para. 16-001)

> … if A under an expectation created or encouraged by B that A shall have a certain interest in land, thereafter, on the faith of such expectation and with the knowledge of B and without objection by him, acts to his detriment in connection with such land, a Court of Equity will compel B to give effect to such expectation.
>
> (*Taylors Fashions Ltd* v. *Liverpool Victoria Trustees Ltd* [1982] QB 133 at [144])

For example, in the case of *Van Laetham* v. *Brooker & Caradoc Estates* [2006] 2 FLR 495 a cohabitant, who had been given a number of evasive excuses as to why a property was not held in joint names, believed that they had an interest in the property and acted to their detriment in reliance upon that belief. The owner had deliberately failed to disabuse them of their mistaken belief and accordingly a proprietary estoppel had arisen.

Accordingly, the doctrine/remedy is aimed at preventing a person from insisting on their strict legal rights where:

- a representation, promise or assurance of sufficient clarity is made that the claimant has or will acquire rights in respect of specified property;
- there has been reliance on it by the claimant;
- there is a not insubstantial detriment to the claimant in consequence of their reasonable reliance, i.e. reliance on the promise or assurance with a sufficient link between the promise and the conduct constituting the detriment (the promise or assurance does not have to be the sole inducement) (*Suggitt* v. *Suggitt* [2011] EWHC 903 (Ch));
- unconscionability arises: 'that equity is concerned to prevent unconscionable conduct permeates all the elements of the doctrine … the court must look at the matter in the round' (*Gillett* v. *Holt* [2000] 2 FLR 266).

However, while the above elements of a proprietary estoppel are useful for the purposes of analysis and structured decision-making, they are not to be treated as watertight compartments and it is essential to consider them all together in one evaluation (*Davies* v. *Davies* [2014] EWCA Civ 568).

Furthermore, in *Habberfield* v. *Habberfield* [2019] EWCA Civ 890 it was held that whether an equity has been raised is a retrospective exercise undertaken from the time when the promisor goes back on the promise, and it is wrong to concentrate on one event only in the course of a long history of dealing.

2.5.2 Representation/promise/assurance

A claimant relying on proprietary estoppel must show a clear and unequivocal assurance in relation to the family home in order to raise an equity in their favour. A representation will not give rise to a remedy if it is uncertain in its content. The relevant question is what the claimant would reasonably have understood the legal owner to mean by their words and acts.

A representation may give rise to a misapprehension on the part of a party which is not shared by the legal owner. Accordingly, unlike with a constructive trust there is no requirement for a common intention.

While an assurance from the legal owner as to some future rights in land can be express or impliedly made, such assurance, however, must be a sufficiently clear one; what was clear, however, depended upon the context. The court has to take a broad approach in order to establish whether it would be unconscionable for a party to renege on something which they had allowed or encouraged another individual to believe (*Thorner* v. *Major* [2009] UKHL 18 – the first case in which the House of Lords has upheld a claim for proprietary estoppel since 1866!).

Thus, the assurance has to be viewed contextually so that the relevant question is what the claimant would reasonably have understood the legal owner to mean by their words and acts:

> [The] promise must be unambiguous and must appear to have been intended to be taken seriously. Taken in its context, it must have been a promise which one might reasonably expect to be relied upon by the person to whom it was made.
>
> (*Walton* v. *Walton* (unreported) 14 April 1994)

For example, in *Bennett* v. *Bennett* (unreported) 18 May 1990, the Court of Appeal held that a mere verbal statement by the legal owner that he 'didn't want [the claimant] out' could not have been reasonably understood by her as an assurance that she could remain for the rest of her life. The statement simply suggested that the legal owner was prepared to let her stay in the property for the time being and that he would, therefore, have the right to ask her to leave on reasonable notice.

A similar conclusion was reached in *Bostock* v. *Bryant* (1990) 61 P&CR 23, where the claimant was told by her uncle: 'don't worry about the future, you'll be alright'. This was held by the Court of Appeal to be too vague to amount to an assurance that she could live in the house as long as she wished.

In *Horsford* v. *Horsford* [2020] EWHC 584 (Ch) no irrevocable assurances had been made to the claimant son. Statements that he would inherit had been equivocal. They could have been only statements of intention, with the defendant parents having authority and freedom to act how they thought best from time to time, and subject to issues of fairness and an approximation of equality between the siblings. Furthermore, he did not suffer any significant detriment in reliance on any assurance that he would inherit the farm, or his expectation to that effect.

Jennings v. *Rice* [2002] EWCA Civ 159 held that in cases where the claimant's expectations were uncertain, or where the court was not satisfied that the high level of the claimant's expectations was fairly derived from the assurances relied upon, the court could still take the claimant's expectations as a starting point.

However, it is not entirely clear what the court is to do with the expectation. Perhaps it can be mooted that where there is such ambiguity then that ambiguity should not deprive a person who reasonably relied on it (an objective test), but perhaps such relief should be accorded on the basis of the least beneficial interpretation.

2.5.3 Specified property

The assurance given must also relate to readily identified property.

To be entitled to a remedy based on proprietary estoppel, the person seeking such remedy must have an expectation of a 'certain interest in land' (*Yeomans Row Management Ltd* v. *Cobbe* [2008] UKHL 55).

For example, a promise made to give 'financial security during my life and financial security on my death' did not represent an assurance of having an interest in any particular asset (*Layton* v. *Martin* [1986] 2 FLR 227).

In *Coombes* v. *Smith* [1986] 1 WLR 808 an assurance given by the defendant to his female cohabitee that he would always 'provide her with a roof over her head' was held insufficient to constitute a representation that she was legally entitled to security of tenure against his wishes.

Similarly, a statement to the effect that the claimant would never want for anything was held insufficient to give rise to an estoppel (*Lissimore* v. *Downing* [2003] 2 FLR 308).

See also *James* v. *Thomas* [2007] EWCA Civ 1212, in which the phrases 'this will benefit us both' and 'you will be well provided for' were held not to constitute a promise of some property interest but merely a representation that the parties were making their life together as man and wife.

However, a promise that a person may be allowed to stay in a house for as long as he or she wishes raised or potentially raised an equity in that person's favour (*Greasley* v. *Cooke* [1981] 1 WLR 1306).

Equally, a promise that 'it'll all be yours one day' was regarded as sufficiently linked to the subject property to justify a claim to it by way of estoppel (*Wayling* v. *Jones* [1995] 2 FLR 1029).

In *Hammond* v. *Mitchell* [1991] 1 WLR 1127, the words spoken were: 'Don't worry about the future because when we are married, it will be half yours anyway and I'll always look after you'. These expressions were held to give rise to a common intention that the claimant was to be entitled to a beneficial share in the property registered in her male partner's sole name.

In *Southwell* v. *Blackburn* [2014] EWCA Civ 1347 the Court of Appeal held that the legal owner's assurance that the claimant 'would always have a home and be secure in this one' and that she 'would have the sort of security that a wife would have, in terms of accommodation at the house' was enough to support the finding that she would have security of rights of occupation in the house which would be recognised even in the event of the breakdown of the parties' relationship.

2.5.4 Detrimental reliance

Although detriment need not be financial, the claimant may fail if any benefits accruing to them as a consequence of the relationship outweigh the detriment suffered.

The concept of detriment in proprietary estoppel is not a narrow or technical one. The assurances relied upon do not have to be the sole inducement for the conduct; it is sufficient if they are an inducement:

> It is the detrimental reliance which makes the promise irrevocable and leads to the conclusion, at the end of a broad enquiry, that repudiation of the assurance is unconscionable.
>
> (*Southwell* v. *Blackburn* [2014] EWCA Civ 1347 at [20])

Whether the claimant suffered detriment must be judged at the point where the person who gave the assurance seeks to go back on it, and whether the detriment is sufficiently substantial must be judged by whether it would be unjust or inequitable to allow the assurance to be disregarded (*Davies* v. *Davies* [2014] EWCA Civ 568).

Davies v. *Davies* [2016] EWCA Civ 463 suggested that it would be a useful working hypothesis to use a sliding scale by which the clearer the expectation, the greater the detriment; and the longer the passage of time during which the expectation was reasonably held, the greater would be the weight that should be given to the expectation.

Whether there is detrimental reliance is an evaluative judgment. It has to be judged in the round.

Ultimately the question is whether, looking at all the relevant circumstances in the round, it would be unconscionable for the promise or assurance not to be kept.

In *Southwell* v. *Blackburn* [2014] EWCA Civ 1347 the detriment to the woman was that she had given up her secure home in which she had invested. It was the detrimental reliance which made the promise irreversible and led to the conclusion that, at the end of a broad enquiry, repudiation of the assurance was unconscionable.

2.5.5 Unconscionable conduct

Being an equitable remedy, proprietary estoppel is concerned with preventing unconscionable conduct and as such the court must look at the matter in the round.

Unconscionability permeates all the elements of proprietary estoppel rather than being a discrete feature of it.

2.5.6 Guidance from the Court of Appeal

Southwell v. *Blackburn* [2014] EWCA Civ 1347 reiterated the principles of proprietary estoppel as follows:

- a representation, if it is to found a claim in proprietary estoppel, must be clear and equivocal;

- the principle of proprietary estoppel requires a broad approach;
- the promise has to be of a right in relation to identified land;
- detriment is not a narrow or technical concept;
- detriment need not consist of the expenditure of money or other quantifiable financial detriment so long as it is something substantial;
- the evaluation of detriment to the promisee which is not exclusively financial is not an exercise in financial accounting;
- the need to show detriment must be approached as part of a broad enquiry as to whether repudiation of an assurance is or is not unconscionable in all the circumstances;
- unconscionability is not a watertight element in the estoppel but rather is a feature which permeates all its elements;
- there must be a sufficient causal link between the assurance relied on and the detriment asserted;
- the issue of detriment must be judged at the moment when the person who has given the assurance seeks to go back on it;
- whether the detriment is sufficiently substantial is to be tested by whether it would be unjust or inequitable to allow the assurance to be disregarded – that is, again, the essential test of unconscionability;
- the detriment alleged must be pleaded and proved:· proprietary estoppel does not look forward into the future and guess what might happen. It looks backwards from the moment when the promise falls due to be performed and asks whether, in the circumstances which have actually happened, it would be unconscionable for the promise not to be kept.

Davies v. *Davies* [2016] EWCA Civ 463, while pointing out that any case based on proprietary estoppel was fact-sensitive, set out a number of relevant legal propositions as follows:

1. The question of whether an equity has been raised and, if so, how to satisfy it, must be considered retrospectively from when the promise is due to be performed, and by asking whether it would be unconscionable for a promise not to be kept either wholly or in part.
2. The ingredients necessary to raise an equity are:

    - an assurance of sufficient clarity;
    - reliance by the claimant on that assurance; and
    - detriment to the claimant in consequence of their reasonable reliance.

3. No claim based on proprietary estoppel can be divided into distinct compartments. So, the quality of the assurances may influence the issue of reliance. Further, reliance and detriment are often intertwined, and, 'whether there is a distinct need for a "mutual understanding" may depend on how the other elements are formulated and understood'.
4. Detriment need not consist of a quantifiable financial detriment so long as it is something substantial. This issue must be approached as part of a 'broad

inquiry as to whether repudiation of an assurance is or is not unconscionable in all the circumstances'.

5. There must be a sufficient link between the assurance relied on and the detriment asserted. The question is whether (and if so to what extent) it would be unjust to allow the person who has given the assurance to go back on it. The essential test is that of unconscionability.
6. The essence is to do what is necessary to avoid an unconscionable result.
7. The court must weigh the detriment suffered against any benefits enjoyed as a consequence of the reliance.
8. Proportionality lies at the heart of the doctrine of proprietary estoppel, so that if the expectation is disproportionate to the detriment, the court should satisfy the equity in a more limited way.
9. In deciding how to satisfy the equity the court has to exercise a broad judgmental discretion, but the discretion is not unfettered and it must be exercised on a principled basis and does not entail what has been memorably called a 'portable palm tree'.

2.5.7 Inter-relationship between proprietary estoppel and trust law

We have already touched on this in relation to what was said in *Stack* v. *Dowden* regarding express declarations of trust:

> No one now doubts that such an express declaration of trust is conclusive *unless varied by subsequent agreement or affected by proprietary estoppel* [emphasis added].

Why would it be that an express declaration of trust could be overridden by proprietary estoppel?

Well, unlike trust law proprietary estoppel is an equitable remedy aimed at achieving justice for the wronged party and preventing the wrongdoer benefiting from their wrong.

In *Clarke* v. *Meadus* [2010] EWHC 3117 (Ch) the argument – that an express declaration within a deed was capable of being overridden by proprietary estoppel in favour of the claimant as a result of promises and representations made after the deeds were executed – was accepted.

Thus, formal documents setting out a party's beneficial interest are not immutable or incapable of being affected by subsequent events amounting to proprietary estoppel.

Is there any difference between how we approach cases of proprietary estoppel and constructive trust?

In *Oxley* v. *Hiscock* [2004] EWCA Civ 546, it was contended by Lord Justice Chadwick that to a large extent there was no difference between an argument based upon constructive trust as opposed to one based upon proprietary estoppel:

> Once it is recognised that what the court is doing in cases of this nature, is to supply or impute a common intention as to the parties' respective shares (in circumstances in which

> there was, in fact, no common intention) on the basis of that which, in the light of all the material circumstances (including the acts and conduct of the parties after the acquisition) is shown to be fair it seems to mee very difficult to avoid the conclusion that an analysis in terms of proprietary estoppel will necessarily lead to the same result; and that it may be more satisfactory to accept that there is no difference, in cases of this nature, between constructive trust and proprietary estoppel. (at [66])

However, in *Stack* v. *Dowden* [2007] 1 FLR 1858 Lord Walker disagreed:

> ... I am now rather less enthusiastic about the notion that proprietary estoppel and 'common interest' constructive trusts can or should be completely assimilated. Proprietary estoppel typically consists of asserting an equitable claim against the conscience of the 'true' owner. The claim is a 'mere equity'. It is to be satisfied by the minimum award necessary to do justice... which may sometimes lead to no more than a monetary award. A 'common intention' constructive trust by contrast is identifying the true beneficial owner or owners and the size of their beneficial interests. (at [37])

This has been further backed up in the case of *Q* v. *Q* [2008] EWHC 1974 (Fam) where it was held that proprietary estoppel and constructive trust remain distinct concepts as there is a significant difference between the nature of reliefs available under either concept.

Under proprietary estoppel the court has to decide 'the minimum equity to do justice' between the parties in the particular circumstances of the case (*Crabb* v. *Arun DC* [1976] Ch 179 at [198]) whereas a constructive trust leads to a declaration of beneficial ownership.

However, that said, in the circumstances of *Q* v. *Q* the relief under either doctrine produced the same result, much in the same way as in *Stack* v. *Dowden* under the respective doctrines of constructive and resulting trust (see **Chapter 3**).

See also *Yaxley* v. *Gotts* [2000] Ch 162; *Herbert* v. *Doyle* [2010] EWCA Civ 1095; *Thorner* v. *Major* [2009] UKHL 18; [2009] 1 WLR 776; *Farrar* v. *Miller* [2018] EWCA Civ 172.

2.5.8 Quantifying the award in a successful claim

As we have seen, proprietary estoppel requires a clear representation or assurance which is relied upon, and indeed in all the circumstances it is reasonable to rely upon, in consideration of which there has been detriment to the person so reliant of sufficient substance to justify an equitable remedy. There must also be a sufficient link between the promises relied upon and the conduct which constitutes the detriment.

Thus, the relevant comparison for the purposes of proportionality is a comparison between detriment and remedy. Expectation is not determinative of the relief to be granted, as the correct question to ask is whether the award is out of all proportion to the detriment, although it will be rare for a claimant to obtain more than their expectation (*Habberfield* v. *Habberfield* [2019] EWCA Civ 890):

> once the elements of proprietary estoppel are established an equity arises. The value of that equity will depend upon all the circumstances including the expectation and the detriment. The task of the court is to do justice. The most essential requirement is that there must be proportionality between the expectation and the detriment.
>
> (*Davies* v. *Davies* [2015] EWHC 1384 (Ch) at [49] quoting from *Jennings* v. *Rice* [2002] EWCA 159)

In summary:

- The value of the equity will depend upon (a) all the circumstances of the case, including (b) expectation and (c) detriment (*Jennings* v. *Rice* [2002] EWCA Civ 159).
- The court must balance the proportionality of the expectation with that of the detriment incurred.

'Proportionality lies at the heart of the doctrine of proprietary estoppel and permeates its every application' (*Henry* v. *Henry* [2010] UKPC 3 at [65]).

- When considering detriment this must be balanced against any relevant benefit enjoyed by the claimant. The court is not simply concerned with financial detriment but looks at all the circumstances in the round.
- When there is a clear understanding between the parties, falling short of a contract:

> In such a case the court's natural response is to fulfil the claimant's expectations. But if the claimant's expectations are uncertain, or extravagant, or out of all proportion to the detriment which the claimant has suffered, the court can and should recognise that the claimant's equity should be satisfied in another (and generally more limited) way.
>
> (*Henry* v. *Henry* [2010] UKPC 3 at [42] quoting from *Jennings* v. *Rice* [2002] EWCA 159)

In *Moore (By His Litigation Friend)* v. *Moore* [2018] EWCA Civ 2669 it was held that even if a case does display the 'consensual character falling not far short of an enforceable contract' (at [27] quoting from *Jennings* v. *Rice* [2002] EWCA 159), the court is still exercising an equitable discretion, which enables it to take into account a wide range of circumstances which may temper the outcome.

In essence, a successful claimant may be awarded the interest they believed they would acquire or, if the circumstances dictate, a lesser interest.

- The question of preventing unconscionable conduct permeates all considerations (*Gillett* v. *Holt* [2001] Ch 210).
- The end result must be a just one having regard to the assumption made by the party asserting the estoppel and the detriment which they have experienced (*Sledmore* v. *Dalby* (1996) 72 P&CR 196).

2.5.9 Practice points

The case of *Davies* v. *Davies* [2014] EWCA Civ 568 emphasised that proprietary estoppel claims require a holistic approach and that therefore split trials are not a good idea.

Furthermore, in many cases there is a clear tactical advantage of pleading, in addition to a main claim to a constructive trust, an alternative case based on proprietary estoppel, particularly if one may struggle in establishing a common intention.

2.6 RELINQUISHING A BENEFICIAL INTEREST

We have concentrated on circumstances where one is seeking to establish a beneficial interest in property; however, equally it is possible to enter into a document expressing the intention not to have such an interest, either at the outset of a transaction (an express declaration of non-beneficial interest) or at a later date.

Wallbank & Wallbank v. *Price* [2007] EWHC 3001 (Ch) is a case which illustrates how a party can relinquish their beneficial interest in a property (here with an informal written document). The assertion of undue influence as to relinquishment was rejected.

CHAPTER 3

Stack v. Dowden [2007] UKHL 17

3.1 INTRODUCTION

At the outset it must be emphasised that *Stack* v. *Dowden* was a joint names case where there was no express declaration of trust: had there been – as we have seen previously – the matter would not have reached what is now the Supreme Court at all.

It is also important to note that on the main issue before the court the conclusions of their Lordships were the same. However, the way in which they arrived at them was distinctly different.

Lord Neuberger (the minority view) chose the resulting trust route, whereas Baroness Hale and Lord Hope chose that of constructive trust as in their view one must take a '"holistic approach" to quantification, undertaking a survey of the whole course of dealing between the parties and taking account of all conduct which throws light on the question what shares were intended' (at [61] citing the Law Commission's paper on *Sharing Homes* (2002) at [4.27]). This approach would be more appropriate in the context of cohabitants and more properly reflective of the realities of what couples in close personal relationships would have in all probability intended, as opposed to a strict arithmetical approach based on financial contributions to the purchase price.

One possible outcome of this for practitioners is that if the resulting trust route achieves much the same result as would the constructive trust route, then the former is more likely to prove much more attractive and cost effective in terms of case preparation than the latter, as its arithmetical approach is clearly simpler than that of the more holistic constructive trust route.

However, be warned; one size does not necessarily fit all and much will depend upon the facts of the individual case.

To put it briefly, *Stack* v. *Dowden* can be broken down as follows:

1. First of all, a distinction must be drawn between those cases where the property is held in joint names and those where the property is held in the sole ownership of only one party.
2. One then has to determine where the burden of proof lies if a party wishes to assert that the beneficial ownership is different from the legal ownership:

> The onus is upon the person seeking to show that the beneficial ownership is different from the legal ownership. So in sole ownership cases it is upon the non-owner to show that he has any interest at all. In joint ownership cases, it is upon the joint owner who claims to have other than a joint beneficial interest. (at [56])

3. It is then for the party who is arguing that the beneficial interest is different from that shown on the legal title to prove it on the facts of the case.
4. In undertaking this task, the court must have regard to the *whole course of dealings* between the parties in relation to the property.

So, let us consider these issues in turn.

3.2 JOINT NAMES CASES

In joint names cases, the questions to be answered are as follows:

1. Did the parties intend their beneficial interests to be different from their legal interests?
2. If they did, in what way and to what extent?

Baroness Hale said at the outset:

> The issue before us is the effect of a conveyance into the joint names of a cohabiting couple, but without an explicit declaration of their respective beneficial interests, of a dwelling house which was to become their home. (at [40])

With respect to this it was said:

> ... at least in the *domestic consumer context*, a conveyance into joint names indicates both legal and beneficial joint tenancy, unless and until the contrary is proved [emphasis added]. (at [58])

Thus, the beneficial interest mirrors the legal interest and a presumption is created that if the legal title is shared equally then so must be the beneficial interest. Note the qualification as to the 'domestic' context as opposed to a business context.

Baroness Hale continues:

> The burden will therefore be on the person seeking to show that the parties did intend their beneficial interests to be different from their legal interests, and in what way. (at [68])

Lord Walker regarded this as:

> ... a considerable burden on whichever of them asserts that their beneficial interests are unequal, and do not follow the law. (at [14])

Furthermore, not only is such an evidential task 'not lightly to be embarked upon', but cases where such submissions succeed will be 'very unusual' (at [68]).

Thus, the court came to the following conclusions:

1. Where the property is in joint names the onus will be on the person seeking to show that the beneficial interest is different from the legal ownership.
2. This may be shown by ascertaining the parties' shared intentions (*'actual, inferred or imputed'*) in respect of the property in the light of their whole course of conduct in relation to it (per Baroness Hale at [60]).
3. It is preferable to pose the question as to what shares were *intended* rather than what is considered fair.
4. The parties' intentions can change over time.
5. The parties can be equal joint owners even though their financial contributions to the purchase were unequal.

A number of issues flow from this:

1. Firstly, there is reference to actual intentions, in other words that which is expressed orally. Then there are intentions that can be inferred from conduct. More controversially, there is also reference to intentions that can be imputed, as referenced in *Oxley*.
2. Secondly, the notion of fairness as propounded by *Oxley* is jettisoned, hence the fact that parties can be joint beneficial owners even though they may have contributed to the property in equal shares.

   Such a presumption in joint names cases is at odds with the presumption that arises under a resulting trust which now appears to be relegated to a remedy in cases where the property is in one person's name only (see **4.3**).
3. Thirdly, the parties' intentions are not set in stone. They can change over time, thus giving birth to the concept of an 'ambulatory constructive trust' which will be discussed later and which itself is ripe for extensive legal arguments.

Following on from this, *Fowler* v. *Barron* [2008] EWCA Civ 377 applied the presumption established in *Stack* v. *Dowden* to establish that a property acquired in joint names without any declaration of trust is to be treated as owned in equal shares, even though one party contributed far more in financial terms to the cost of the property than the other:

> Where there has been no express agreement, arrangement or understanding between the parties, the court has to search for their inferred common intention. In an ordinary domestic case, the conveyance of property into the parties' joint names suggests that the parties intended to be joint sharers of the property in the absence of cogent evidence to suggest otherwise, and therefore there is a strong presumption that their beneficial interests were intended to be equal. The burden rests on the party challenging that presumption to show that the parties should be taken to have intended that their beneficial interests should be different from their legal interests. (at [51])

> It provides a default rule that, unless and until the contrary is proved, joint tenants in this context are treated as joint legal and beneficial owners. If the contrary were not proved, the mere fact that the property was transferred into their joint names would be enough to give both parties an equal beneficial share. (at [34])

A clear warning, therefore, for those who deal with ordinary domestic conveyancing transactions.

The mere fact of placing a property in joint names, without an express declaration, is to create a strong presumption – in the absence of cogent evidence to the contrary – that the beneficial interests are held equally.

The mere fact that the parties have contributed to its acquisition in unequal shares will not normally be sufficient to rebut that presumption.

The onus therefore will be on the party asserting that the property is owned other than in equal shares to show, on the civil standard of proof, that they had a shared intention to own it in different shares. That onus, as we have seen, will not be an easy one to discharge.

In the case of *Adekunle* v. *Ritchie* [2007] EW Misc 5 the TR1 did not contain any express declaration of trust.

There was, however, a Form 62 restriction entered on the proprietorship register which in essence severed the joint tenancy. It read as follows (as per the normal entry in such circumstances):

> No disposition by one proprietor of the land (being the survivor of joint proprietors and not being a Trust corporation) under which capital money arises is to be registered except under an Order of the Registrar or the Court.

Although it was held that the restriction did not amount to an express declaration of trust (see *Huntingford* v. *Hobbs* [1993] 1 FLR 736) it was held that the restriction may be of some assistance in determining the intentions of the parties in light of their 'whole course of dealings'.

That case also reinforced the view that it would only be in 'very unusual' circumstances that the beneficial interest in the property would be found to be different from the legal interest, and therefore the normal course would be for the beneficial ownership to follow the legal ownership.

3.2.1 Investment property

We have seen the qualification that Baroness Hale referred to in relation to the presumption that applies to property acquired in the domestic consumer context.

However, the presumption of equal beneficial ownership has been held to be displaced in circumstances where the property was purchased not as a home but as an investment property (*Laskar* v. *Laskar* [2008] EWCA Civ 347; *Adekunle* v. *Ritchie* [2007] EW Misc 5) (i.e. in a commercial other than a domestic context as supported by Lord Hope in *Stack* v. *Dowden*).

In such circumstances, and in the absence of any relevant discussions between the parties to the contrary, it was held in *Laskar* that the proper approach was to determine the parties' respective beneficial shares, not by reference to constructive trust doctrine, but by a strict application of resulting trust theory:

> ... it would not be right to apply the reasoning in *Stack* v. *Dowden* to such a case as this, where the parties primarily purchased the property as an investment for rental income and capital appreciation, even where their relationship is a familial one. (at [17])

However, in *Marr* v. *Collie (Bahamas)* [2017] UKPC 17 it was held that the presumption that a conveyance into joint names indicates both legal and beneficial joint tenancy unless and until the contrary is proved should not be confined exclusively to a domestic setting.

In doing so, it held that *Laskar* was not authority for the proposition that the principle applies only in the domestic consumer context:

> Where a property is bought in the joint names of a cohabiting couple, even if that is as an investment, it does not follow inexorably that the 'resulting trust solution' must provide the inevitable answer as to how its beneficial ownership is to be determined. Lord Neuberger did not intend to draw a strict line of demarcation between, on the one hand, the purchase of a family home and, on the other, the acquisition of a so-called investment property in whatever circumstances that took place. It is entirely conceivable that partners in a relationship would buy, as an investment, property which is conveyed into their joint names with the intention that the beneficial ownership should be shared equally between them, even though they contributed in different shares to the purchase. Where there is evidence to support such a conclusion, it would be both illogical and wrong to impose the resulting trust solution on the subsequent distribution of the property. (at [49])

> ... save perhaps where there is no evidence from which the parties' true intentions can be identified, the answer is not provided by the triumph of one presumption over another. (at [54])

The answer lies in the context:

> If it is the unambiguous mutual wish of the parties, contributing in unequal shares to the purchase of property, that the joint beneficial ownership should reflect their joint legal ownership, then effect should be given to that wish. If, on the other hand, that is not their wish, or if they have not formed any intention as to beneficial ownership but had, for instance, accepted advice that the property be acquired in joint names, without considering or being aware of the possible consequences of that, the resulting trust solution may provide the answer. (at [54])

Of course, the initial intention (or lack thereof) at the time of purchase may change. That was the reason the House of Lords in *Stack* v. *Dowden* emphasised the examination of the whole course of conduct of the parties.

3.3 SOLE NAME CASES

In sole name cases, as with joint names cases, there are two questions which need to be answered. But in this case, they are as follows:

1. Was it intended that the parties should share the beneficial interest in a property which was conveyed to only one of them?

2. If it was so intended, in what proportions was it intended that they share the beneficial interest?

Again, the burden of proof lies with the party who wishes to show that the beneficial interest differs from the legal interest.

Thus, in sole name cases, a two-stage enquiry is normally required, as to: firstly, the existence of a beneficial interest and secondly, its extent.

This is to be contrasted with joint ownership cases as it is normally only the second-stage enquiry that needs to be undertaken, it having already been established, by the mere fact that a person's name is on the legal title, that they have a share; it is merely the quantum that may be in dispute.

With sole name cases, if the claimant falls at the first hurdle in establishing a share at the outset, then it's game over!

Where such a beneficial interest can be established, from a constructive trust perspective, the court adopted the formulation set out by Chadwick LJ in *Oxley* v. *Hiscock*, save that the attribute of 'fairness' was held not to be an appropriate yardstick in determining entitlement and was thus dispensed with:

> … the search is … for the result which … the parties must, in the light of their conduct, be taken to have *intended* … the court [may not] abandon that search in favour of the result which the court considers *fair* [emphasis added]. (at [61])

As with the quantification of the second question posed in joint ownership cases, one must:

> search … to ascertain the parties' shared intentions, *actual, inferred* or *imputed*, with respect to the property in the light of their *whole course of conduct in relation to it* [emphasis added]. (at [60])

Neuberger LJ was himself unhappy with the phrase used in *Oxley* as to 'the whole course of dealing … in relation to the property'.

He felt that it was too limited and imprecise, as it gave insufficient focus to dealings which cast light on the beneficial ownership, and the fact that all aspects of the relationship can be relevant in the court's assessment of the parties' intentions. He felt that the court should:

> undertake a survey of the whole course of dealing between the parties … taking account of all conduct which throws light on the question what shares were intended. (at [145])

Thus, many more factors other than financial contributions may be relevant in determining the parties' true intentions.

Thus, Lord Bridge's dicta in *Lloyds Bank* v. *Rosset* – that where there is no evidence of the parties having reached an agreement as to their intentions but a common intention may be inferred from their conduct, and that only direct contributions to the payment of the mortgage will suffice – is no longer a correct statement of the law.

The rationale in *Stack* v. *Dowden* was subsequently followed in the Privy Council decision of *Abbott* v. *Abbott* [2008] 1 FLR 1451 where it endorsed the view set out in *Stack* v. *Dowden* at [34] that the court should take:

a wide view of what is capable of counting as a contribution towards the acquisition of a residence, while remaining sceptical of the value of alleged improvements that are really insignificant, or elaborate arguments (suggestive of creative accounting) as to how the family finances were arranged. Lord Walker went as far as to say that he 'would include contributions in kind by way of manual labour, provided that they are significant'. (at [36])

Thus – and this is where there is an advantage over the resulting trust method – a relatively small contribution can result in a not insubstantial share on a constructive trust basis.

Having said this, Rimer LJ in *Thompson* v. *Hurst* [2011] EWCA Civ 537, when granting permission to appeal, queried how far a claimant has to go to establish an interest if they have made no direct financial contribution to the deposit or the mortgage in sole ownership cases.

3.4 IMPUTATION

Neuberger LJ in *Stack* v. *Dowden*, while accepting that an intention may be inferred, rejected the concept of imputing an intention:

> An inferred intention is one which is objectively deduced to be the subjective actual intention of the parties, in the light of their actions and statements. An imputed intention is one which is attributed to the parties, even though no such actual intention can be deduced from their actions and statements, and even though they had no such intention. Imputation involves concluding what the parties would have intended, whereas inference involves concluding what they did intend. (at [126])

It involves:

> a hypothetical negotiation between the actual parties, or what reasonable parties would have agreed. (at [127])

Thus, although the court can legitimately 'infer' a common intention from the actions and behaviour of co-owners, to 'impute' an intention is to attribute to the parties something which cannot be deduced from their statements or actions.

In *Kernott* v. *Jones* [2010] EWCA Civ 578 the reference of Baroness Hale to 'imputation' was further questioned on the basis that the court cannot invent an 'intention' where one cannot be inferred:

> I accordingly do not myself interpret *Stack* as having intended to enable the courts to find, by way of the imputation route, an intention where none was expressly uttered nor inferentially formed. (at [77])

Of course, that leaves open the question as to what to do in such an eventuality, i.e. where there is no actual express or inferred common intention. Must we resort to the equitable remedy of proprietary estoppel?

Furthermore, is not the resulting trust doctrine imputing an intention that the parties themselves may never have intended in respect of their respective shares? (For answers to this see the Supreme Court decision of *Jones* v. *Kernott* at **Chapter 4**.)

3.5 FAIRNESS

Following *Stack* v. *Dowden*, *Fowler* v. *Barron* [2008] EWCA Civ 377 further emphasised that in determining disputes concerning beneficial interests in property the court's role was not to determine what was fair but to determine the parties' shared intentions – actual, inferred or imputed – with regard to the property in the light of their whole course of conduct in respect of it.

This was reiterated in the case of *Morris* v. *Morris* [2008] EWCA Civ 257 where again it was held that the court's task was not to find a fair outcome for the parties but to ascertain the outcome which reflects what they must themselves have intended. The court was to take a holistic view of the party's conduct so far as it illuminated their shared intentions about the ownership of the property.

Such conduct included, but was not limited to, the financial contributions the parties made towards the acquisition of the property or the repayment of any loan raised for such purpose:

> in a family context, many more factors than financial contributions may be relevant to defining the parties' true intentions [including] ... the reasons why the home was acquired in the joint names, the purpose for which the home was acquired, the nature of their relationship and whether they had children for whom they had a shared responsibility to provide a home.
>
> (*Fowler* v. *Barron* [2008] EWCA Civ 377 at [56])

However, *Laskar* v. *Laskar* is interesting in that while commenting that although 'fairness' is not the basis upon which the court reaches a decision in these kinds of cases, it held that it was not unhelpful to see whether the outcome arrived at seemed unjust (perhaps not dissimilar to the approach in matrimonial cases in relation to the yardstick of equality and the overarching aim of fairness):

> It is sensible to stand back and see whether that looks a fair result ... it does seem to me that it is not unhelpful to see whether the outcome ... seems unjust, because if it is, it may be worth revisiting the reasoning. (at [33])

However, in the case of *Hameed* v. *Qayyum* [2009] EWCA Civ 352 it was held that in determining the necessary common intention to give rise to a constructive trust, the court had to consider the result that the parties must have intended to achieve as opposed to what might have been considered fair.

Again, in *Thomson* v. *Humphrey* [2010] 2 FLR 107 Warren J made it clear that cases of this nature have to be determined on strict legal principles, not by imposing some standard of fairness. A claimant who seeks to establish a beneficial interest must show that it was intended that they should have a share:

> Whether the conclusion I have reached is one that could be seen subjectively or objectively as fair or not, is not a matter for this court. That is a matter for law reform.

The issue I had with *Stack* v. *Dowden* is this: while I can understand that the court can find an actual intention as expressed between the parties as to their beneficial interests which may lend itself to an unfair outcome, this is less the case when one goes down the route of inference or imputation. Is a court really going to infer or impute an intention as to the sharing of the beneficial interest which on the face of it appears unfair?

The answer to this will have to await that of *Jones* v. *Kernott* (see **Chapter 4**).

3.6 A NON-EXHAUSTIVE CHECKLIST

In *Stack* v. *Dowden* Baroness Hale helpfully sets out a non-exhaustive checklist as to what to look out for in arriving at a determination as to the parties' intentions:

1. Advice given at the time of transfer

This is where the conveyancing file comes into its own. Hopefully, the conveyancer at the time of instructions would have kept contemporaneous attendance notes and letters setting out comprehensively the advice given and the instructions received.

It goes without saying that instructions provided in consequence of advice given and set out in such attendance notes will prove critical in establishing the intentions of the co-owners as to how they intended to share their beneficial interests.

Such attendance notes and correspondence will inevitably be among the documents included in any trial bundle.

2. Discussions shedding light on intentions

This is, of course, a key facet of a constructive trust based upon express discussions. However, not only do such discussions have to be proved to have taken place, but there is also the issue of context and interpretation.

The case of *James* v. *Thomas* [2008] 1 FLR 1598 provides an example of how communications between the parties during the 'whole course of dealing' between them can be open to interpretation.

In this specific case statements that the improvements to the property would 'benefit them both' made at a time when the parties were living together as husband and wife, and when it was intended that they would do so for the foreseeable future, were held could be interpreted as meaning that the improvements would be reflected in an improvement to their quality of life as opposed to an acknowledgment of a proprietary interest.

Similarly, the defendant's representation that the claimant would be well provided for in the event of their death was held not to be a representation as to proprietary entitlement in the property but a representation as to what would be the position after the defendant's death on the assumption that they were still living together at that time.

What of excuses as to why the property is not vested in joint names?

On this subject *Curran* v. *Collins* [2015] EWCA Civ 404 said this:

> … it cannot be right that the giving of a reason why someone is not on the title deeds inevitably leads to the inference that it must have been agreed that they would have an interest in the property. (at [69])
>
> … the mere giving of a 'specious excuse' necessarily or even usually leads to an inference that the person to whom the excuse is given can reasonably regard herself as having an immediate entitlement to an interest in the property in question. (at [74])

Thus, whether it is reasonable to draw the inference of a common intention depends on all the circumstances, and an excuse will not be held to be inferential evidence of the requisite intention unless the inference is one that can reasonably be drawn by the person to whom the statement is made.

3. Reasons for purchasing in joint names

4. Any reason for a joint tenancy being preferred

5. Purpose for which the home is acquired

6. Nature of the parties' relationship

It must be emphasised that in cohabitant disputes the court is not concerned with issues such as the welfare of any dependent children or the needs of the respective parties as is the case under the Matrimonial Causes Act 1973.

Indeed, as indicated previously, the court is not concerned as to what may or may not be fair as between the parties as to their respective beneficial interests, but is concerned solely as to the parties' intentions and dealings between them which have a bearing on those intentions.

7. Whether there are any children for whom the home is provided

This is relevant in so far as the Trusts of Land and Appointment of Trustees Act (TOLATA) 1996, s.15(1)(b) and (c) is concerned (see **Chapter 6**) and may be relevant not only as to the issue as to whether or not the property should be sold pursuant to s.14 of the Act but also as a possible indicator in so far as the question of the parties' intentions is concerned as to the way the property was intended to be held:

> The court, in executing the trust should regard the primary object as being to provide a home and not a sale. Steps should be taken to preserve it as a home for the remaining partner and children but giving the outgoing partner such compensation, by way of a charge or being bought out, as is reasonable in the circumstances.
>
> (*Williams* v. *Williams* [1976] Ch 278 at [285])

See also *Re Evers Trust* [1980] 1 WLR 1327.

8. Financing of the purchase

Under the resulting trust solution, in any assessment of a claim for a declaration as to the extent of the parties' interest in a property, the respective financial contributions of each of them will be conclusive unless there is evidence to the contrary to shift that presumption.

An audit trail will need to be provided as to the financing of the purchase, together with documentary evidence (e.g. bank accounts and the completion statement located on the conveyancing file).

9. Financing of other major expenditure on the property

This area is not without difficulty.

Subsequent substantial improvement by one of the parties to the property may on its own create or enhance a beneficial share even in the absence of any financial contribution to the initial purchase or subsequent mortgage instalments (see *Bernard* v. *Josephs* [1982] 1 Ch 391; *Burns* v. *Burns* [1984] FLR 216; *Passee* v. *Passee* [1988] 1 FLR 263; *Pettitt* v. *Pettitt* [1970] AC 777):

> indirect contributions, such as making improvements which added significant value to the property ... ought to be taken into account as well as financial contributions made directly towards the purchase of the property. (*Stack* at [12])

This leads to the contention that the shares as originally proposed at the outset of the purchase of the property have subsequently been altered due to a subsequent significant and substantial contribution to improvement work. As Baroness Hale states:

> There may also be reason to conclude that, whatever the parties' intentions at the outset, these have now changed. An example might be where one party has financed (or constructed himself) an extension or substantial improvement to the property, so that what they have now is significantly different from what they had then. (at [70])

As previously mentioned, this gives rise to the concept of an ambulatory constructive trust, for which see *Jones* v. *Kernott* at **Chapter 4**.

This will, of course, need to be substantiated by corroborative evidence, including bank statements as to the financing of the same, and valuation evidence to show the variation in value attributable to the work undertaken.

On the issue of subsequent improvements courts tend to take an 'added value' approach to the valuation of a party's share: namely, to ascertain the value of the property at the date immediately preceding the making of the improvement and then to identify what addition to the value of the property was due to that improvement. The share of the party who made the improvement should then be treated as enlarged by a proportionate amount corresponding to the increase in value represented by the improvement (*Re Nicholson (deceased): Nicholson* v. *Perks* [1974] 1 WLR 476). (This is a type of resulting trust calculation but based on value output as opposed to contribution input; also contrast the calculation in *Re Pavlou* [1993] 2 FLR 751 – equitable accounting.)

In the case of *James* v. *Thomas* [2008] 1 FLR 1598, while accepting that common intention as to beneficial shares in property necessary to found a constructive trust can be inferred from evidence of the parties' conduct during the 'whole course of dealings' in relation to the property – and that such common intention could be formed any time before, after or during the acquisition of the property itself – in the absence of an express post-acquisition agreement it was held that the court would be slow to infer from conduct alone that the parties intended to vary their beneficial interest established at the time of the initial acquisition and as was said in *Morris* v. *Morris* [2008] EWCA Civ 257 at [25]:

> the court should be cautious before finding that the activities of a wife or a cohabitant can only be explained on the footing that she believes that she was acquiring an interest in land.

This case therefore clearly follows the more restrictive approach in *Lloyds Bank plc* v. *Rosset* [1990] 2 FLR 155 where it was stated that express discussions as to shared ownership had to occur prior to the acquisition of the property itself, and that those occurring at a later date could only be considered in exceptional cases.

Accordingly, any inference of agreement as to post-acquisition change of ownership will not readily be drawn from conduct alone in the absence of evidence of an express agreement.

This was further supported in the case of *Mirza* v. *Mirza* [2009] EWHC 3 (Ch) where again it was reiterated that a claim under a resulting or constructive trust has to be founded on the actual or *imputed* intention of the parties. In the absence of an express post-acquisition agreement, the court would be slow to infer from conduct alone that the parties intended to vary existing beneficial interests established at the time of acquisition.

Indeed, in *Stack* v. *Dowden* Lord Neuberger opined that compelling evidence was required to infer change, and such evidence would normally 'involve discussions, statements or actions subsequent to the acquisition' (at [138]).

The issue as to beneficial interests under a joint tenancy changing over time was dealt with more comprehensively in the case of *Kernott* v. *Jones* [2010] EWCA Civ 578.

The key question in this case was as follows:

> Where; (1) an unmarried couple has acquired residential accommodation in joint names, which by common agreement was held by them beneficially in equal shares as at the date of their separation, and; (2) one party ... thereafter; (a) continues to live in the property; and; (b) assumes sole responsibility for its continuing acquisition and maintenance ... can the court properly infer an agreement post separation that the parties' beneficial interests in the property alter. (at [6])

In that case a couple purchased a property as joint tenants (albeit with no express declaration of trust). The relationship ended. The man moved out and purchased a house in his name, for which he was solely responsible. The woman remained in occupation of the property and was solely responsible for it for 15 years! (presumably so that she could continue to provide a home for the dependent children). The man thereafter claimed his share in the property.

It was common ground that the beneficial interests in the jointly owned property were held in equal shares. The live issue before the court was, however, whether – and if so to what extent – the parties' respective interests in the property were changed thereafter.

In the High Court (on appeal from the County Court) Nicholas Strauss QC held (following HHJ Dedman in the court below) that the conduct of the parties following the breakdown of their relationship did show that their intentions had changed (or could be taken as having changed) since they purchased the property due to a substantial change in circumstances (as opposed to the rules applicable to equitable accounting (see **Chapter 5**)).

After the split the parties had maintained separate finances to an even more marked degree than the couple in *Stack* v. *Dowden* and the judge inferred from those facts that they no longer intended equal beneficial ownership. The presumption of equal beneficial ownership between joint tenants was therefore rebutted.

In the absence of any express declaration as to how the shares in the beneficial interest had changed, it was therefore open to the court to decide what was fair and reasonable and it accordingly awarded a larger share to the woman based upon the facts in this case (note the reference to fairness (see **3.5**)):

> Whatever the beneficial interests may be at the time of acquisition, a trust may be 'ambulatory' i.e. the intentions of the parties as regards their interests in the property may change, or be taken as having changed, over time ... But ... there is little guidance ... as to the circumstances in which the presumption of equality will be displaced or how, if it is, the altered amounts are to be assessed.
>
> (*Jones* v. *Kernott* [2009] EWHC 1713 (Ch) at [26])

Thus, while the court cannot override the stated intention of the parties and impose its own views (irrespective of the notion of fairness), where those intentions are not expressed the court can impute what those intentions might be by deciding what is fair and just:

> In my view, what the majority in *Stack* held was only that the court should not override the intention of the parties, in so far as that appears from what they have said or from their conduct, in favour of what the court itself considers to be fair ... the court must not impose its view. (at [30]) ... To the extent that the intention of the parties cannot be inferred, the court is free ... to impute a common intention to the parties. Imputing an intention involves ... attributing to the parties an intention which they did not have, or at least did not express to each other. The intention is one which the parties 'must be taken' to have had. It is difficult to see how this process can work, without the court supplying, to the extent that the intention of the parties cannot be deduced from their words or conduct, what the court considers to be fair. In particular ... if there is evidence of conduct from which it is right to conclude that the parties intended their respective shares to alter ... but

> none to indicate how, the only available criterion by which to assess the extent of the alteration is what is objectively fair, and the only available judge of that is the court. (at [31])
>
> In my view, despite the absence of any communication by either party to the other of any actual intention, the judge was right to impute to the parties an intention that their beneficial interests should be altered to take account of changes in the circumstances from how they stood at the time that they parted, and that, in the absence of any indication by words or conduct as to how they should be altered, the appropriate criterion was what he considered to be fair and just. The parties' interests were 'ambulatory' … (at [49])

Thus, since the parties had no discernible intentions as to the amount of the adjustment, they had to be taken to have intended that it should be whatever was fair and reasonable or just.

So the reference in *Stack* v. *Dowden* [2007] UKHL 17, [2007] 2 AC 432 to the intentions of the parties being 'actual, inferred or imputed' indicated that it was open to the court to attribute to the parties a common intention that they did not have, or at least had not expressed to each other.

The Court of Appeal, however, followed *Stack* v. *Dowden* in holding that there was nothing indicative as to there being a common intention to displace the presumption of the parties' initial interests being equal, by virtue of the fact that the property was initially conveyed in the parties' joint names. A full examination of the facts would be unlikely to lead to a result different from the legal title unless those facts were very unusual. The mere passage of time was insufficient to do so.

Such an intention had to be expressed or inferred but could not be imputed; the imposition of an objectively perceived 'fair' solution was not an available option in TOLATA 1996 claims which offer merely a declaratory remedy:

> If this appellant and this respondent had truly intended that the appellant's beneficial interest in the property should reduce post separation, or if the property was to belong to the respondent when the appellant acquired his own house, they should have so decided and acted accordingly by adjusting their beneficial interests in the property. (at [62])

Interestingly, Rimer LJ provided quite a cogently argued critique of *Stack* v. *Dowden* as follows:

(a) The presumption of equal beneficial ownership and the 'heavy burden' required to discharge it meant that:

> … a bid by a joint purchaser to establish a greater beneficial interest than a joint interest will involve the steepest of climbs, usually resulting in a failure to attain the summit. (at [72])

However, in *Stack* v. *Dowden* the shares ascribed to the parties provided a departure from equality (65:35) on the basis that the facts of the case were 'exceptional' because the parties had kept their finances separate and there were greater contributions from one of the parties. Rimer LJ questioned how such facts of themselves made the case exceptional.

(b) Furthermore, in *Stack* v. *Dowden*:

> The search is to ascertain the parties' shared intentions, actual, inferred or imputed, with respect to the property in the light of their whole course of conduct in relation to it. (at [60])

In relation to this Rimer LJ observed:

> In most cases such a quest may well be elusive, because if the parties actually had any such intention, they would have voiced it; and if they did not voice it, that will probably be because they did not have one, with the consequence that there will be no basis for inferring otherwise. (at [76]) ... it is possible that she was suggesting ... the court to ascribe to the parties an intention that they neither expressed nor inferentially had: in other words, that the court can invent an intention for them. That, however, appears unlikely, since it is inconsistent with Baroness Hale's repeated reference to the fact that the goal is to find the parties' intentions, which must mean their real intentions. (at [77])

In his view the court has no jurisdiction to 'impute' an intention that the parties did not in reality have.

Thus, another seminal case went to the Supreme Court on 4 May 2011 in order to clarify and develop the reasoning in *Stack* v. *Dowden*, the key questions being:

- Was there sufficient evidence from which the trial judge could infer that the parties held the beneficial interest other than jointly?
- If so, was the trial judge entitled to *infer* or *impute* that the parties held the equity in particular proportions?

Other considerations included the issue of fairness in so far as its inter-relationship with imputation is concerned if there is insufficient evidence to draw any inference as to the parties' intentions as derived from their conduct.

A side issue was also whether the 'whole course of dealings' between the parties when looking at their conduct should be restricted to their course of dealings in relation to the property or if a wider approach should be taken (see *Oxley* v. *Hiscock* and Neuberger LJ's views in *Stack* v. *Dowden*), and could such a trust be ambulatory (that is, capable of variation over time) and if so in what circumstances.

There was also the question of what, if any, the role of equitable accounting played in the particular circumstances of the case (see **4.4**).

10. How the parties arranged their finances

It may be that the way in which the parties have arranged their finances during their relationship also provides an indication as to their intentions concerning their share of the beneficial ownership.

In *Stack* v. *Dowden*, for instance, the fact that the parties kept their finances separate added to the suggestion that they did not intend their beneficial interests in the property to be equal, notwithstanding the fact that the property was held jointly.

11. Responsibility for the discharge of the mortgage and outgoings on the house

While repayments of mortgage instalments may be of minor significance and in themselves may not be sufficient to establish a beneficial interest if they can be explained away – for example as payments in lieu of rent – payments (particularly those of a substantial capital payment) to reduce the mortgage capital may be interpreted differently so as to indicate a change of intention between the parties as to their beneficial shares.

12. Mercenary considerations

The post-*Stack* v. *Dowden* case of *Laskar* v. *Laskar* [2008] EWCA Civ 347 held that in the particular circumstances of that case the primary purpose of the purchase was not in the 'domestic consumer context' but in a commercial 'investment property' context.

Accordingly, it was held that it would not be right to apply the reasoning in *Stack* v. *Dowden* to a case where the parties primarily purchased the property as an investment for rental income and capital appreciation, even where the relationship was a familial one (in that case mother and daughter). Even if the presumption were to apply it was held in that case that the presumption would have been rebutted given the circumstances.

In *Erlam* v. *Rahman* [2016] EWHC 111 (Ch) the principles of *Stack* v. *Dowden* were not applied because it was not a 'domestic' case; the properties were acquired for investment purposes and therefore the court applied the stricter resulting trust analysis.

Has this therefore opened the door for future arguments, with one party attempting to assert that the transaction is a commercial venture as opposed to a purely domestic one and vice versa in order to provide justification one way or another to depart from or to adhere to the constructive trust regime propounded by *Stack* v. *Dowden*? (Contrast, however, *Agarwala* v. *Agarwala* [2013] EWCA Civ 1763.)

However, in *Wodzicki* v. *Wodzicki* [2017] EWCA Civ 95 it was held that the resulting trust principles should apply even though this was a non-commercial situation, as there was nothing close about the relationship between the parties in this matter despite their being members of the same family.

Conversely, *Marr* v. *Collie (Bahamas)* [2017] UKPC 17 (see **3.2.1**) held that if it is the unambiguous mutual wish of the parties, contributing in unequal shares to the purchase of property, that the joint beneficial ownership should reflect their joint legal ownership, then effect should be given to that wish.

If, however, that is not their wish, or if they have not formed any intention as to beneficial ownership, but had accepted advice that the property be acquired in joint names, without considering or being aware of the possible consequences of that, the resulting trust solution may provide the answer.

The presumption that a conveyance into joint names indicates both legal and beneficial joint tenancy unless and until the contrary is proved should not be confined exclusively to a domestic setting, although if the conveyance occurs where the parties are only involved in a personal relationship, that would make it easier to infer that such was the intention.

The intention of the parties is still a crucial factor where there is a commercial dimension to the acquisition of the property. Where additional evidence is available in the form of testimony from the parties themselves as to their intentions when the property was acquired, this can rebut the presumption of a resulting trust.

Where a property is bought in the joint names of a cohabiting couple, even if that is as an investment, it does not follow inexorably that the resulting trust solution must provide the inevitable answer as to how its beneficial ownership is to be determined.

CHAPTER 4

Jones v. Kernott [2011] UKSC 53

4.1 INTRODUCTION

The appeal to the Supreme Court gave it the opportunity to revisit the decision of *Stack* v. *Dowden* [2007] UKHL 17.

At the outset, the Supreme Court reiterated the presumption of joint beneficial ownership in cases where a property is owned in the parties' joint names.

In cases where the property is in joint names:

> The presumption is that the parties intended a joint tenancy both in law and in equity. But that presumption can of course be rebutted by evidence of a contrary intention, which may more readily be shown where the parties did not share their financial resources. (at [25])

In relation to cases where the property is held in the name of only one party:

> The first issue is whether it was intended that the other party have any beneficial interest in the property at all. If he does, the second issue is what that interest is. There is no presumption of joint beneficial ownership. But their common intention has once again to be deduced objectively from their conduct. (at [52])

See *Oxley* v. *Hiscock* [2004] EWCA Civ 546 at **2.4**.

Such a presumption was justified on the basis that:

- Purchasing property in joint names indicates an 'emotional and economic commitment to a joint enterprise' (at [19]).
- There are practical difficulties in analysing respective contributions to the property over long periods of cohabitation ('whole course of dealing').
- It is to be expected that joint transferees would have spelled out their beneficial interests if they intended them to be different from their legal interests, and cases in which the burden will be discharged will be very unusual (a trap for sloppy conveyancing transactions).

This presumption, however, may be rebutted by evidence that it was not, *or ceased to be* (ambulatory constructive trust), the common intention of the parties to hold the property jointly (e.g. by not sharing their financial resources as in *Stack* v. *Dowden*).

It seems that following this decision the court will be more readily prepared to infer this where (as in *Stack* v. *Dowden*) the parties do not share, or mingle, their financial resources.

In the absence, however, of clear evidence of intention, a question arises as to when the court can infer such intention and when the court can, instead, impute an intention.

As previously outlined, an inference is drawn where an actual intention is objectively deduced from the dealings and conduct of the parties; an imputation is one attributed to the parties by the court itself having regard to the 'whole course of dealing' between the parties.

The Supreme Court emphasised, however, that the search is primarily to ascertain the parties' actual intentions, express or inferred, but if it is clear that the beneficial interests are shared – but impossible to infer a common intention as to the proportions in which they are shared – the court will have to impute an intention to the parties which they may never have had.

Thus, the Supreme Court has now confirmed that where it is not possible to determine the parties' intentions as to quantification of their beneficial ownership by way of actual express intentions made orally one to the other, or inferred from their conduct, judges can impute an intention based on a 'fair' outcome.

From this the following principles can be derived:

1. The starting point where a family home is bought in joint names is that the parties own the property as joint tenants in law and equity in equal shares, i.e. equity follows the law; in sole name cases, however, there is no such presumption as to such sharing (see *Oxley* v. *Hiscock* [2005] Fam Law 211).
2. That presumption can be displaced by showing:
   - that the parties had a different common intention at the time when they acquired the home; or
   - that they later formed the common intention that their respective shares would change (ambulatory constructive trust).
3. Common intention, if it can be inferred, is to be objectively deduced from the conduct and dealings between the parties:

   > ... the relevant intention of each party is the intention which was reasonably understood by the other party to be manifested by that party's words or conduct notwithstanding that he did not consciously formulate that intention in his own mind or even acted with some different intention which he did not communicate to the other party.
   >
   > (Lord Diplock in *Gissing* v. *Gissing* [1971] AC 886 at [906])

4. Where it is clear that they:
   - had a different intention at the outset; or
   - had changed their original intention, but it is not possible to ascertain

by direct evidence, or by inference, an actual intention as to their respective shares;

then the court is entitled to impute an intention that each is entitled to have that share:

> which the court considers fair having regard to the whole course of dealing between them in relation to the property. (at [51])

'The whole course of dealing … in relation to the property' should be given a broad meaning, enabling a similar range of factors to be taken into account as may be relevant to ascertaining the parties' actual intentions (thus confirming the wider interpretation of the phrase and the matters to be taken into account).

5. Each case will turn on its own facts; financial contributions are relevant but there are many other factors which may enable the court to decide what shares were either intended or fair (see **3.5**).

The starting point, therefore, must always be what the parties actually intended themselves, irrespective of the concept of fairness. The court cannot impose a solution which is contrary to what the evidence shows that they actually intended.

On the facts of the case the court relied on the finding of fact at first instance that the parties' intentions as regards the property had changed after their separation; as such, therefore, there was no need for the court to impute an intention to the parties.

4.2 INFERENCE VERSUS IMPUTATION

The judgment also contains a historical derivation of the concepts of inference and imputation:

> Unless it is possible to infer from the conduct of the spouses at the time of their concerted action in relation to acquisition or improvement of the family asset that they did form an actual common intention as to the legal consequences of their acts upon the proprietary rights in the asset the court must impute to them a constructive common intention which is that which in the court's opinion would have been formed by reasonable spouses.
>
> (*Pettitt* v. *Pettitt* [1970] AC 777 at [823])

Reasonable spouses will intend only what is fair:

> … there is a wide gulf between inferring from the whole conduct of the parties that there probably was an agreement, and imputing to the parties an intention to agree to share even where the evidence gives no ground for such an inference. If the evidence shows that there was no agreement in fact then that excludes any inference that there was an agreement. But it does not exclude an imputation of a deemed intention if the law permits such an imputation.
>
> (*Gissing* v. *Gissing* [1971] AC 886 at [897])

(See also the earlier analysis of *Jones* v. *Kernott* while in the High Court at **3.6**.)

In *Jones* v. *Kernott* in the Supreme Court the majority expressed the view that, despite their conceptual differences, there was no real practical difference between inferring and imputing (Lady Hale, Lord Walker, Lord Collins):

> Subjective intentions can never be accessed directly, so the court must always direct itself to a consideration of the parties' objective intentions through a careful consideration of the relevant facts. The point is that the imputation/inference distinction may well be a distinction without a difference with regard to the process of determining parties' intentions. It is not that the parties' subjective intentions are irrelevant but rather that a finding as to subjective intention can only be made on an objective basis.
>
> (at [34] quoting from an article by Nick Piska, 'Intention, Fairness and the Presumption of Resulting Trust after *Stack* v *Dowden*' (2008) 71 MLR 120)

Lord Collins succinctly put it thus: 'one person's inference will be another person's imputation' and it would be difficult to imagine a scenario where in the absence of an express agreement the court would infer a shared or common intention which is unfair.

In my respectful view this has to be correct. Consider the following:

- A finding of express discussions as to what the parties' intentions are in relation to their beneficial shares is exactly that, a finding based on the actual evidence as to who said what irrespective of whether the outcome is fair.
- An inference as to beneficial shares based on conduct entails the court putting itself in the shoes of the parties and deciding what they did in fact intend. However, as the court is yet to be gifted with retrospective telepathy this is a judgment call and clearly the court is unlikely to reach a decision which on the facts is manifestly unfair as that would undoubtedly lead to an appeal.
- Similarly, with imputation, how can one really categorically infer what the parties' unspoken intentions were unless the evidence is clear? Isn't imputation basically inference from the opposite angle, two sides of the same judicial coin? That is, a court looks at the conduct of the parties over the whole course of dealing and draws out of it what it thinks the parties must have intended, applying the concept of what is perceived as being fair, and by applying its own objective analysis of the parties' subjective intentions. Is it not that what happens in judge-craft is that inference and imputation meet somewhere in the middle?

The minority disagreed (Lord Kerr, Lord Wilson).

Lord Kerr pointed out that it was somewhat artificial to say an intention is being imputed when what the court is actually doing is deciding what is fair in light of the whole course of dealing with the property, which is wholly unrelated to ascertainment of the parties' intentions. The parties will almost certainly never have had that intention at all.

He thought it would be better to say that if an intention cannot be deduced from the parties' conduct, then the court will divide the beneficial interests to achieve a fair result without reference to what the parties intended or would/should have intended.

However, he conceded that the 'language of imputing intention has entered the lexicon of this area of law and it is probably impossible to discard it now'.

Lord Kerr was also concerned that the concept of inferring intention should not be strained:

> It is hardly controversial to suggest that the parties' intention should be given effect to where it can be ascertained and that, although discussions between them will always be the most reliable basis on which to draw an inference as to that intention, these are not the only circumstances in which that exercise will be possible. There is a natural inclination to prefer inferring an intention to imputing one. If the parties' intention can be inferred, the court is not imposing a solution. It is, instead, deciding what the parties must be taken to have intended and where that is possible it is obviously preferable to the courts enforcing a resolution. But the conscientious quest to discover the parties' actual intention should cease when it becomes clear either that this is simply not deducible from the evidence or that no common intention exists. It would be unfortunate if the concept of inferring were to be strained so as to avoid the less immediately attractive option of imputation. In summary, therefore, I believe that the court should anxiously examine the circumstances in order, where possible, to ascertain the parties' intention but it should not be reluctant to recognise, when it is appropriate to do so, that inference of an intention is not possible and that imputation of an intention is the only course to follow. (at [72]) …
>
> As soon as it is clear that inferring an intention is not possible, the focus of the court's attention should be squarely on what is fair and, as I have said, that is an obviously different examination than is involved in deciding what the parties actually intended. (at [75])

Per Lord Wilson:

> … although its preference is always to collect from the evidence an expressed or inferred intention, common to the parties, about the proportions in which their shares are to be held, equity will, if collection of it proves impossible, impute to them the requisite intention. (at [84])

This latter statement in reference to equity sounds dangerously close to providing a solution based on equitable principles as opposed to trust law.

Following on from this analysis we now seem to have the following line of reasoning in descending order in arriving at a decision as to a party's beneficial interest:

1. Express declarations of trust.
2. Express constructive trust.
3. Constructive trust inferred through conduct.
4. Constructive trust through imputation as to what is a fair outcome having regard to the whole course of dealing between the parties.

4.3 DEATH OF RESULTING TRUST IN JOINT OWNERSHIP

Jones v. *Kernott* sounded the death knell in relation to the imposition of a resulting trust in joint names cases:

> There is no presumption that the parties intended that the beneficial interest be shared in proportion to their financial contributions to the acquisition of the property. (at [60])

> The time has come to make it clear, in line with *Stack* v. *Dowden* (see also *Abbott* v. *Abbott* [2007] UKPC 53, [2007] 2 All ER 432), that in the case of the purchase of a house or flat in joint names for joint occupation by a married or unmarried couple, where both are responsible for any mortgage, there is no presumption of a resulting trust arising from their having contributed to the deposit (or indeed the rest of the purchase) in unequal shares. The presumption is that the parties intended a joint tenancy both in law and in equity. But that presumption can of course be rebutted by evidence of a contrary intention, which may more readily be shown where the parties did not share their financial resources. (at [25])

Thus, a resulting trust (the doctrine itself being one of imputation of an intention to the parties) is now only likely to arise in cases where the property is in one person's name or is acquired as an investment property (*Laskar* v. *Laskar*, but see **3.2.1** and **3.6**).

4.4 WHAT ROLE FOR EQUITABLE ACCOUNTING?

Given the main finding in *Jones* v. *Kernott* that the intentions of the parties did in fact change (ambulatory constructive trust – whole course of dealing in relation to the property) there was no scope for further accounting, and in any event this would have involved quite a disproportionate effort. Some would say that this somewhat confuses the issue when analysing what we mean when we speak about equitable accounting (see **Chapter 5**), and the potential impact this decision has on this equitable remedy in cases of lengthy separation.

A possible defence is perhaps it was the specific facts of *Jones* v. *Kernott* that we need to consider:

- Upon separation the parties attempted to sell the home but without success. A joint life policy was surrendered and the proceeds split which enabled the man to buy elsewhere thus concentrating his investment on a new venture to the detriment of the family home and the children:

  > They separated in October 1993. No doubt in many such cases, there is a period of uncertainty about where the parties will live and what they will do about the home which they used to share. This home was put on the market in late 1995 but failed to sell. Around that time a new plan was formed. The life insurance policy was cashed in and Mr Kernott was able to buy a new home for himself. He would not have been able to do this had he still had to contribute towards the mortgage, endowment policy and other outgoings on 39 Badger Hall Avenue. The logical inference is that they

> intended that his interest in Badger Hall Avenue should crystallise then. Just as he would have the sole benefit of any capital gain in his own home, Ms Jones would have the sole benefit of any capital gain in Badger Hall Avenue. Insofar as the judge did not in so many words infer that this was their intention, it is clearly the intention which reasonable people would have had had they thought about it at the time. But in our view it is an intention which he both could and should have inferred from their conduct. (at [48])

This is the potential problem when relying on ambulatory constructive trust in preference to the process of equitable accounting, at least in separation cases and possibly generally.

Parties will be looking for a 'smoking gun', a key event in the 'whole course of dealing' between themselves either during the relationship or following its termination and their subsequent separation, in which to seek to argue either for an increased share in the equity for themselves or, conversely, for a reduced share for the other party.

4.5 DEVELOPMENTS POST-JONES V. KERNOTT

The first reported appellate decision post-*Jones* v. *Kernott* was *Geary* v. *Rankine* [2012] EWCA Civ 555.

This reiterated the position that where a property is vested in a party's sole name the first issue to be decided is whether the non-owning party has a beneficial interest at all (the first stage or primary question in *Oxley* v. *Hiscock*).

However, and more importantly, it reiterated that at this first stage one has to ascertain the parties' 'actual' shared intention (i.e. an intention common to both parties), whether expressed orally or inferred objectively from their conduct.

At this stage there is no room for imputation, as this only arises when one moves on to the second-stage question as to computation, provided one surmounts the first hurdle (the secondary question):

> Whether the beneficial interests are to be shared at all is still a question of a party's actual shared intentions. An imputed intention only arises where the court is satisfied that the parties' actual common intention, express or inferred, was that the beneficial interest would be shared but cannot make a finding about the proportions in which they were to be shared. (at [19])

This case also confirmed that a common intention constructive trust can also be based on a change of intention subsequent to the purchase of the property. Thus, the species of trust known as an ambulatory constructive trust (intentions changing over time) looks as if it is very much here to stay.

Shortly thereafter, *Thompson* v. *Hurst* [2012] EWCA Civ 1752 also confirmed that at the 'Stage I' enquiry (did the parties intend to share the property beneficially?) the court can look only to actual common intention expressed in words or inferred from conduct.

It is only at the 'Stage II' enquiry (quantification of the beneficial interests) that imputation of intention is permissible.

In *Capehorn* v. *Harris* [2015] EWCA Civ 955 the court reaffirmed that where an asset is owned in law by one cohabitant but another claims a beneficial interest in it, a two-stage analysis is called for to determine whether a common intention constructive trust arises:

- Firstly, the person claiming the beneficial interest must show that there was an agreement that they should have a beneficial interest in the property.
- Secondly, if such an agreement can be shown to have been made but there is no agreement on the extent of the interest, the court may impute an intention that the person was to have a fair beneficial share in the asset. In such a case the court may assess the quantum of the fair share in the light of all the circumstances:

> There is an important difference between the approach applicable at each stage. At the first stage, an actual agreement has to be found to have been made, which may be inferred from conduct in an appropriate case. At the second stage, the court is entitled to impute an intention that each person is entitled to the share which the court considers fair having regard to the whole course of dealing between them in relation to the property. A court is not entitled to impute an intention to the parties at the first stage in the analysis. (at 17])

However, in *Graham-York* v. *York (Personal Representative of the Estate of Norton Brian York)* [2015] EWCA Civ 72 the Court of Appeal reiterated that there are nonetheless restrictions on imputing a fair solution:

> It is essential, in my judgment, to bear in mind that, in deciding in such a case what shares are fair, the court is not concerned with some form of redistributive justice. Thus it is irrelevant that it may be thought a 'fair' outcome for a woman who has endured years of abusive conduct by her partner to be allotted a substantial interest in his property on his death.
>
> The plight of Miss Graham-York attracts sympathy, but it does not enable the court to redistribute property interests in a manner which right-minded people might think amounts to appropriate compensation.
>
> Miss Graham-York is 'entitled to that share which the court considers fair having regard to the whole course of dealing between them in relation to the property'. It is these last words, which I have emphasised, which supply the confines of the enquiry as to fairness. (at [22])

Finally, *Barnes* v. *Phillips* [2015] EWCA Civ 1056 again reiterated that:

> ... imputation is not permissible at the stage of determining whether there has been a common change of intention. (at [25])

It is impermissible, therefore, for the court to impute to the parties a common intention (which they never actually had) either:

- in the case of a jointly registered property, to rebut the presumption of joint beneficial ownership; or

- in the case of a property registered in a sole name, at the Stage I enquiry of whether to share ownership at all.

Several decisions at first instance have also followed suit, subject to a couple which seem to have departed from the now established law.

In *CPS* v. *Piper* [2011] EWHC 3570 (Admin) Holman J reiterated that, at the primary stage, the parties' common intention was to be deduced objectively from their entire conduct.

At the quantification stage, however, in the absence of direct evidence or inference, it was open to the court to impute an intention as to the size of the parties' respective interests by asking what was fair having regard to their whole course of dealing.

In *Aspden* v. *Elvy* [2012] EWHC 1387 (Ch), again a single ownership case, HHJ Behrens proceeded to impute an intention (but only at the assessment stage) as to the parties' respective shares, in the absence of express discussions, by reference to what was fair having regard to the whole course of dealing between them.

In *Re Ali* [2012] EWHC 2302 (Admin), another sole name case, Dobbs J also confined the process of imputation (where necessary) to the second stage of the computation enquiry. So far as the acquisition stage was concerned, this was to be determined solely by reference to the parties' common intention (either express or inferred).

Interestingly, in *Thompson* v. *Hurst* [2012] EWCA Civ 1752 (see **3.3**) it was held that given that the property was not held in joint names there could be no scope for a legal presumption of joint beneficial ownership even where, but for the advice of the mortgage adviser, the property would have been held jointly.

The court held that it cannot approach quantification on the hypothetical basis of what might have been.

In *Quaintance* v. *Tandan* [2012] EWHC 4416 (Ch) the court inferred that – by walking away and leaving no forwarding address – the defendant wanted nothing more to do with the claimant or the property. Although there was an unsigned declaration of trust from around the time of the purchase, which meant that their initial intentions must have been to hold in equal shares, their common intention had changed, thus providing an example of an ambulatory constructive trust.

Contrast this, however, with the earlier case of *Roy* v. *Roy* [1996] 1 FLR 541 wherein it was made clear that the parties would be bound by a declaration of trust in the transfer even if they had not signed it, unless there was a successful claim for rescission or rectification.

In *Thandi* v. *Sands* [2014] EWHC 2378 (Ch) it was held that the starting point is – in the absence of evidence to the contrary – that the beneficial ownership in properties followed the legal interest. The burden of proof to show a different beneficial ownership is on the person asserting it. Such evidence must be convincing. In so far as an interest is said to arise by way of a common intention trust, the whole of the circumstances must be looked at to determine whether such an interest exists.

The court pointed out that the relevant intention may be found from express words spoken or written, or by inference from the actions of the parties, but that in deciding what inferences are to be drawn from conduct, the relevant conduct must be looked at as a whole:

> The task of the court is (almost) always to find the actual intention of the parties, the first point of reference being what they had said, orally or in writing, as to that intention … If there was no expression of intention, the court may make inferences from their conduct, such as payment of or towards the purchase price. The inference is however (save in exceptional cases where an intention may be imputed even though there is no evidence that it was actually held) of actual intention. (at [74])

Note, however, the error made at the Stage I enquiry regarding the reference to imputation which clearly now only arises at Stage II, and to that extent the observation made by Mostyn J in *Bhura* v. *Bhura (No.2)* [2014] EWHC 727 (Fam) to the contrary is wrong in collapsing the traditional two-stage analysis into just one test – namely, 'what are the parties' beneficial shares?' – such that intention may be imputed throughout the entire exercise in order to achieve fairness and not just at the point of determining quantum.

CHAPTER 5

Equitable accounting

5.1 INTRODUCTION

So far we have been dealing with ascertaining the appropriate shares in respect of beneficial entitlement between two co-owners.

Equitable accounting is the process whereby such sums as adjudged due to the co-owners are adjusted in order to produce a fair outcome having regard to the sums they have each received or expended in relation to the property:

> ... Equity developed the doctrine of 'equitable accounting' to facilitate the striking of the balance between the co-owners. This consisted of a body of (non-binding) guidelines or rules of convenience aimed at achieving justice between the co-owners. The thrust of these guidelines was that, where it is just to do so, co-owners may be given credit for monies paid and expenditure incurred on the jointly owned property, a co-owner in sole occupation of property may be charged with or required to give credit to his co-owner for an occupation rent and these credits may be offset against each other.
>
> (*Murphy* v. *Gooch* [2007] EWCA Civ 603 at [10])

This does not involve an alteration in the actual shares in which the property is held, but is a personal remedy between the beneficiaries calculated at the time when the property is sold and is a discretionary exercise:

> What can at least be said is that an exercise of equitable accounting is not to be confused with an enquiry as to the extent of the parties' respective beneficial interests in the property in question. Questions of equitable accounting only arise once the extent of the parties' beneficial interests has been determined, since the requirement to account (where it exists) is a reflection of and derives from those beneficial interests.
>
> (*Wilcox* v. *Tait* [2007] 2 FLR 871)

This latter statement explains why in *Jones* v. *Kernott* equitable accounting did not feature at all, albeit that it is often recognised that the duty to account generally only arises after separation when the common purpose of the trust between the parties comes to an end.

As was held in *Clarke* v. *Harlowe* [2007] 1 FLR 1, in the ordinary case of cohabitation, equitable accounting begins at the date of separation because, in general, payments for outgoings or improvements prior to the date of separation is in accordance with the arrangements between the parties and the common purpose of the implied trust.

Ordinarily therefore, the common purpose of the implied trust subsists whilst the relationship subsists, and whilst the ordinary arrangements for the discharge of the outgoings are in place there is no breach or failure by any one of the parties to honour any obligation owed to the other and consequently no room or reason for equitable accounting.

After the relationship ends however, and the parties separate, the common purpose of the implied trust has generally come to an end, no common arrangements between the parties survive, and each ought to discharge his or her proportionate share of the outgoings, with appropriate accounting on the sale of the property in the event of any failure to honour that obligation. At that stage there are no common arrangements between the parties with the result that each ought to discharge his or her proportionate share of the outgoings.

There is thus, at that time, an obligation on each of the parties. If one party fails to honour their obligation, an appropriate account can be taken on the sale of the property. As is clear from the authorities, the account can include an obligation to pay an occupation rent:

> In general, payment for outgoings or improvements prior to the date of separation is in accordance with the arrangements between the parties and the common purpose of the implied trust. There is no breach or failure to honour those arrangements and thus no room for equitable accounting. There may however be exceptional cases where it can clearly be shown that one or other of the parties is in breach of the arrangements to pay for specified improvements or outgoings. In such a case I do not see why there should not be equitable accounting even though the parties are not separated. (at [39])

Note the latter qualification. Furthermore:

> ... in the ordinary cohabitation case it is open to the court to infer from the fact of cohabitation that during the period of cohabitation it was the common intention of the parties that neither should thereafter have to account to the other in respect of expenditure incurred by the other on the property during that period for their joint benefit. Whether the court draws that inference in the given case will, of course, depend on the facts of that case ... in an ordinary cohabitation case equitable accounting is only likely to come into play in respect of the period following the termination of the relationship between the co-owners. However, there can be no absolute rule as to that.
>
> (*Wilcox* v. *Tait* [2007] 2 FLR 871)

Again, note the qualification in the final paragraph. In essence this highlights the nature of this discretionary remedy in achieving overall fairness which is the main focus of any equitable jurisdiction, be it equitable accounting or proprietary estoppel.

The normal subject matter of equitable accounting usually involves the following:

- receipt of rent or other profits (occupation rent);

- the payment of mortgage instalments; and
- expenditure on improvements and repairs.

We will deal with each of these in turn.

5.2 OCCUPATION RENT

Where, as often is the case, one beneficial owner is in sole occupation of the property to the exclusion of the other, the court can order the payment of an occupation rent from the occupant to the non-occupying owner commensurate with their beneficial entitlement, i.e. a person with a 50 per cent interest should pay 50 per cent of the reasonable rental income by way of occupation rent (see for example *Akhtar* v. *Hussain* [2012] EWCA Civ 1762).

It is a question of fact in each case whether a person who has left the property has been excluded from it (see *Davis* v. *Jackson* [2017] 1 WLR 4005).

It has previously been suggested that a joint owner who *elects* to vacate the property of their own volition cannot, by doing so, then make the other liable for an occupation rent.

In the circumstances of the breakdown of a relationship, however, one could in response to this argue for what is in essence a 'constructive exclusion' – by virtue of the other party's behaviour or, indeed, given the very fact that the relationship has broken down – that it would be unreasonable to expect the parties to continue to reside together under the same roof.

This seems to be the suggestion in the case of *Re Pavlou* [1993] 2 FLR 751 where it was held that an occupation rent would be allowed wherever it was necessary to do equity to the case, and that where there was a separation, an occupation rent would not be payable if the party in occupation would welcome the other back, but would be *prima facie* payable by the party remaining in occupation after a divorce petition had been presented.

As, of course, the issue of presenting a divorce petition is not possible in cases where the parties are not married, by analogy surely the same principle must apply where the relationship has 'irretrievably broken down'.

Thus, an occupation rent can arise not only where the co-owner in occupation has excluded or restricted the other party's right to occupy, but also in any other case where it is necessary to do broad justice as between the parties (see *Byford* v. *Butler* [2003] EWHC 1267 (Ch); *Suttill* v. *Graham* [1977] 1 WLR 819; *Akhtar* v. *Hussain* [2012] EWCA Civ 1762).

5.2.1 What, therefore, is the appropriate rent?

In the case of *Dennis* v. *McDonald* [1982] Fam 63 Purchas LJ, when asked to decide between (1) rack rent, (2) a percentage of the value of the property, and (3) a fair rent, held that the appropriate figure would be a 'fair rent', worked out pursuant to the principles of the then Rent Act 1977 (although it could be argued that the level of occupation rent should now be equated to that of the current market rent for the property in question).

In *Re Barcham* [2008] EWHC 1505 (Ch) a single joint expert's opinion was obtained on the level of the open market rental value of the property.

Note also that the separation can be consensual – see *Murphy* v. *Gooch* [2007] EWCA Civ 603.

5.3 MORTGAGE PAYMENTS AND OTHER OUTGOINGS

As is often the case, the occupying cohabitant will usually continue to meet the mortgage instalments and other outgoings to stave off potential repossession or the accrual of debt, putting their occupation of the property at risk.

While the party in occupation cannot normally seek credit for the payment of the outgoings (as they are required to meet such payments in order to enable them to enjoy the facilities the property has to offer), they will normally be allowed credit for the *relevant proportion* of the mortgage instalments paid on behalf of the non-occupying party (see *Bernard* v. *Josephs* [1982] Ch 391).

A distinction, however, must be drawn between reducing the mortgage by paying off all or part of the capital and simply paying the mortgage interest.

A party who, upon separation, makes payments reducing the capital element of the mortgage will usually be entitled to a credit for such reduction.

The reason for this is that such payments increase the value of the equity of redemption so that the payments are to the benefit of both parties (see *Re Pavlou* (above)).

As far as mortgage interest payments are concerned there is the potential for a swings-and-roundabouts argument as to the non-occupying party receiving an occupation rent from the occupying party, as against the occupying party receiving a contribution to the relevant proportion of the mortgage interest payments.

It is not hard to see what happens next as a neat solution to this situation.

In order to avoid any unnecessary costs in litigating the issues as to equitable accounting in respect of ongoing mortgage interest payments generally, as against occupation rent, it is normal, in practice, for the occupation rent payments due to the non-occupying party to be set off against the relevant proportion of the mortgage interest payments due from the non-occupying party on a *quid pro quo* basis, particularly where the amounts are so similar such that a forensic exercise would be a waste of time or completely disproportionate (see the example of such a broad-brush approach in *Re Richards (A Bankrupt)* [2009] EWHC 1760 (Ch)).

Thus, the mortgage interest [in full] will normally be the sum an occupying party should pay for his use and occupation (see *Leake* v. *Bruzzi* [1974] 2 All ER 1196; *Suttill* v. *Graham* [1977] 3 All ER 1117; *Murphy* v. *Gooch* [2007] EWCA Civ 603).

However, one must not be tempted into seeing this as a 'one size fits all' solution, particularly in cases where the mortgage is substantial or, in the alternative, extremely low, as this may not equate to a true reflection of the market rent. Each case will be fact-dependent and, of course, the issue of proportionality must always be borne in mind:

> That practice is not ... a rule of law to be applied in all circumstances irrespective of, on the one hand, the amount of the mortgage debt and the instalments paid, and on the other hand, the value of the property and the amount of the occupation rent that ought fairly to be charged. It is a rule of convenience ...
>
> (*Re Gorman* [1990] 2 FLR 284)

5.4 EXPENDITURE ON IMPROVEMENTS

The remaining occupier will also normally be entitled to credit for the relevant proportion of improvements and redecorations carried out by them which add to the value of the property (but not mere maintenance or the acquisition of contents).

This can either be for one-half of the value of the expenditure itself or for the increase in the value of the property brought about by those improvements, whichever is the lesser:

> I must make it clear of course that, in deciding as I do that the wife is entitled as against the trustee in bankruptcy to credit for one half of any repairs or improvements, there has to be an inquiry as to the amount expended and the increase, if any, in the value of the property thereby realised. Much expenditure on property is not reflected in any increase in value, and most expenditure on property results in a much smaller increase in value than the amount expended. The wife will be entitled, as against the trustee in bankruptcy, to credit only for one half of the lesser of the actual expenditure and any increase in the value realised thereby.
>
> (*Re Pavlou* [1993] 1 WLR 1046 at [1049])

In such circumstances, all that usually is required is a broad approach to the valuation of those improvements (see *Passee* v. *Passee* [1988] 1 FLR 263).

Expenditure on improvements, however, will only be taken into account provided they are commenced as from the date of separation. The reason for this is that it is at the time of separation that the common purpose of the trust created by the cohabitants would have ceased (see *Clarke* v. *Harlowe* [2007] 1 FLR 1).

However, as seen earlier, *Jones* v. *Kernott* may have clouded this issue in relation to ambulatory constructive trusts following separation. There is also a query as to the issue of consensual and jointly funded post-separation improvements.

5.5 REPAIRS

In *Re Barcham* the trustee conceded that they would be liable for half the value of repairs carried out by Mrs Barcham post Mr Barcham's bankruptcy.

Thus, the same principle applying to improvements would appear to apply in respect of post-separation repairs carried out by the occupying cohabitant which would fall to be shared according to the beneficial interests.

5.6 FUTURE DEVELOPMENTS: NON-PAYMENT OF CHILD SUPPORT

In *Barnes* v. *Phillips* [2015] EWCA Civ 1056 the court cited, with approval, the *obiter dicta* of Strauss J at first instance in *Jones* v. *Kernott*, that failure to contribute to the maintenance of children was a factor that could legitimately be taken into account.

Despite the fact that the Court of Appeal had left this issue to one side in that case, Wall LJ observed that the defendant's failure to maintain the children might well be relevant were he to seek to charge the claimant for her occupation of the property and were the process of equitable accounting to be applied between them.

Indeed, in *Jones* v. *Kernott* in the Supreme Court, much was made as to the man's failure to meet his obligations in relation to the property and the children.

5.7 A PRACTICAL APPLICATION OF THE PRINCIPLE

An example of equitable accounting in practice can be seen in the case of *Re Pavlou* [1993] 2 FLR 751.

The facts of the case were as follows:

- H left in January 1983.
- W stayed, paying the mortgage and funding repairs and improvements.
- H was made bankrupt in March 1987.
- W and the trustee agreed to sell the house. The issue was equitable accounting.

The court held as follows:

1. W should be credited with one-half of the increase in value resulting from expenditure on repairs, etc. or one-half of the actual expenditure, if less.
2. W should be credited with one-half of the increase in equity due to her payment of the capital element of the mortgage.
3. Occupational rent (which W was *prima facie* liable to pay) should be set off against the interest elements of the mortgage payments she had made (they were broadly the same).

5.8 IS EQUITABLE ACCOUNTING AFFECTED OR ALTERED BY STACK V. DOWDEN?

Stack v. *Dowden* also provided a shift in how equitable accounting should be dealt with when compared to previous case law.

The majority in the House of Lords treated the issue of equitable accounting as being governed by TOLATA 1996, ss.12–15.

Lord Neuberger and Baroness Hale, however, adapted the pragmatic stance that while the court's powers of equitable accounting should be exercised in accordance with TOLATA 1996, the outcome would rarely be different from that which would have resulted from the application of equitable principles as established by earlier authority.

However, in future applications before the court, while the results may well ultimately be similar, arguments will now have to be based fairly and squarely on the criteria set out in TOLATA 1996.

That said, subsequent cases have held that TOLATA 1996 itself does not provide for an all-exclusive regime rendering previous common law principles inapplicable, such that ss.12–15 of TOLATA 1996 do not replace the doctrine of equitable accounting (see *French* v. *Barcham* [2008] EWHC 1505 (Ch); *Davis (As Trustee in Bankruptcy of Jackson)* v. *Jackson* [2017] EWHC 698 (Ch)).

Perhaps, therefore, it is now appropriate to look at TOLATA 1996.

CHAPTER 6

Trusts of Land and Appointment of Trustees Act 1996

6.1 RIGHTS TO OCCUPY AND THE REGULATION OF THAT OCCUPATION

It might be worth just taking a brief canter through the relevant sections of TOLATA 1996 itself.

Section 6 provides that for the purpose of exercising their functions, trustees have the powers of an absolute owner but should have regard to the rights of beneficiaries when exercising those functions, and the use of those powers should not contravene any other legal or equitable rules.

Section 7 allows (with the consent of the beneficiaries) trustees to partition land between beneficiaries with undivided shares and for the payment of any necessary equality money.

Section 12 of the Act provides for a party's right to occupy a property in which they have a beneficial interest.

Section 13 then goes on to give the trustees of the property in question the power to regulate the exercise of that right of occupation. It is worth quoting the relevant parts of s.13 in full (emphasis added):

> **13 Exclusion and restriction of right to occupy**
>
> (1) Where two or more beneficiaries are … entitled under section 12 to occupy land, the trustees of land may exclude or restrict the entitlement of any one … of them.
>
> (2) Trustees may not …
>
> (a) unreasonably exclude any beneficiary's entitlement to occupy land, or
> (b) restrict any such entitlement to an unreasonable extent.
>
> (3) The trustees of land may, from time to time, impose reasonable conditions *on any beneficiary in relation to his occupation of land* by reason of his entitlement under section 12.
>
> (4) The matters to which trustees are to have regard in exercising the powers conferred by this section include –
>
> (a) the intentions of the person or persons … who created the trust,
> (b) the purposes for which the land is held, and
> (c) the circumstances and wishes of each of the beneficiaries who is … entitled to occupy the land …

(5) The conditions which may be imposed on a beneficiary ... include, in particular, conditions requiring him –

(a) to pay any outgoings or expenses in respect of the land, or
(b) to assume any other obligation in relation to the land or to any activity which is or is proposed to be conducted there.

(6) Where the entitlement of any beneficiary to occupy land ... has been excluded or restricted, the conditions which may be imposed on any other beneficiary ... include, in particular, conditions requiring him to –

(a) make payments by way of *compensation* to the beneficiary whose entitlement has been excluded or restricted, or
(b) forgo any payment or other benefit to which he would otherwise be entitled under the trust so as to benefit that beneficiary.

(7) The powers conferred on trustees by this section may not be exercised –

(a) so as [to] prevent any person who is in occupation of land ... from continuing to occupy the land, or
(b) in a manner likely to result in any such person ceasing to occupy the land,

unless he consents or the court has given approval.

(8) The matters to which the court is to have regard in determining whether to give approval ... include the matters mentioned in subsection (4)(a) to (c).

It is a moot point that the principles set out in s.13(5) and (6) appear not to apply to a beneficiary who is not in occupation of the property in question as they may only be imposed under s.13(3) 'on any beneficiary in relation to his occupation of land'.

14 Applications for order

(1) Any person who is a trustee of land or has an interest in property subject to a trust of land, may make an application to the court for an order under this section.
(2) On an application for an order under this section, the court may make any such order –

(a) relating to the exercise by the trustees of any of their functions ... or,
(b) declaring the nature or extent of a person's interest in property subject to the trust,

as the court thinks fit.

...

Section 15 of the Act then goes on to set out the matters to which the court is to have regard when exercising its powers under s.13.

In essence, ss.12, 13 and 14 regulate who is to live in the property, who pays what to whom and make provision for the court to order the sale of any property held on trust. This includes property held not only on an express trust (where the property is held jointly) but also where there is an adjudged resulting or constructive trust.

Any person who is regarded as beneficially entitled to a property can make an application to the court for an order for sale and/or a declaration as to their beneficial entitlement.

However, under the statute the court cannot adjust the shares; it can only declare what they are, although adjustment may subsequently be made by virtue of equitable accounting.

In addition to ordering or preventing a sale, and declaring the nature or extent of a person's interest in the property, the court can also make orders in relation to the exercise of the trustees' functions and can give directions as to the exercise of a party's right to occupy as set out in ss.12 and 13 above, including the payment of an occupation rent, which was the point made in *Stack* v. *Dowden*.

It will be seen, however, that the court has no power under s.14 to order one beneficiary under a trust of land to sell or transfer their beneficial interest to another beneficiary.

Section 14(2)(a), which confers the relevant power, provides only that:

> ... the court may make any such order ... relating to the exercise by the trustees of any of their functions ... as the court sees fit.

The direct disposal of a beneficiary's interest, whether upon sale to another beneficiary or otherwise, is quite simply not a function of a trustee of land as provided for in the Act:

> It is, in my judgment, no part of the functions of trustees of land to deal with or dispose of beneficial interests under the trust, whether by sale or otherwise, at least not directly.
>
> (*Bagum* v. *Hafiz* [2015] EWCA Civ 801 at [17])

However, although there is no power under s.14 to order or direct that one beneficiary under a trust of land should sell or transfer their beneficial interest to another beneficiary, the court does have jurisdiction to order trustees to sell a co-owned property upon terms such that one beneficiary has a right to a pre-emptive bid at a price determined by the court, failing which it can be sold on the open market with all the beneficial owners at liberty to bid.

The justification for this is that s.14(2) gives the court the widest discretion to make orders relating to the exercise by the trustees of any of their functions, as long as the court has regard to the matters set out in s.15. Thus, the court is not rigidly constrained by principles of equity and is given a wider ambit in which to make decisions than a trustee without an order of the court:

> I consider that the clear object and effect of sections 14 and 15 is to confer upon the court a substantially wider discretion, exercised upon the basis of wider considerations, than might be enjoyed by the trustees themselves, acting without either the consent of their beneficiaries or an order of the court.
>
> (*Bagum* v. *Hafiz* [2015] EWCA Civ 801 at [23])

Accordingly, in circumstances where beneficiaries are in dispute with one another as to what should be done with trust property, the court is not rigidly constrained by the rules of equity which may constrain the trustees themselves, and may make provision accordingly for an option to buy (see *Bagum* v. *Hafiz* [2015] EWCA Civ

801; *Chaston & Arnold* v. *Chaston* [2018] EWHC 1672 (Ch); *In the Matter of the Estate of Roger John Kingsley* [2020] EWCA Civ 297).

The practical outcome of this, therefore, is that the court has the power to order a sale of a property, giving one beneficiary the opportunity to purchase at a value to be determined by the court on expert valuation evidence where the beneficiaries are in dispute with one another.

This is also supported by s.15(3) whereby the court can have regard to, but is not bound by, the wishes of the majority of beneficiaries in the event of a dispute.

Section 15 sets out the matters relevant in determining applications under s.14, and again this section is set out in full (emphasis added):

> **15 Matters relevant in determining applications**
>
> (1) The matters to which the court is to have regard in determining an application for an order under section 14 include –
>
> (a) the *intentions* of the person or persons … who created the trust,
> (b) the *purposes* for which the property subject to the trust is held,
> (c) the *welfare of any minor who occupies* or might reasonably be expected to occupy any land subject to the trust as his home, and
> (d) the *interests of any secured creditor* of any beneficiary.
>
> …
>
> (3) In the case of any other application … the matters to which the court is to have regard also include the *circumstances and wishes of any beneficiaries* of full age and entitled to an interest in possession in property subject to the trust …
>
> …

It is important to note that the factors set out in s.15 are non-exhaustive and the court may consider any other matters that it considers relevant, thus providing for the all too familiar maxim 'all the circumstances of the case' scenario, and thus giving the court maximum flexibility having regard to the 'whole course of dealing between the parties'.

CHAPTER 7

Practice and procedure

7.1 PRACTICE

7.1.1 Taking instructions

In the event of a TOLATA 1996 dispute, it is vital to take detailed instructions from the client more particularly in relation to the following matters:

- The history of the relationship including when the parties met, when they started living together, whether they were engaged and the history of ownership of the property, either jointly or in sole names.
- Whether a declaration of trust, cohabitation agreement, separation deed or any other document was signed in relation to the property.
- Whether there was an oral agreement or mutual understanding as to the ownership of the property and whether there are any witnesses to corroborate this.
- How the purchase of the property was funded.
- Whether there is a mortgage, and if so in whose name and who pays it.
- Who is responsible for paying the utility bills.
- Whether there have been any renovations or other improvements and how they were funded.
- Whether an agreement or understanding could be implied through the parties' financial contributions, such as contributions to the mortgage or renovations or otherwise through their conduct.
- Whether there were any acts of detriment on the part of either party, for example a sacrifice of one party's secure housing to live with the other.

7.1.2 Initial action

If it is established that the property is held jointly, one's first task will be to ascertain how the property is so held. We have already seen that there are two ways in which an equitable interest in land may be held, i.e. either as joint tenants or as tenants in common.

The main reason for doing this is because of what is known as the right of survivorship which attaches to a party holding property as a joint tenant.

In the case of tenants in common, if one such owner should die, their share in the property will pass under their will or the laws of intestacy.

However, if a joint tenant dies, the other joint tenant acquires their interest in the property automatically upon death of the other through the rule of survivorship.

A joint tenancy, however, can be brought to an end and converted into a tenancy in common by what is known as 'severance'.

Therefore, when initially instructed in a case whereby the property is held on a joint tenancy, you will need to advise the client as to severing the joint tenancy, as clearly in the majority of cases the client will want to ensure that, should they die, their share in the property does not automatically pass to the other co-owner.

The most common method of severing a joint tenancy is by notice in writing to the other joint tenant pursuant to the Law of Property Act (LPA) 1925, s.36(2).

A notice that is not communicated to the other joint tenant, or is in some way conditional or unclear, will not have the effect of severing the joint tenancy.

Service of the notice is governed by the provisions of LPA 1925, s.196. Section 196(4) operates as a deeming provision in cases where the notice is sent by registered post and which is not subsequently returned by the postal operator.

The notice is also effective if left at the recipient's last known address even if they do not actually receive it (LPA 1925, s.196(3); *Kinch* v. *Bullard* [1999] Fam Law 738).

Once a severance has been effected, in order for the severing party to protect their interest you will also need to file an application for a restriction pursuant to the Land Registration Act (LRA) 2002, s.43(1)(c) (Form SEV).

At one and the same time, as is the case with divorcing clients, you should also advise your client as to the good sense in making or amending their will – an ideal cross-selling or marketing opportunity.

What of the situation as to a non-owning cohabitant? In this situation, in order to protect them from a subsequent sale or transfer of interest above their head, the interest of the non-owning party should be protected by registration of a restriction to ensure that the payment of the purchase money is made to at least two trustees (see Land Registration Rules 2003, SI 2003/1417, rule 94(1)(b) and (2)). Note, the registration of a notice is not available to protect interests under a trust of land (LRA 2002, s.33).

A restriction is '... an entry in the register regulating the circumstances in which a disposition of a registered estate or charge may be the subject of an entry in the register' (LRA 2002, s.40(1)).

A restriction will have the effect of freezing the register by preventing any dealings in the property (LRA 2002, s.40(2)(a)) either indefinitely or for a set period (LRA 2002, s.40(2)(b)) or require certain conditions to be met, for example the applicant being notified and requiring their consent to any entry on the register (LRA 2002, s.40(3)).

The registrar also has power to enter a restriction upon the title to the property if it appears to them necessary or desirable in order to protect a right or claim in relation to the registered property (see LRA 2002, s.42(1)).

An applicant who is not the legal owner and does not have the owner's consent must have a 'sufficient interest in the making of the entry' (LRA 2002, s.43).

Rule 93 of the Land Registration Rules 2003 lists 23 classes of persons regarded as having a sufficient interest; the list includes a person with an interest under a trust of land (Land Registration Rules 2003, rule 93(a)).

A cohabitant, therefore, who has a beneficial interest in a property, thus has a sufficient interest in which to seek a restriction (Land Registration Rules 2003, rule 93).

In relation to such disputes, therefore, LRA 2002, s.43(1) expressly provides that a person who has a 'sufficient interest' in a property may apply for a restriction.

The appropriate Land Registry application form is Form RX1 which must be accompanied by a statement providing full details of the applicant's interest and how it arose (Land Registration Rules 2003, rules 92(3), 93).

For an express trust the trust document itself should be lodged or Form RX1 should set out brief details about it.

For resulting and constructive trust claims Form RX1 should set out brief details of the type of claimed trust interest and how it arose.

Estoppel-based claims affect the legal estate and may be protected by a notice (LRA 2002, s.116).

The appropriate wording for the restriction is as follows:

> No disposition by a sole proprietor of the registered estate (except a trust corporation) under which capital money arises is to be registered unless authorised by an order of the court.

In cases where the claimant can establish a good arguable case that there is a real risk of dissipation, a freezing order may also be sought pursuant to the Senior Courts Act 1981, s.37(1) by way of the Civil Procedure Rules 1998 (CPR), rule 25.1(1)(f) and the relevant Practice Direction (PD25A).

Consideration should also be given to contacting the mortgage lender to place a dispute indicator on its records, in order to prevent one party from drawing down on the mortgage in the event that there is a facility to do so, thus reducing the equity.

7.2 PRE-ACTION STEPS

7.2.1 Pre-action protocols

Most types of litigation under the CPR have what are known as pre-action protocols which set out certain steps that are required to be taken as a matter of good practice *before* proceedings are issued.

The rationale behind pre-action protocols is to encourage more pre-issue contact between the parties, with a view to the early exchange of information to facilitate settlement without recourse to the court process.

This normally entails the early notification of a claim, setting down fully the basis upon which it is made, prompt and collaborative disclosure of documentary evidence, the joint selection of and agreed instructions to any necessary expert and the encouragement of negotiation and settlement, including the use of alternative dispute resolution (ADR).

The common objective of all pre-action protocols is:

- to encourage the exchange of early and full information to assist in the resolution of the dispute;
- to enable the parties to avoid proceedings by agreeing a settlement before commencement of proceedings through negotiation and mediation;
- to support the efficient management of proceedings where litigation is necessary.

While there are a number of pre-action protocols there is no specific pre-action protocol that deals with TOLATA 1996 claims. Notwithstanding this, the court will have expected the parties, in accordance with the overriding objective, to have acted reasonably in exchanging information and documents relevant to the claim and generally in trying to avoid the necessity of commencing proceedings.

That said, the Practice Direction – Pre-Action Conduct and Protocols, which applies in cases where there is no specific pre-action protocol, provides as follows:

> Litigation should be a last resort. As part of a relevant pre-action protocol or this Practice Direction, the parties should consider whether negotiation or some other form of ADR might enable them to settle their dispute without commencing proceedings. (para.8)

Accordingly, therefore, a good template before commencing proceedings should consist of the following.

7.2.1.1 Claimant provides details of the prospective claim

It is always appropriate for a claimant to write a letter before action even if there is no reasonable expectation that there would be any sensible response.

The letter of claim should give sufficient and concise details to enable the prospective defendant to understand and investigate the claim without requiring any further extensive information.

It should enclose copies of any essential documents which are relied upon and call for a prompt acknowledgment and a full written response within a reasonable period (normally between 14 and 28 days).

The letter should set out the basis of the claim, a clear summary of the facts upon which the claim is based, what the claimant seeks from the defendant and, if the claim can be quantified, an explanation as to how the amount sought has been calculated.

The following points might be useful when considering what to include:

- A chronological background to the relationship (e.g. any engagement) including details relevant to the acquisition of the property that is the subject of the dispute.
- The financial arrangements of the parties, both generally and in relation to the purchase.
- Any agreement, arrangement or understanding which the parties had in relation to the ownership of the property that is the subject of the dispute.
- Discussions had between the parties and their context, including potential third party witnesses to such discussions.
- Contributions to the acquisition of the property and any subsequent home improvements, in both money and money's worth.
- Acts of detriment or reliance in relation to the agreement or understanding (detriment must be pleaded and proved (*Gillett* v. *Holt* [2000] 2 FLR 266)).

The letter should also set out what will happen should a response not be received within the stated period which will usually be the threat of court proceedings and costs sanctions.

If any necessary documents cannot be enclosed with the letter before action to corroborate that which is set out then it should identify the same and ask for copies of those essential documents which the other side might have possession of.

The letter should also enquire of the other side as to whether or not they would be willing to enter into mediation or any other form of ADR procedure and to draw the other side's attention to the court's potential power to impose sanctions for failure to engage in any such pre-action negotiations.

7.2.1.2 Defendant's response

The recipient of such a letter should acknowledge it within 14 days of receiving it and should state when a full written response is likely to be given, and may request further documentation to enable a full response to be given.

The full written response, when it comes, should state whether or not the claim is accepted in whole or in part and make proposals for settlement; or if a claim is not accepted, give detailed reasons why it is not, identifying which of the claimant's contentions are accepted and which are in dispute and the basis of that dispute.

The letter should also enclose copies of any essential documents which the defendant relies upon and any copy documents requested by the claimant, or explain why they are not available.

The letter should also ask for copies of any further additional essential documentation which the defendant does not have and wishes to obtain. The claimant should comply with any such requests within as short a period of time as is practicable or explain why such documents cannot be provided.

Equally, the defendant will need to set out their position in respect of mediation or other alternative resolution procedure.

Failure to comply with these steps may result in the court, among other things:

- ordering the non-compliant party to pay the costs of the other party;
- ordering the non-compliant party to pay interest on any judgment awarded against it;
- depriving the non-compliant party of any interest on a judgment if they are successful; and
- staying the proceedings until compliance with the rules has been satisfied.

It is only after these steps have been taken and negotiations or mediation flounder that proceedings should commence, and only then after an overall review of the outstanding issues and respective positions of the parties and consequential risk/benefits analysis in order to see whether proceedings are unavoidable.

7.2.2 Pre-action disclosure

As we have seen, under the pre-action protocol the receipt of the letter of claim gives rise to the obligation to exchange relevant information and documentation.

If a defendant fails to provide disclosure within the spirit of the protocol, the claimant can apply for disclosure pre-issue.

7.2.2.1 Disclosure before proceedings start against a prospective party

Disclosure before proceedings start

31.16

(1) This rule applies where an application is made to the court under any Act for disclosure before proceedings have started.

(2) The application must be supported by evidence.

(3) The court may make an order under this rule only where –

- (a) the respondent is likely to be a party to subsequent proceedings;
- (b) the applicant is also likely to be a party to those proceedings;
- (c) if proceedings had started, the respondent's duty by way of standard disclosure, set out in rule 31.6, would extend to the documents or classes of documents of which the applicant seeks disclosure; and
- (d) disclosure before proceedings have started is desirable in order to –
  - (i) dispose fairly of the anticipated proceedings;
  - (ii) assist the dispute to be resolved without proceedings; or
  - (iii) save costs.

(4) An order under this rule must –

- (a) specify the documents or the classes of documents which the respondent must disclose; and
- (b) require him, when making disclosure, to specify any of those documents –
  - (i) which are no longer in his control; or
  - (ii) in respect of which he claims a right or duty to withhold inspection.

(5) Such an order may –

(a) require the respondent to indicate what has happened to any documents which are no longer in his control; and
(b) specify the time and place for disclosure and inspection.

Standard disclosure – what documents are to be disclosed

31.6 Standard disclosure requires a party to disclose only –

(a) the documents on which he relies; and
(b) the documents which –

(i) adversely affect his own case;
(ii) adversely affect another party's case; or
(iii) support another party's case; and

(c) the documents which he is required to disclose by a relevant practice direction.

Application is made by way of a Part 23 notice, supported by evidence which can be either within the application itself or contained in a separate witness statement.

The remedy is discretionary, but before the court will consider the discretionary aspects of whether to make an order as to pre-action disclosure, the jurisdictional threshold also has to be crossed as set out in rule 31.16(3).

The factors that the court must consider as set out in rule 31.16(3) are as follows:

1. Is the respondent likely to be a party to subsequent proceedings?
2. Is the applicant likely to be a party to those proceedings?
3. Would the requested documents have been disclosable by the respondent had proceedings been issued by way of standard disclosure (i.e. a party's own documents in support of their case or documents adverse to their case or supporting the other parties)?
4. Is it desirable to allow pre-action disclosure to:

   (a) dispose fairly of the anticipated proceedings;
   (b) assist the dispute to be resolved without proceedings; or
   (c) save costs?

The issue as to whether the applicant and respondent are likely to be parties to subsequent proceedings is often not in dispute.

'Likely' means 'might well' or something less than 'probable' (*Jet Airways (India) Ltd* v. *Barloworld Handling Ltd* [2014] EWCA Civ 1311).

There is no requirement under the rule to establish that the commencement of proceedings is likely (*Herbert Black* v. *Sumitomo Corp* [2001] EWCA Civ 1819).

Difficulties can arise as to whether the requested documents would be disclosable pursuant to standard disclosure and whether or not it is desirable for the court to allow pre-action disclosure.

The burden rests with the applicant to establish that the scope of standard disclosure would extend to the pre-issue requested documents, by showing it is more probable than not that the documents are within the scope of standard disclosure in regard to the issues that are likely to arise. If the applicant is unable to surmount this hurdle the application must fail.

Attempting to obtain pre-action disclosure of documents that will not in due course be subject to standard disclosure by simply calling for classes or categories of documents is not permissible:

> Applications for pre-action disclosure are not meant to be a mini-trial of the action and should be disposed of swiftly and economically. Elaborate arguments are to be discouraged.
>
> (*Smith* v. *Secretary of State for Energy and Climate Change* [2013] EWCA Civ 1585 at [39])

Generally, when considering an application under CPR rule 31.16, the court does not need to (and should not) embark upon a consideration of difficult legal issues.

Such applications are in the nature of case management decisions requiring the judge to take a broad view of the merits of the potential claim, but not necessitating an investigation into legally complex and debatable potential defences. The situation, of course, would be different if a defendant can show beyond argument that a claim was hopeless or non-justiciable, or if disclosure of the documents themselves raised non-justiciable issues.

While it is inappropriate, therefore, in a pre-action application for disclosure for the court to embark on a detailed analysis of the substantive issues, the court must be able to identify the issues in the case to be able to determine the application:

> the court must be clear what the issues in the litigation are likely to be i.e. what case the claimant is likely to be making and what defence is likely to be being run so as to make sure the documents being asked for are ones which will adversely affect the case of one side or the other, or support the case of one side or the other.
>
> (*Black* v. *Sumitomo Corp* [2001] EWCA Civ 1819 at [76] quoting from *Bermuda* v. *KPMG* [2001] EWCA Civ 269)

The court must ask itself: does the request fall within the definition of standard disclosure? If the request for documents is narrow and the documents will help determine the issues it is more likely that the request will be granted. If what is requested is well beyond the scope of standard disclosure then it is likely that the request will be refused.

A reasonable search for such documents is required under CPR rule 31.7. So, what is a reasonable search?

> ... a search which was conducted in good faith and was fair and proportionate to the case in hand, given the number of documents involved, the nature and complexity of the case, the ease and expense of retrieval and the significance of any document likely to be located, would be a reasonable search ... The deficiencies relied upon have to be so significant that it can be said that a reasonable search simply had not happened.
>
> (*Smailes* v. *McNally* [2013] EWHC 2882 (Ch))

A reasonable search must be tailor-made to the value and significance of the likely product of the search. If the value of such evidence is not likely to be high then the search should be correspondingly limited.

The accompanying practice direction states that parties should act in a reasonable and proportionate manner considering the complexity of the matter and the amount at stake (PD31A, para.2).

The factors relevant in deciding the reasonableness of a search include the following:

- the number of documents involved;
- the nature and complexity of the proceedings;
- the ease and expense of retrieval of any particular document; and
- the significance of any document which is likely to be located during the search.

An application for pre-action disclosure thus has to be highly focused and should not encompass categories of documents that would simply prove to be relevant, if at all, as part of the background, let alone documents that might merely lead to a train of enquiry.

The extent of discovery thus has to be assessed on a case-by-case basis. The court will therefore consider the features of the case with a view to making an order tailored to achieving a just outcome, which includes limiting costs as far as possible:

> ... the more focused the complaint and the more limited the disclosure sought in that connection, the easier it is for the court to exercise its discretion in favour of pre-action disclosure ...
>
> (*Black* v. *Sumitomo* [2001] EWCA Civ 1819 at [95])

but:

> The more diffuse the allegations, however, and the wider the disclosure sought, the more sceptical the court is entitled to be about the merit of the exercise.
>
> (*Black* v. *Sumitomo* [2001] EWCA Civ 1819 at [95])

As to the desirability of ordering pre-action disclosure an applicant has to show that, at the very least, they have a *prima facie* arguable case:

> In considering whether to make an order, among the important considerations are the nature of the loss complained of, the clarity and identification of the issues raised by the complaint, the nature of the documents requested, the relevance of any protocol or pre-action inquiries, and the opportunity which the complainant has to make his case without pre-action disclosure...
>
> (*Assetco plc* v. *Grant Thornton UK LLP* [2013] EWHC 1215 (Comm) at [17])

In summary, therefore, the following principles apply:

- The court may only make an order if all of the matters set out in CPR rule 31.16(3)(a)–(d) are satisfied.
- Whether disclosure is 'desirable' within CPR rule 31.16(3)(d) involves a two-stage process comprising jurisdictional and discretionary aspects.

- The jurisdictional threshold is a low one; the fact that it has been passed might throw a little light on the manner in which the discretion should be exercised.
- The order can only be made in respect of documents that will be within the documents disclosable under standard disclosure. It is not sufficient that they might be so.
- The court has warned against ordering pre-action disclosure to encourage fishing expeditions. The broader and more diffuse the issues, the less likely it will be that an order will be made.
- It is for the applicant to identify their cause of action and demonstrate that they have a real prospect of success.

7.2.2.2 Disclosure before proceedings start against a non-party

This is regulated by CPR rule 31.17.

The questions before the court in these circumstances are:

- Are the documents sought likely to support the case of one party or adversely affect the case of another? If so
- are the documents sought necessary to dispose of the claim fairly or save costs?

The first requirement is that any documents sought must be shown to be likely to support or adversely affect the case of one or other party. Thus, the question to be asked in each case is whether they are likely to help one side or the other.

The word 'likely' in this context has been considered in the Court of Appeal and is taken to mean that the document or documents 'may well' assist (*Three Rivers District Council* v. *Governor and Company of the Bank of England (No. 4)* [2003] 1 WLR 210).

The second requirement is that disclosure of the documents sought is 'necessary' in order to dispose fairly of the claim or to save costs. This only arises for consideration if the first requirement has been met. Unless the documents are relevant in that sense, it is not necessary to address the test of necessity.

There is also a residual discretion on the part of the court whether or not to make such an order even if the first two requirements have been met. It is at this stage that broader considerations come into play, such as where the public interest lies and whether or not disclosure would infringe third-party rights in relation, for example, to privacy or confidentiality. If so, the court must conduct a careful balancing exercise.

In any event, the court has a clear obligation to ensure, if necessary of its own motion, that this intrusive jurisdiction is not used inappropriately, even by consent. In exercising its responsibility, the court may well be assisted by submissions made on behalf of any third party, the protection of whose interests must be considered.

7.2.2.3 Costs of pre-action disclosure

CPR rule 46.1(2)–(3) set out the general costs position in so far as applications for pre-action disclosure are concerned:

> (2) The general rule is that the court will award the person against whom the order is sought that person's costs –
>
> (a) of the application; and
> (b) of complying with any order made on the application.
>
> (3) The court may however make a different order, having regard to all the circumstances, including –
>
> (a) the extent to which it was reasonable for the person against whom the order was sought to oppose the application; and
> (b) whether the parties to the application have complied with any relevant pre-action protocol.

The general rule, therefore, is that the applicant will pay the respondent's costs of the application and of complying with the order as to pre-action disclosure. However, the court has a discretion to make a different order and in so doing the court must have regard to all the circumstances including:

- genuine doubts as to entitlement;
- the extent to which it was reasonable for the respondent to oppose the application; and
- whether the parties have complied with the pre-action protocol.

In the case of *Cattles Ltd* & Anor v. *Pricewaterhouse Coopers LLP* [2011] EWHC 2714 (Comm) it was held that the intended defendant could recover their costs up until the date when their refusal to provide the requested documents became unreasonable.

The costs of the application, if not agreed, will be summarily assessed. It is thus vital that a costs schedule is filed and served, as the court cannot make an order for 'costs in the case' as there are no proceedings on foot.

7.3 PROCEDURE ON COMMENCING A CLAIM

This is really where we get outside the comfort zone for family lawyers, as any application under TOLATA 1996 must be made in accordance with that alien creature known as the Civil Procedure Rules 1998 (CPR).

This alone is enough to strike fear into the heart of many a family lawyer as their knowledge of the CPR is probably limited. However, fear not, as the all-familiar Family Procedure Rules 2010 are very much based on their civil counterparts.

As far as the rules themselves are concerned, there are three main strands of importance for those who practise within the civil jurisdiction:

- Knowledge of the rules of court.
- Adherence to those rules and compliance with the court's orders.
- Conduct of litigation in accordance with the overriding objective.

The first thing to perhaps emphasise is the provisions of CPR rule 1.1 which permeates the whole ethos of the Civil Procedure Rules and is known as the 'overriding objective'.

The importance of this is set out in CPR rule 1.3, which states that not only are the parties themselves required to assist the court in furthering the 'overriding objective', but through CPR rule 1.4, the court itself is required to further the overriding objective by actively managing cases (active case management).

7.3.1 What is the overriding objective?

The overriding objective requires all cases to be dealt with justly and at proportionate cost, as set out in CPR rule 1.1(2):

> (2) Dealing with a case justly and at proportionate cost includes, so far as is practicable –
>
> (a) ensuring that the parties are on an equal footing;
> (b) saving expense;
> (c) dealing with the case in ways which are proportionate –
>
> (i) to the amount of money involved;
> (ii) to the importance of the case;
> (iii) to the complexity of the issues; and
> (iv) to the financial position of each party;
>
> (d) ensuring that it is dealt with expeditiously and fairly;
> (e) allotting to it an appropriate share of the court's resources, while taking into account the need to allot resources to other cases; and
> (f) enforcing compliance with rules, practice directions and orders.

The rules therefore emphasise:

- the centrality of dealing with cases at proportionate cost; and
- the fact that the overriding objective requires the court to place weight on enforcing compliance.

Active case management includes:

1. Encouraging parties to co-operate with each other in the conduct of the proceedings.
2. Identifying the issues.
3. Deciding promptly which issues need full investigation and trial and disposing summarily of others.
4. Deciding the order in which issues are to be resolved.

5. Encouraging the parties to use an ADR procedure if the court considers that appropriate and facilitating the use of such procedure if the court considers this appropriate.
6. Helping the parties to settle the whole or part of the case.
7. Fixing timetables or otherwise controlling the progress of the case.
8. Considering whether the likely benefits of taking a particular step justify the cost of taking it.
9. Dealing with as many aspects of the case as possible on the same occasion.
10. Dealing with the case without the parties needing to attend at court.
11. Making use of technology.
12. Giving directions to ensure that the trial of a case proceeds quickly and efficiently.

7.3.2 Court's case management powers

The court discharges its obligations under CPR rule 1.4 by the use of its case management powers as set out in CPR Part 3: these powers are in addition to any other powers given to the court by any other rule, practice direction or other enactment.

The court's general case management powers are set out in CPR rule 3.1 and provide a judge with a formidable arsenal of 'powers' to facilitate case management:

The court's general powers of management

3.1

(1) The list of powers in this rule is in addition to any powers given to the court by any other rule or practice direction or by any other enactment or any powers it may otherwise have.

(2) Except where these Rules provide otherwise, the court may –

(a) extend or shorten the time for compliance with any rule, practice direction or court order (even if an application for extension is made after the time for compliance has expired);
(b) adjourn or bring forward a hearing;
(bb) require that any proceedings in the High Court be heard by a Divisional Court of the High Court;
(c) require a party or a party's legal representative to attend the court;
(d) hold a hearing and receive evidence by telephone or by using any other method of direct oral communication;
(e) direct that part of any proceedings (such as a counterclaim) be dealt with as separate proceedings;
(f) stay the whole or part of any proceedings or judgment either generally or until a specified date or event;
(g) consolidate proceedings;
(h) try two or more claims on the same occasion;
(i) direct a separate trial of any issue;
(j) decide the order in which issues are to be tried;
(k) exclude an issue from consideration;

(l) dismiss or give judgment on a claim after a decision on a preliminary issue;
(ll) order any party to file and exchange a costs budget;
(m) take any other step or make any other order for the purpose of managing the case and furthering the overriding objective, including hearing an Early Neutral Evaluation with the aim of helping the parties settle the case.

Dealing with the latter point of judge-led early neutral evaluation (ENE) Norris J noted in *Seals* v. *Williams* [2015] EWHC 1829 (Ch) that:

> The advantage ... over mediation itself is that a judge will evaluate the respective parties' cases in a direct way and may well provide an authoritative (albeit provisional) view of the legal issues at the heart of the case and an experienced evaluation of the strength of the evidence available to deploy in addressing those legal issues. The process is particularly useful where the parties have very differing views of the prospect of success and perhaps an inadequate understanding of the risks of litigation itself. (at [3])

The court went on to find a jurisdictional basis for ordering ENE, even if the parties did not consent, as the court has the power to:

> take any other step or make any other order for the purpose of managing the case and furthering the overriding objective, including hearing an Early Neutral Evaluation with the aim of helping the parties settle the case.
>
> (CPR rule 3.1(2)(m))

This was further endorsed in *Lomax* v. *Lomax (Referral to Early Neutral Evaluation)* [2019] EWCA Civ 1467.

ENE is a process which assists with the fair and sensible resolution of a case and is very much part of the court process. Of course, family practitioners will be very familiar with this terminology which is very much akin to a financial dispute resolution (FDR)-type hearing.

To these powers must also be added the powers to:

- impose conditions on a party (CPR rule 3.1(3)(a));
- specify the consequence of failure to comply with an order (CPR rule 3.1(3)(b));
- vary or revoke orders (CPR rule 3.1(7));
- strike out a case (CPR rule 3.4);
- impose and give relief from sanctions (CPR rules 3.1(3)(b), 3.8 and 3.9);
- rectify errors (CPR rule 3.10).

As to the latter rule, in particular:

> CPR rule 3.10 is a beneficial provision to be given a very wide effect. It can be used beneficially where a defect has no prejudicial effect to the other party and to prevent the triumph of style over substance ... the most important question in determining whether CPR rule 3.10 applies is whether there has been an error of procedure which might otherwise invalidate a procedural step ... Another important factor to consider is whether the defendant has suffered any prejudice as a result of the procedural error ... Whether the defect was the fault of the applicant is considered, but it is a subsidiary factor.
>
> (*Dory Acquisitions Designated Activity Co* v. *Frangos* [2020] EWHC 240 (Comm) at [76])

The court can exercise any of its case management powers on its own initiative (CPR rule 3.3).

However, where the court proposes to make an order on its own initiative it must give any person who is likely to be affected by the order an opportunity to make representations within a specified period. Such opportunity should be set out on the face of the order itself (CPR rule 3.3(2), (5), (6)).

Note, the parties are assumed to have been content with such an order if no application is made to vary it or no appeal lodged within 14 days of service. Therefore, if not happy, act quickly; you are given an automatic right to do so.

Upon considering such representations the court will give due weight to the decision of the judge who dealt with the matter without a hearing, and the party seeking to challenge the order must be able to identify a good reason for disagreeing with it (*R (on the Application of Kuznetsov)* v. *London Borough of Camden* [2019] EWHC 3910 (Admin)).

Another trap for the unwary is that where the court sends out notification that a fee is due (e.g. fees due on filing of the directions questionnaire (DQ) and listing questionnaire (LQ) (Hearing Fee); see **7.3.4.1** and **7.3.4.8**), the case will automatically be struck out without further order if that fee is not paid in time, along with a deemed order as to costs where there is such a strike-out as a result of non-payment.

7.3.3 Costs management/budgeting

> In modern litigation, with the emphasis on proportionality, there is a requirement for parties to make an assessment at the outset of the likely value of the claim and its importance and complexity, and then to plan in advance the necessary work, the appropriate level of person to carry out the work, the overall time which would be necessary and appropriate to spend on the various stages in bringing the action to trial and the likely overall cost.
>
> (*Jefferson* v. *National Freight Carriers plc* [2001] 2 Costs LR 313 at [321])

CPR rules 3.12–3.18 and the accompanying practice direction PD3E set out procedural rules in relation to costs budgeting, through the medium of costs management conferences and the making of costs management orders, which apply to all Part 7 multi-track cases (see **7.3.4.3**).

PD3E provides a strong steer in favour of costs management in Part 8 proceedings as well where there is a real risk of disproportionate costs being incurred in relation to applications under the Trusts of Land and Appointment of Trustees Act 1996.

The purpose of costs management is:

> that the court should manage both the steps to be taken and the costs to be incurred by the parties to any proceedings (or variation costs as provided in rule 3.15A) so as to further the overriding objective.
>
> (CPR rule 3.12(2))

Its purpose is to enable the court to manage both the steps to be taken and the costs to be incurred at each phase of the proceedings so as to further the overriding objective by the making of what are known as costs management orders.

In its simplest form costs management involves each party, early in the proceedings, producing an estimate of how many hours are likely to be spent – and by which seniority of lawyer – on each stage of their action from pre-issue of the claim until trial.

The budgets are then approved by a judge at a hearing, if proportionate to the remedy being sought. If not, the judge can amend them, for example by reducing the amount of hours to be spent on a particular task.

The court will generally make a costs management order to record the extent to which budgets have been agreed/approved with appropriate revisions.

Once such an order has been made the court will then control budgets in respect of recoverable costs.

Budgets may also be updated during the life of the action and parties will need to keep each other and the court informed of subsequent revisions.

The case, therefore, will be managed by reference to the approved budgets and, when the court assesses the costs liability of the losing party at the end of the case, the costs in the latest agreed/approved costs budget will generally be taken to represent the costs recoverable on the basis of a standard assessment:

> The primary function of the budget is to ensure that the costs incurred are not only reasonable but proportionate to what is at stake in the proceedings. If, as is the intention of the rule, budgets are approved by the court and revised at regular intervals, the receiving party is unlikely to persuade the court that costs incurred in excess of the budget are reasonable and proportionate to what is at stake.
>
> (*Henry* v. *News Group Newspapers Ltd* [2013] EWCA Civ 19 at [28])

Costs management conferences are intended to run alongside case management conferences, their purpose being to consider whether the budgeted costs fall within the range of reasonable and proportionate costs as, when making any case management decision, the court must have regard to any available budget.

The question is: does the court decide the directions first and then set the budget in light of that or does the court set the budget first and then give directions consistent with it (a linear approach)?

The favoured approach appears to be a more holistic process and hybrid one of running the two side by side, i.e. by deciding the budget; constructing directions that will meet the budget; hearing submissions on the ultimate result; and then, standing back, adjusting the budget accordingly to arrive at a final figure.

Costs budgets in Form H (which comprises a self-calculating spreadsheet) must be prepared, exchanged and agreed or approved by the court at the case management conference.

Costs budgets are defined in the glossary to the Civil Procedure Rules as:

> An estimate of the reasonable and proportionate costs (including disbursements) which a party intends to incur in the proceedings.

It is important to emphasise that the court is setting the budget for each phase of the litigation; therefore, a figure needs to be set for each of the following phases:

- Pre-action
- Issue/pleadings
- Costs management conference (CMC)
- Disclosure
- Witness statements
- Experts' reports
- Pre-trial review (PTR)
- Trial preparation
- Trial
- Alternative dispute resolution (ADR)
- Contingencies

A few points in relation to the above are worthy of mention.

Costs already incurred on a particular phase should always go in the 'costs incurred' column for each phase so as to avoid double counting. Accordingly, the first phase of pre-action costs is simply the repository of a small number of matters that do not fit into another phase.

Always complete the assumptions column for each individual phase, as these are likely to be particularly important in the case of later variations to the costs budget.

However, only those assumptions that significantly affect the level of costs should be included in the budget.

As for contingencies:

> The first point to make about contingencies is that they must involve work that does not fall within the main categories on Precedent H. Secondly, in order for work to qualify as a contingency it must be possible to identify to the opposite party and the court what that work would be. … Thirdly, there is the important issue of how likely it needs to be that the work will be required, before it can properly be included as a contingency. … In my judgment work should be included as a contingency only if it is foreseen as more likely than not to be required. (at [70]) … If work that falls outside one of the main categories is not thought probable, it can reasonably and should be excluded from the budget. The time and costs involved in estimating how much work would cost are not easily justified if the work is no more than a possibility or is unlikely. If work identified as a contingency is included in a budget but not considered probable by the court no budget for it should be approved. (at [71])
>
> (*Yeo* v. *Times Newspaper* [2015] EWHC 209 QB)

Where the costs budget does not exceed £25,000, or the claim is less than £50,000, only page one of Precedent H need be completed.

The budget must be dated and verified by a statement of truth and signed by a senior legal representative of the party.

Following on from this the parties must produce budget discussion reports in order to try to achieve consensus and agreement of budgets. A format for the budget discussion is annexed to PD3E.

Costs budgets must be prepared, exchanged and filed by all parties, except litigants in person, in cases worth less than £50,000 with their directions questionnaire (see **7.3.4.1**) and in all other cases not less than 21 days before the CMC.

The budget discussion report (Precedent R) must be filed not less than seven days before the CMC.

The budget discussion report requires each party to comment on the costs budget of the other and obliges the parties to adopt a realistic attitude to the other side's budget and assist in identifying real disputes between them on costs.

The practice of putting forward unrealistically low figures for the opposing party's costs in the hope that the District Judge will reach a figure somewhere in the middle is to be deplored (*Findcharm Ltd* v. *Churchill Group Ltd* [2017] EWHC 1108 (TCC).

The recoverable costs of preparing Form H, save in exceptional cases, cannot exceed the greater of £1,000 (or 1 per cent of the approved budget), and all other recoverable costs of budgeting and costs management cannot exceed 2 per cent of the approved budget.

If the parties can agree their respective budgets the court cannot go behind that agreement, so wherever possible it is always better to agree budgets.

If the budget is reasonable and proportionate it should be agreed by the other party, or approved by the court, possibly after making appropriate revisions, at the case/costs management conference (CCMC) when directions for progressing the case will also be given.

Note, the court can only approve a budget that relates to costs to be incurred, not those costs which have already been incurred.

The focus of a judge making a costs management order is on estimating the costs reasonably and proportionately to be incurred in the future.

Note, the court does not approve or disapprove hourly rates when budgeting costs; it simply approves an amount which it is reasonable, necessary and proportionate for a party to incur for each of the phases of the litigation – with the exception, of course, of the incurred costs.

If the incurred costs appear to be disproportionate, the judge may want to order a breakdown of those costs prior to the case/costs management conference.

The court is not undertaking an advanced mini detailed assessment or micro-managing the work but considering 'whether the budgeted costs fall within the range of reasonable and proportionate costs' (PD3E, para.12).

Thus:

> … parties and their solicitors can no longer conduct litigation in a manner which does not keep the proportionality of the costs being incurred at the forefront of their minds at all times. (at [44])
>
> It is no longer acceptable – if it ever was – for parties to pursue issues or applications that have no real impact on the issues that are central to the dispute. Further, it is no longer acceptable for solicitors to carry on a war of attrition by correspondence, whether instructed to do so or not: it is the parties who are the subject of the duty in CPR 1.3, not merely … their solicitors. (at [45])

> Whilst English law is an adversarial process, that goes to the issues in the case, not to every aspect of the procedure. Parties to litigation ... are expected to conduct that litigation in the manner that is most expeditious and economical. Bringing the right issues to trial in the most economical fashion, and taking steps to ensure that the costs are kept at a level that is proportionate to what is at stake, is to be at the heart of the process. (at [47])
>
> Unreasonableness, intransigence and the taking of every point must in my view now be regarded as unacceptable, because conducting litigation in that way flies in the face of the overriding objective as it is now formulated. These habits must disappear from the landscape of litigation... If they do not, offending litigants must expect to bear the costs. (at [48])
>
> If access to justice is to have any real meaning, then the aim of keeping costs to the reasonable minimum must become paramount. Procedural squabbles must be banished and a culture of co-operative conduct introduced in their place. This will not prevent contentious issues from being tried fairly: on the contrary it should promote it. (at [49])
>
> (*Gotch* v. *Enelco Ltd* [2015] EWHC 1802 (TCC))

Once a costs management order is made the court thereafter controls the parties' budgets in respect of recoverable costs. An approved budget can only be varied with court approval (unless it is agreed between the parties).

Amended budgets (using Precedent T – which readily identifies under which phases revision is being sought and by how much) should be submitted to the other party for agreement where there are significant developments in the litigation that warrant revisions. If the amendments are not agreed, they will need to be submitted to the court, with a note of the changes made, with reasons and the objections of the other parties, for the court to approve, vary or disapprove.

The court, upon receipt of the same, may approve, vary or disallow the proposed variation, or may list for a further CMC (in other words, the court may deal with variation as a paperwork exercise, but presumably subject to the usual right for a party to challenge any decision by an application to vary or set aside within seven days of receipt of the order).

CPR rule 3.15A provides that:

- Revision is mandatory if there is a significant development in the litigation that warrants it and may result in budgets being increased or decreased.
- A party must certify that, if the variation sought is an increase, the additional costs did not appear in the previous approved/agreed budget or any earlier permitted variation to it.
- Precedent T, the last approved/agreed budget and an explanation of any disagreement between the parties on the sought variation must be submitted to the court promptly.

When the court makes an order for variation it may vary the budget in respect of costs incurred after the previous costs management order, but prior to the variation order. This is an exception to the general rule at CPR rule 3.17(3) which provides that the court may not approve costs incurred up to and including the date of the costs management hearing.

Sharp v. *Blank* [2017] EWHC 3390 (Ch) gave the following guidance on the term 'significant developments':

> Significance must be understood in light of the claim – its size, complexity and the manner in which the litigation has unfolded – and also from the likely additional costs that have been, or are expected to be, incurred. … (at [33])
>
> One momentous event may be significant for these purposes, but a series of events that, taken singly or together, may not be. … Although it is likely to be helpful to consider developments by reference to the phases in the budget they affect, whether a development is significant must be looked in the way it affects the litigation as a whole. (at [35])
>
> … when the court is considering whether there have been significant developments, the court should look at the totality of the related developments. (at [61])

An increase in the trial timetable is not, of itself, sufficient to justify an approved increase in a costs budget. Applications for specific disclosure, which lead to the disclosure of large numbers of documents, may amount to a significant development capable of justifying revision of a costs budget.

> … a mistake in the preparation of a budget, or a failure to appreciate what the litigation actually entailed, will not usually permit a party to claim later there has been a significant development because the word 'development' connotes a change to the status quo that has happened since the budget was prepared. If the mistake could have been avoided, or the proper nature of the claim understood at the time the budget was prepared, there has been no change or development in the litigation. By contrast, if the claim develops into more complex and costly litigation than could reasonably have been envisaged, that may well be the result of one or more significant developments. (at [37])

See also *Al-Najar* v. *The Cumberland Hotel (London)* [2018] EWHC 3532 (QB) at [8]:

> (a) Whether a development is 'significant' is a question of fact which depends primarily on the scale and complexity of what has occurred.
> (b) If what has occurred is something that should reasonably have been anticipated by the party seeking to revise its budget, then that party will probably be unable to label it significant or, for that matter, a development.
> …
> (d) As a matter of policy, it seems to me that the bar for what constitutes a significant development should not be set too high because, otherwise, parties preparing a budget would always err on the side of caution by making over-generous (to them) assessments of what was to be anticipated.

Following on from the above observations, *Murray* v. *Neil Dowlman Architecture Ltd* [2013] EWHC 872 (TCC) makes it plain that it will be, bar special circumstances, extremely difficult to persuade the court that inadequacies or mistakes in the preparation of a budget, which is then approved by the court, should be subsequently revised or rectified:

> The courts will expect parties to undertake the costs budgeting exercise properly first time around, and will be slow to revise approved budgets merely because, after the event, it is said that particular items had been omitted or undervalued. (at [17])

Thus, get your budget right first time and if needs be consider assistance from your costs draughtsperson.

If interim applications are made which reasonably were not included in a budget, then the costs should be treated as additional.

At the end of the case, an agreed or approved budget cannot be exceeded and can only be challenged on detailed assessment if a party can establish that there was 'good reason' to exceed the budgeted amount for the work included in that budget.

Thus, a costs budget is an instrument for the management of costs and an important reference point in any subsequent detailed assessment.

'Good reason' is nowhere defined in the rules. Thus, it is extremely important that costs budgets are both a reasonable and an accurate estimate of the total likely costs of the case.

This will be particularly relevant in constructive trust cases where the costs of the proceedings may very quickly swallow up what equity there might otherwise be available:

> As to what will constitute 'good reason' in any given case I think it much better not to seek to proffer any further, necessarily generalised, guidance or examples. The matter can safely be left to the individual appraisal and evaluation of costs judges by reference to the circumstances of each individual case.
>
> (*Harrison* v. *University Hospitals Coventry & Warwickshire NHS Trust* [2017] EWCA Civ 792 at [44])

> ... the starting point must be that the approved budget is intended to provide the financial limits within which the proceedings are to be conducted and that the court will not allow costs in excess of the budget unless something unusual has occurred. Whether there is good reason to depart from the approved budget in any given case, therefore, is likely to depend on, among other things, how the proceedings have been managed, whether they have developed in a way that was not foreseen when the relevant case management orders were made, whether the costs incurred are proportionate to what is in issue and whether the parties have been on an equal footing.
>
> (*Henry* v. *News Group Newspapers Ltd* [2013] EWCA Civ 19 at [18])

A word of warning – in the absence of a Form H the costs of the defaulting party are assumed to be an amount comprising the court fees only for which relief from sanctions will need to be sought (see CPR rule 3.9 at **7.3.4.13**).

7.3.3.1 An aide-mémoire

1. Budgets must be filed by the date specified in the notice of proposed allocation (CPR rule 26.3(1)), or, if no such date is specified, with the directions questionnaires, or 21 days before the first CMC.

2. Budgets must be in Form H and comply with PD3E, para.6. Form H is downloadable and self-calculating. Start as soon as instructed and collaborate with the other side.
3. Budgets must be dated and signed with a statement of truth.
4. The costs of preparing budgets must not exceed the higher of £1,000 or 1 per cent of the approved budget. All other recoverable costs of the budgeting and cost management process shall not exceed 2 per cent of the approved budget.
5. Budgets must be complete, considered and provide for all contingencies.
6. Budgets should be exchanged and filed and at the first CMC the court will make a costs management order as follows:

   (a) If budgets are *agreed* between the parties the court will record the agreement, and the extent of it.
   (b) If budgets are *not agreed* the court will review and revise the total figures of each phase of the proceedings to be incurred in order to make them within a range which is reasonable and proportionate.

7. The court may not 'approve' costs incurred before the date of the budget (unless they are agreed) but may record its comments on them and will take them into account when considering the reasonableness and proportionality of all subsequent costs in relation to that phase, having regard to the phases of the litigation.

   Note, irrespective of whether or not the court makes a costs management order, it may record on the face of any case management order any comments it has about the incurred costs which are to be taken into account in any subsequent assessment proceedings.
8. The judge will control the parties' budgets in respect of recoverable costs and manage that case having regard to the parties' budgets and the costs involved in any procedural step.
9. Any party which fails to file a prescribed budget will be treated as having filed a budget comprising only the appropriate court fees.
10. Parties may revise their budgets upwards or downwards if significant developments in the litigation warrant such revisions. Such amended budgets must be submitted to other parties for their agreement. In default of agreement, the amended budgets must be submitted to the court, together with a note of:

    (a) the changes made and the reasons for those changes; and
    (b) the objections of any other party.

    The court may approve, vary or disapprove the revisions.
11. When assessing costs on the standard basis the court will:

    (a) have regard to the receiving party's last approved or agreed budget for each phase of the proceedings; and
    (b) not depart from such approved or agreed budget unless satisfied there is good reason to do so.

12. Self-represented litigants are not required to prepare a budget but shall nevertheless be provided with a copy of the represented party's.

    Note *Campbell* v. *Campbell* [2016] EWHC 2237 (Ch) held that the court has jurisdiction to order a litigant in person to produce a costs budget and to make a costs management order in relation to litigant in person costs.

7.3.4 Commencing proceedings

The County Court has unlimited jurisdiction to hear and determine applications made under TOLATA 1996, s.14 and indeed, this is the level of court that will normally hear such applications (County Courts Act 1984, s.23(b)).

The application itself must be made to the court for the district in which the defendant resides or carries on their place of business or the district in which the property is situated.

Transfer to the High Court should only be appropriate if the issues are very complex or there are very significant sums of money involved.

A claim should only be commenced in the High Court if justified by one or more of the following:

- financial value;
- complexity;
- importance of the claim to the general public.

If issued in the High Court the claim can be issued either in the Chancery or Family Division.

In most cases regarding cohabitants I would suggest that the Family Division is utilised unless the case turns on the finer points of strict trust law or involves subsidiary issues, such as rescission or rectification of the title deeds on the grounds of fraud, mistake or undue influence.

Cases involving difficult issues of undue influence or fraud might also be more suitable for the High Court.

Moreover, if any party wishes to apply for ancillary remedies such as freezing orders and seizing orders then such orders themselves can only be made within the High Court jurisdiction.

Under the CPR, there are two types of claims procedure: Part 7 claims and Part 8 claims.

The majority of property ownership disputes will fall within the Part 7 procedure, as the Part 8 procedure should ordinarily only be used where the claim itself is unlikely to involve a substantial dispute of fact.

Bearing in mind that most of these cases deal with the extent of a party's beneficial interest in property it will be more likely than not that there will be a significant factual dispute and therefore the Part 7 procedure should be used (although do not worry if you issue under the wrong part as the court can always correct matters by treating it as if issued under the correct one on the occasion of the first directions hearing).

An example of where the Part 8 procedure might be used is where the issue as to beneficial entitlement is not in dispute, and a co-owner merely seeks to enforce a sale of the property to realise their share and/or to take an equitable account by way of adjustment to those shares.

A Part 7 action is commenced on Form N1, while a Part 8 action is commenced on Form N208.

Whichever claim form is used it must contain a statement of truth.

The proceedings themselves are deemed to have commenced when the claim form is issued by the court, which will be the date placed on it by the court office.

Once issued, the claim form must be served within four months.

7.3.4.1 Part 7 procedure

The appropriate claim form for this part is Form N1.

The particulars of claim must either be included within the claim form itself or be set out in a separate self-contained document, which must be served with the claim form or served separately within 14 days after the claim is issued.

If the particulars of claim are not contained in or filed and served with the claim form there must be a statement within the claim form itself stating that the particulars of claim will follow.

The claimant thus has three choices:

1. File and serve the claim form incorporating the particulars.
2. File and serve the claim form with the particulars contained in a separate document.
3. File and serve the claim form, and serve the particulars following on from that within 14 days.

In all but the simplest cases it is advisable for the particulars to be contained within a separate document to enable the claim to be pleaded in sufficient detail.

Both the claim form and particulars must be served within four months of issue.

Both the claim form itself and the particulars, and indeed any witness statements, must be endorsed with a statement of truth as these documents constitute evidence before the court.

The claim form itself should set out brief details of the claim, together with a concise statement of the nature of the claim and the remedy sought.

The claimant should identify the issues and the extent of the dispute between the parties, without going into excessive detail. The claim thus must be concise and formulate a cause without background facts or evidence.

Moreover, the function of the statement of case is to define the issues upon which the court is invited to adjudicate. The setting out of a party's case is essential to a fair hearing, enabling the other party to know what points are in issue, what documents to disclose, what evidence to call and how to prepare for trial. A party should not be exposed to issues and arguments of which they had no fair warning (*The Prudential Assurance Company* v. *HM Revenue & Customs* [2016] EWCA Civ 376).

The particulars of claim must set out a concise statement of the facts on which the claimant relies. They should identify the issues and the extent of the dispute between the parties, making clear the general nature of the case being advanced.

It is important that a proper distinction is made between a concise statement of facts and recitation of the evidence upon which it is sought to prove such facts, the latter of which should be contained in subsequent witness evidence.

CPR rule 16 and the relevant Practice Direction (PD16: see in particular paras.7.3–7.5) set out specifically what must be included in the particulars of claim in cases of this nature.

Uppal v. *Uppal* [2006] EWCA Civ 1595 at [20] emphasises the importance of properly constituted pleadings:

> In my view the judge should have stuck to the case as it was pleaded ... In my view he was wrong to go outside the pleaded case.

Where the claim is based upon a **written agreement**, a copy of the document(s) constituting the agreement should be attached to or served with the particulars of claim.

Where the claim is based upon an **oral agreement**, then the particulars of claim should set out the words used and state by whom and to whom and when and where they were spoken.

Where the claim is based upon an **agreement by way of conduct**, the particulars of claim must specify the conduct relied on and by whom and when and where the act constituting the conduct took place and what the act that took place was.

If the parties have owned previous properties, the history of that ownership should also be set out.

In addition, all sources of funds for the purchase price of those properties should be identified, as should details of repayments of the mortgage and other outgoings. This is particularly pertinent to claims presented on the basis of a resulting trust.

The claim form and accompanying documents, together with sufficient copies for service, must be filed at court together with the requisite fee.

The court will issue the claim and return copies for service together with a response pack and notice of issue.

When the claim form is served, it must be accompanied by:

- a form for defending the claim;
- a form for admitting the claim;
- a form for acknowledging service of the claim.

The acknowledgment of service itself must provide for the defendant's date of birth and the address for service must state the full postcode unless the court otherwise orders.

The time for service of the defence is 14 days after service of the particulars of claim, or 28 days if an acknowledgment is filed.

However, this period can be extended by up to 28 days provided both parties agree in writing. The court must be informed if this is the case. If a longer period is required an application using the Part 23 procedure will be required, setting out in full the reasons why such further period is required.

The defence when filed and served must provide a comprehensive response to the claim and can also include a counterclaim. As for the contents of the defence generally see CPR rule 16.5.

In their defence the defendant must state:

- which of the allegations in the particulars of claim they deny;
- which allegations they are unable to admit or deny but which they require the claimant to prove; and
- which allegations they admit.

Where the defendant denies an allegation:

- they must state their reasons for doing so; and
- if they intend to put forward a different version of events from that given by the claimant, they must state their own version.

Once a defence is filed a court officer will provisionally decide the 'track' which appears to be most suitable for the claim, and serve on each party a notice of proposed allocation requiring the parties to complete, file and serve a directions questionnaire (DQ) (Form N181 for the fast track or multi-track) together with the appropriate allocation fee (in the case of the claimant, or the defendant if a counterclaim) and, if a case appears suitable for allocation to the fast track or multi-track, require the parties to file proposed directions by the date specified in the notice.

The court will usually only allocate to a track and thereafter give procedural directions when all parties have filed their directions questionnaires.

If neither party files a DQ there is a mandatory provision that the court will issue a seven day unless order with the sanction that failure to comply will result in the claim, defence and any counterclaim being treated as struck out without further order.

If only one party fails to file a DQ the court may allocate, if there is sufficient information, order an allocation hearing (beware of subsequent penalisation for the necessity of such a hearing on the defaulting party) or make an unless order against the defaulting party.

The completion of a DQ is something that should be done with care. It is read by the District Judge and its contents will determine:

- the correct track allocation;
- whether a stay will be imposed;
- whether the case is transferred to another court; and
- whether the matter is listed for a case/costs management conference (CCMC) or the court makes directions of its own initiative.

Paragraph 2.3 of PD26 states that the parties should consult one another and co-operate in completing the DQs and that they should 'try to agree the case management directions which they will invite the court to make' (see also CPR rule 29.4).

Do, therefore, try to agree a comprehensive set of directions as opposed to each sending your own versions. If any directions are not agreed state what they are and why they are being sought or opposed, as the case may be.

The majority of allocation directions are undertaken administratively. CPR PD26, para.6.1 moreover states that:

> The court will only hold an allocation hearing on its own initiative if it considers that it is necessary to do.

If both parties so request it is common for cases to be stayed for one month (or more) to enable the parties to explore the possibility of a resolution through mediation or otherwise, in accordance with the overriding objective.

If agreed, the court will issue a standard N24 stay order with consequential directions for the parties to inform the court if matters are agreed for which a consent order can be filed, whether a further stay is required and if so how long, or if the matter remains contested and if so what directions are needed to progress the matter through to trial.

It is thus extremely important to keep the court informed by way of an agreed joint letter for a further stay if needed, or agreed directions prior to the end of the stay period if matters cannot be agreed. Diarise the end of the stay as a key date accordingly.

If a stay is not appropriate, then the court will allocate the case to a track and give consequential directions which, as stated above, the parties should seek to agree by submission of a draft order with their direction questionnaires. (Note the appendix to PD28 contains some suggested standard directions for the fast track, and it might also be useful to try and obtain your local court's 'tick box' standard directions form to use as a template.)

7.3.4.2 Service

CPR Part 6 contains provisions regarding service.

There is no definition of 'service' in Part 6. However, the glossary to the CPR refers to 'steps required by rules of court to bring documents used in court proceedings to a person's attention'.

The fact that the person has or has not received the document does not necessarily mean that that person has or has not been served.

Service is usually effected by the court unless the court orders otherwise or the claimant elects to effect service.

Rule 6.3 prescribes the permitted methods of service:

- For individuals the address for service is their usual or last known place of residence. It is therefore incumbent on a claimant to take reasonable steps to ascertain the defendant's address for service. Service can also be effected by personal service.
- If the claimant is unable to discover the correct address, then service can be effected at an alternative place or by an alternative method; if so make an application.
- However, if the claimant still cannot ascertain the current address or any alternative place or method they are still entitled to serve at the 'last known address'.
- There must be a specific agreement to serve by email and/or fax and the defendant or their solicitors *must* have confirmed in writing that they are willing to accept such service.
- Where the defendant's solicitors have notified the claimant in writing that they are instructed to accept service of the claim, service *must* be effected on the defendant's solicitors and any other form of service will not be valid.
- Service by such method, however, cannot be inferred merely because the solicitor is acting for the defendant; there must be express authority to that effect.
- Although CPR rule 6.15 gives the court the power to retrospectively sanction service which has otherwise been bad this can only be done if there is a good reason to do so.

Service of the claim form is dealt with in CPR rule 7.5.

Service of the claim form outside the four-month period is dealt with by CPR rule 7.6(3); it is a discretionary exercise. The words of CPR rule 7.5(1) are mandatory, and the procedure for extension is strict.

As a matter of common sense, the court will always want to know why the claim form was not served within the specified period. The weaker the reason for not serving on time, the more likely it is that the application will be refused.

The relevant legal principles governing the court's approach to an application under CPR rule 7.6(2) are to be found in the judgments of the Court of Appeal in *Hashtroodi* v. *Hancock* [2004] EWCA Civ 652, *Collier* v. *Williams* [2006] EWCA Civ 20 and *Bayat* v. *Cecil* [2011] EWCA Civ 135.

It is important to note, however, that this provision does not apply to the particulars (*Totty* v. *Snowden* [2001] 4 All ER 577) as these are dealt with by CPR rule 3.1(2)(a).

The criteria governing an extension of time for service of particulars of claim are significantly less stringent than those relating to extending time for service of the claim form. Thus, as a matter of good practice, it is better to serve the claim form within time and apply to extend service of the particulars rather than serve neither.

Where there is no reason for the failure to serve the claim form within the time allowed other than incompetence, neglect or oversight on the part of the claimant or their legal representative, this will be a powerful reason for refusing to grant an extension of time, although not an absolute bar (*Hashtroodi* v. *Hancock* [2004] EWCA Civ 652).

The court will be required to consider how good a reason there was for the failure to serve in time. The stronger the reason, the more likely the court will be to grant an extension. This involves making a judgment about the reason why service has not been effected within the relevant four-month period.

If the application is made before the expiry of the time limit the court has a general discretion in accordance with the overriding objective. However, there must at least be some attempt to effect service.

Defendants must consider issues of service before filing the acknowledgment; if they don't they cannot then go on to argue the point later, including any argument as to challenging an application for extension of time (see CPR Part 11).

7.3.4.3 The tracks

CPR rule 26.8 sets out those matters which the court must consider when deciding which track to allocate the case to:

Matters relevant to allocation to a track

26.8

(1) When deciding the track for a claim, the matters to which the court shall have regard include –

- (a) the financial value, if any, of the claim;
- (b) the nature of the remedy sought;
- (c) the likely complexity of the facts, law or evidence;
- (d) the number of parties or likely parties;
- (e) the value of any counterclaim or other Part 20 claim and the complexity of any matters relating to it;
- (f) the amount of oral evidence which may be required;
- (g) the importance of the claim to persons who are not parties to the proceedings;
- (h) the views expressed by the parties; and
- (i) the circumstances of the parties.

Under the Civil Procedure Rules, there are three tracks:

- the small claims track;
- the fast track; and
- the multi-track.

The **small claims track** is the normal track for claims valued at no more than £10,000.

The **fast track** is the normal track for cases with a financial value of between £10,000 and £25,000 and where the trial itself is likely to take no more than one day, and oral expert evidence is limited to one per party and in no more than two disciplines.

The **multi-track** is the normal track for all other cases.

It is the norm for these types of cases to be allocated to the multi-track, not only because of the likely value of the claim but also because – other than the simplest of cases – they are likely to take more than one day of court time.

Upon allocation, the court will either:

- give directions for case management and set a timetable; or
- fix a case management conference.

As discussed earlier, the parties themselves are encouraged to agree directions, and indeed the majority of case management directions will be dealt with by way of a telephone conference.

The CMC should be attended by a legal representative who is familiar with the case and the issues involved and have sufficient authority to deal with any issues that are likely to arise, including potential settlement of the case.

Directions will usually involve:

- disclosure and inspection of documents;
- exchange of witness statements; and possibly
- expert evidence.

If an order is sought which is not routinely made at a case management conference then an application notice should be issued in good time for the hearing (PD29, para.5.8(1)).

The following documents must be filed and served before the CMC/CCMCs:

- DQs;
- costs budget in Form H and budget discussion reports in multi-track cases (see **7.3.3**);
- draft directions using the specimen directions template;
- estimates as to costs for any proposed expert evidence;
- disclosure report in multi-track cases (see CPR rule 31.5(3) and **7.3.4.4**).

In addition, the following may also be directed to be filed:

- case summary;
- schedule of issues;
- a breakdown of costs incurred;
- alternative estimates for experts (e.g. on a single joint expert (SJE) basis);
- list of witnesses to be called, indicating:
  - their name;
  - the issues that they will address;
  - the anticipated length of the statement.

The starting point for directions will, of course, be the model directions provided for in the CPR themselves, which if at all possible must be agreed between the parties and submitted to the court at least seven days before the hearing – which, if agreed, may necessitate the vacation of the hearing and save costs.

Each court tends to have its own set of standard directions and it is a good idea to ask your local District Judge to be provided with a copy so that when drawing up agreed directions you are using the template which is used in your own court; they also serve as a useful aide-mémoire.

Accordingly, the first case management conference should be a real event at which the court takes hold of the case and gives directions which will focus the factual evidence, the expert evidence and the disclosed documents on the real issues between the parties through to trial.

More so than in the family jurisdiction there is an emphasis in the civil jurisdiction on the use of remote telephone hearings. Indeed, any allocation hearing, listing hearing, interim application, case management conference or pre-trial review with a time estimate of no more than one hour will be conducted by way of a telephone hearing unless the court orders otherwise. The only exceptions are without notice applications, where the parties are unrepresented or where more than four parties wish to make representations (PD23A, para.6.2).

TELEPHONE HEARINGS: A QUICK GUIDE (PD23A)

- Apply at least seven days in advance for permission if you wish for a hearing to proceed as such (PD23A, para.6.4).
- Submit an agreed case summary, proposed draft order and agreed bundle, including evidence and documents referred to or relied upon (if necessary), at least two days before the hearing (PD23A, paras.6.12 and 9.1).
- The designated legal representative is responsible for arranging the telephone conference for precisely the time fixed by the court (PD23A, para.6.10(1)).
- The hearing must be dealt with by the 'designated legal representative'.
- Introduce yourself before speaking and do not speak over your opponent.
- If talking on a mobile check your signal strength.
- Make sure that the time estimate is adequate.

Unless specifically agreed no one can personally attend the judge during the course of a telephone hearing.

Telephone hearings are more suitable for short decisions dealing with procedural issues rather than where a fully reasoned judgment is required. Difficult cases should not be undertaken by telephone unless there is no alternative; this is particularly so where the judge will need a few minutes to reflect before giving judgment.

So, let us now look at the usual types of directions given at the case management hearing.

7.3.4.4 Disclosure and inspection

CPR rule 31.8(1) provides that a party's duty to disclose documents is limited to documents which are or have been in their control, and rule 31.8(2) provides that for that purpose a party has a document in their control if:

> (a) it is or was in his physical possession;
> (b) he has or has had a right to possession of it; or
> (c) he has or has had a right to inspect or take copies of it.

A party discloses a document by stating that it exists or has existed.

Moreover, CPR rule 31.14(1) gives the right to any party to 'inspect a document mentioned' in a statement of case, witness statement, witness summary or affidavit.

A document need only be 'mentioned' or 'alluded to' or 'referred to' for CPR rule 31.14 to come into play.

When such a document is disclosed, a party has a right to inspect it unless the document is no longer in their control, or they have a right or duty to withhold inspection of it (i.e. public interest or legal privilege applies) or such disclosure would be disproportionate or not otherwise in accordance with the overriding objective.

The presumption will usually be in favour of allowing inspection of disclosed documents unless the court can be persuaded as to any of the above.

Note that for the purposes of determining such an application the court can direct that the party wishing to withhold inspection produce the document to the court.

For example, in relation to ADR, confidentiality applies to the disclosure of documents during the mediation process because the 'without prejudice' privilege applies and contractual confidentiality provisions will usually prevent such disclosure (*Cumbria Waste* v. *Baines Wilson* [2008] EWHC 786 (QB)).

Within civil proceedings the overriding principle is that disclosure will be restricted to that which is necessary in the individual case.

In determining any such issue of proportionality, a court will have regard to whether inspection is necessary for the fair disposal of the application.

The general provisions as to disclosure are dealt with by CPR Part 31.

Case management directions may confine such disclosure to standard disclosure by way of list of documents or specific disclosure under CPR rule 31.12.

'**Standard disclosure**' places upon the disclosing party an obligation to disclose documents upon which they intend to rely as well as those which might adversely affect their case, or support that of the other party (see **7.2.2.1**).

An order for standard disclosure imposes an obligation to search and produce a list (Form N265).

For cases allocated to the multi-track one must also have regard to the requirements of CPR rule 31.5(3)–(8) in relation to a disclosure report.

A disclosure report must estimate:

> the broad range of costs that could be involved in giving standard disclosure in the case, including the costs of searching for and disclosing any electronically stored documents...

CPR rule 31.5(3) provides for the specific contents of this report.

One must also have regard to the menu of possible disclosure orders as provided for by CPR rule 31.5(7) which are as follows:

(a) Dispense with disclosure.
(b) Disclose what you rely upon and request specific disclosure from the other party.
(c) Disclosure on an issue-by-issue basis.
(d) Disclosure where it is reasonable to suppose that a document may contain information which enables the party to advance its own case or to damage the case of another party or which leads to an enquiry with either of those consequences.
(e) Standard disclosure.
(f) Any other appropriate order.

The court, at the case management conference, will decide which of the menu options is appropriate having regard to the overriding objective, the issue of proportionality and the need to limit disclosure to that which is necessary to deal with the case justly, ensuring that the parties also carry out a sufficient search for any e-documents.

To assist in this exercise the disclosure report – verified by a statement of truth and filed and served 14 days before the first case management conference – must set out what documents the parties have, in what form and where they are (CPR rule 31.5(3)). The parties must estimate the costs of such disclosure and select one of the menu options.

Not less than seven days before the case management conference the parties must, in addition, meet or speak to discuss and seek to agree a proposal for disclosure.

Just as with case management directions, if the parties reach agreement and the court considers the proposals are suitable, the proposals may be approved without the need for a hearing.

E-Disclosure in multi-track cases is dealt with by exchanging an Electronic Document Questionnaire (PD31B).

If a party is unhappy with the documents disclosed as being inadequate then they may make an application to the court under CPR rule 31.12 for specific disclosure. An application for specific disclosure is made under CPR Part 23 and is similar to Part 18 of the Family Procedure Rules 2010.

The application must state the order that the court is being asked to make, the documents or class of documents that are sought and must be supported by evidence.

In determining the application, as with all applications before the court, the court will be guided by the overriding objective and will consider all of the circumstances of the case including proportionality.

The relevance of the documents requested will also be analysed by reference to the issues in dispute between the parties.

The court has jurisdiction under CPR rule 31.12 to make an order for specific disclosure at any time, irrespective of whether or not formal disclosure has taken place.

As far as disclosure specific to these types of applications is concerned, an important source of relevant information will be the conveyancing file (e.g. attendance notes, letters giving advice as to beneficial ownership and the completion statement), official copies of the title and more crucially Form TR1/Form 19(JP) and any notice of severance.

Other documents that might prove useful include the mortgage application and offer, the estate agent's initial letter and any proposal forms in respect of insurance/endowment policies (see *Crossley* v. *Crossley* [2005] EWCA Civ 1581).

Bank statements, passbooks and credit card statements may also be relevant if they can show either receipt of monies or payments of mortgage instalments and premiums, household expenditure, repairs and renovations, as well as copy invoices from any suppliers or tradespeople in relation to such repairs or renovations/improvements.

7.3.4.5 Part 18 requests

CPR Part 18 makes provision for the court to order a party to provide clarification on a matter which is in dispute in the proceedings and to give additional information in relation to it.

The purpose of this rule is to ensure that the parties have all the information required to deal with the case efficiently and justly and only relates to matters in dispute:

> ... A request for further information, under CPR 18, arises really as part of the responsibility of the court to manage cases and the parties to co-operate in the just and efficient disposal of the issues between them. The function of a request is to identify the material facts that are going to be relied upon at trial, but not to plead evidence that will be led to prove those facts.
>
> (*Pacific Biosciences of California, Inc* v. *Oxford Nanopore Technologies Ltd* [2018] EWHC 806 (Ch) at [19])

Before making an application to the court for an order under Part 18, the party seeking clarification or information should first serve on the party from whom it is sought a written request for that clarification or information, stating a reasonable timescale in which the response should be received (see PD18 paras.1.3–1.7 as to the format of the request).

In essence, this partially mirrors the process as to questionnaires under the Family Procedure Rules 2010, rule 9.14(5)(c).

The regime for further information to be provided in relation to matters in dispute under CPR Part 18 is based on the tests of 'necessity' and 'proportionality' in relation to a party's ability to prepare their own case and to understand the case they have to meet. It is not a fishing expedition.

7.3.4.6 Expert evidence

There is a popular misconception that the court's permission is required before one instructs an expert; however, a party may instruct as many experts as they like, but they require the court's permission before calling an expert to give oral evidence or putting their report as evidence before the court (CPR rule 35.4(1)).

Expert evidence obtained by a party other than pursuant to a court order or as part of the protocol is obtained at their own risk. Thus, it is always best to seek approval first, particularly when in proceedings.

CPR Part 35 sets out a clear warning that expert evidence will be restricted to that which is reasonably required in order to resolve the proceedings (the former lower standard as previously applied to family cases).

Ask yourself whether the evidence is necessary – in the sense that a decision cannot be made without it – or whether it is of marginal relevance, in which case a balance has to be struck and the proportionality of its admission assessed.

In striking that balance, the court has to take into account such factors as the value of the claim, the effect of a judgment either way on the parties, how the commissioning of the evidence is to be paid for, and any delay likely to be entailed by the production of the evidence.

Key points:

- Is the expert evidence necessary? If the evidence is necessary it should be admitted.
- If it is not necessary then the question is whether the evidence will be of assistance to the court.
- If it is of assistance, then the question is whether it is reasonably required to resolve the proceedings.

Where a party applies for permission to rely upon expert evidence one must identify the field in which they wish to rely upon that evidence, and if practicable the name of the expert upon whom they wish to rely and the related timescale in which the report is to be filed.

One area in which expert evidence will almost certainly be required is in respect of a valuation of the property in dispute, the extent to which any relevant improvements have increased the value and the figure for occupation rent.

In such circumstances this will necessitate appointing a single joint expert (SJE).

As for single joint experts generally, as opposed to each party having their own expert, PD35, para.7 sets out the criteria for determining whether or not a single joint expert should be appointed as follows:

> When considering whether to give permission for the parties to rely on expert evidence and whether that evidence should be from a single joint expert the court will take into account all the circumstances in particular, whether:
>
> (a) it is proportionate to have separate experts for each party on a particular issue with reference to –

    (i) the amount in dispute;
    (ii) the importance to the parties; and
    (iii) the complexity of the issue;

(b) the instruction of a single joint expert is likely to assist the parties and the court to resolve the issue more speedily and in a more cost-effective way than separately instructed experts;
(c) expert evidence is to be given on the issue of liability, causation or quantum;
(d) the expert evidence falls within a substantially established area of knowledge which is unlikely to be in dispute or there is likely to be a range of expert opinion;
(e) a party has already instructed an expert on the issue in question and whether or not that was done in compliance with any practice direction or relevant pre-action protocol;
(f) questions put in accordance with rule 35.6 are likely to remove the need for the other party to instruct an expert if one party has already instructed an expert;
(g) questions put to a single joint expert may not conclusively deal with all issues that may require testing prior to trial;
(h) a conference may be required with the legal representatives, experts and other witnesses which may make instruction of a single joint expert impractical; and
(i) a claim to privilege makes the instruction of any expert as a single joint expert inappropriate.

In TOLATA 1996 claims it is rare to see anything other than there being an appointment of a single joint expert even in cases where fraud is alleged, such as a handwriting expert, unless the property concerned has some unusual features such as potential development value or is of such high value as to lead to a range of values.

Needless to say, all experts appointed by the court owe a duty to the court which takes precedence over any duty they might have to the party appointing them or paying their fees.

The court order appointing the expert should identify the expert or the field of expertise and the issues they are required to address. The court may also limit the amount of the experts' fees and expenses that are recoverable from the other party if the claim were to be ultimately successful.

It will also be extremely rare for the court to allow the expert to attend the final hearing to give oral evidence, as the usual form in which their evidence will be presented will be by way of a written report compliant with CPR Part 35 and the corresponding practice direction, followed by questions, which must be proportionate and be for clarification purposes only (CPR rule 35.6).

As for expert evidence generally, in civil cases see *Kennedy* v. *Cordia (Services) LLP* [2016] UKSC 6 and the *Guidance for the instruction of experts in civil claims* (Civil Justice Council, 2014).

7.3.4.7 Witness statements

When giving directions the court will usually order witness statements to be filed and served, setting out the substance of the oral evidence upon which the parties intend to rely.

The order will normally be for simultaneous exchange of statements. There may be occasions, however, when sequential service will be appropriate, e.g. when the defendant needs to know the precise case advanced by the claimant before being in a position to respond.

CPR rule 32.2(2) provides that the court may give directions in relation to factual evidence in as much as:

- identifying or limiting the issues to which such factual evidence may be directed;
- identifying which witnesses may be called;
- limiting the length or format of witness statements.

Witness statements must comply with the requirements set out in PD32, paras.17–22.

Key points to note are:

- The witness statement should be headed with the title of the proceedings.
- At the top right hand corner of the first page you should include details as to the party on whose behalf the statement is made, the initials and surname of the witness, the number of the statement in relation to that witness, the identifying initials and number of each exhibit referred to and the date the statement was made.
- The witness statement must, if practicable, be in the intended witness's own words.
- The witness statement should state the full name of the witness and their place of residence, or if they are making the statement in their professional capacity it should state the address where they work, their position and the name of their firm or employer.
- Exhibits should be verified and identified by the witness and remain separate from the witness statement.
- It is usually convenient if the witness statement follows the chronological sequence of events, and each paragraph should as far as possible be confined to a distinct aspect of the claim.
- A witness statement should be verified with a statement of truth.
- The statement should be bound securely in a manner which will not hamper filing and each page should be endorsed with the case number and bear the initials of the witness.

A witness statement is also required to indicate that which is within a witness's own knowledge, and the source of any other matters of information or belief.

The importance in the full preparation of witness statements cannot be overstated as in these types of actions the reported decisions are notable in underlining the importance that can often be attached to the minutiae of the parties' respective financial histories.

One can do no better, perhaps, than refer to the words of Waite J in the case of *H* v. *M (Beneficial Interest)* [1992] 1 FLR 229:

> The primary emphasis accorded by the Law in cases of this kind to express discussions between the parties ('however imperfectly remembered and however imprecise their terms') means that the tenderest exchanges of a common law courtship may assume an unforeseen significance many years later when they are brought under equity's microscope and subjected to an analysis under which many thousands of pounds of value may be liable to turn on fine questions as to whether the relevant words were spoken in earnest or in dalliance and whether without representation or intent. This requires that the express discussions to which the Court's initial enquiries will be addressed should be pleaded in the greatest detail, both as to language and as to circumstance. In the Family Division, where there is no procedure for pleadings or particulars, the decree of particularity in which the relevant discussions are asserted in the Claimant's initial Affidavit will be of prime importance for both sides. From the Claimant's point of view, failure to achieve particularity at that stage may cause the claim to flounder for vagueness at the trial, where the Affidavit will stand as their evidence in chief, on which they will be unlikely to be allowed to enlarge orally before they are cross-examined on it. From the Respondent's point of view, they must be entitled, in an area of Law where the nuances of language are all important, to know exactly what case they have to meet.
>
> Particularity will have the further advantage to both sides of enabling the strength of the claim to be assessed by the parties' advisers at an early stage, with sufficient definition to provide a fair basis for reasonable compromise. That will be an especially desirable objective in the case of separating unmarried couples, whose distress or bitterness is often found, paradoxically, to have been increased rather than diminished by the decision not to undertake a commitment to each other in marriage.

From this it can be seen that it is vital that full and detailed instructions are taken at the outset of the retainer, and that a party's case is set out clearly from the start and focuses on the issues that the court will be required to determine.

Generally speaking, a witness statement should contain:

- the name of the person making the statement and their connection to the case;
- the nature of the claim;
- brief background;
- a schedule of issues and what the current position is;
- what is being sought and by whom;
- the reasons put forward in favour of or opposition to the claim.

For constructive trust cases based upon express discussions, for instance, the witness evidence must specifically deal with the following:

- When any relevant conversations took place (a special occasion – anniversary/ birthday).
- Where it took place.
- Were any witnesses present or were they told of such agreement in the immediate aftermath?
- Was anything set down in writing in order to corroborate such an account?

Note also the use of headings to fit in with Baroness Hale's non-exhaustive checklist:

1. Advice given at the time of transfer.
2. Discussions shedding light on intentions.
3. Reasons for purchasing in joint names.
4. Any reason for a joint tenancy being preferred.
5. The purpose for which the home was acquired.
6. The nature of the parties' relationship.
7. Whether there are any children for whom the home is provided.
8. The financing of the purchase.
9. The financing of other major expenditure on the property.
10. How the parties arranged their finances.
11. Responsibility for the discharge of the mortgage and outgoings on the house.
12. Mercenary considerations.

This has been further emphasised in the case of *Thomson* v. *Humphrey* [2009] EWHC 3576 (Ch) where Warren J accentuated the desirability of the parties presenting a fully documented account of the history of their relationship which was reiterated in *Smith* v. *Bottomley and Coach House Properties Ltd* [2013] EWCA Civ 953 where it was held that the evidence presented must match the pleaded case.

> I make clear that I am not suggesting that courts must adopt an inflexible approach to the question of whether or not a particular unpleaded issue may or may not be the subject of investigation at a trial. There will be cases in which it will be obvious that it would be unjust for the court not to entertain and decide a non-pleaded issue: for example, when it is apparent that both sides have come to court ready to deal with it as an issue in the case despite its omission from the pleadings. … such cases are likely to be rare.
> (*Lombard North Central Plc* v. *Automobile World (UK) Ltd* [2010] EWCA Civ 20 at [79])

As can be seen, contested constructive trust cases have the ability to grow in such a way that their costs can quickly become disproportionate to the sums in issue, particularly where one is having to establish an interest, or quantify that interest, having regard to the whole course of dealing between the parties.

7.3.4.8 Additional directions

Further directions that you may come across include the request for the preparation of a case summary, which will be required to be prepared by the applicant and to be agreed, if at all possible, with the other side.

The purpose of the case summary is to assist the court to understand and deal with the issues before it.

It should set out a brief chronology of the claim, the issues of facts which are agreed or in dispute and the evidence required to decide them.

Other directions include the setting down of the matter for trial and the completion of what are known as pre-trial checklists (listing questionnaires (LQs)) (Form N170) and, in more complex cases, a pre-trial review before the trial judge.

The purpose of the pre-trial checklists is to ensure that all directions have been complied with and that the matter is ready for trial. In straightforward cases pre-trial checklists may be dispensed with.

The LQ requires the parties to report on progress, the extent of compliance with directions, any outstanding applications and overall readiness for trial.

It is a requirement for both parties to ensure that the trial timetable is followed and adhered to, and that any difficulties are brought to the court's attention on the occasion of the filing of the pre-trial checklists, if not before.

Accordingly, any applications that need to be made prior to the trial itself should be dealt with at the same time as filing the pre-trial checklists, at the very latest.

On the fast track LQs will need to be filed not less than three weeks, and no more than eight weeks, before the commencement of the trial window.

On the multi-track they should be filed not later than eight weeks before the commencement of the trial window.

In the case of one or other party failing to file the LQs the court can either dispense with them, so as to retain the trial window (unlikely), or deal with the matter by way of an unless order (CPR rules 28.5 (fast track) and 29.6 (multi-track)).

If there are any issues which concern the court following the filing of the checklists the court may list the matter for a pre-trial review (if not already listed).

As for the time estimate for the trial, make sure this is accurate; it is better to overestimate than underestimate.

Note the limitation of a one-day hearing on the fast track. Consider the number of witnesses required (on both sides) and estimate sufficient time to allow for reflection and judgment and any argument on the issue as to costs.

Regarding the trial itself, there is a heavy presumption that there should be no postponement unless circumstances are exceptional and there is no other option; postponement will be an order of the last resort.

The court will also direct for there to be filed at court, prior to the final hearing, an agreed trial bundle which normally comprises copies of the claim form and statements of case, a case summary, schedule of issues and chronology, requests for further information and responses to those requests, the witness statements, experts' reports and any responses to questions raised by any party pursuant to those reports, copies of previous orders made within the proceedings and any other necessary documentation relevant to the trial of the issue. (Note the warning given in *Seagrove* v. *Sullivan* [2014] EWHC 4110 (Fam) regarding bundles getting out of hand.)

Pursuant to CPR PD29, para.4.10(9), where the court feels that it is appropriate, it may give directions for the parties to consider ADR prior to giving any directions:

> The parties shall by [date] consider whether the case is capable of resolution by ADR. If any party considers that the case is unsuitable for resolution by ADR, that party shall be prepared to justify that decision at the conclusion of the trial, should the judge consider that such means of resolution were appropriate, when he is considering the appropriate costs order to make.

> The party considering the case unsuitable for ADR shall, not less than 28 days before the commencement of the trial, file with the court a witness statement without prejudice save as to costs, giving reasons upon which they rely for saying that the case was unsuitable.

Furthermore, many courts are now directing that cohabitant cases are listed for FDR-style hearings pursuant to the court's general case management powers as set out in CPR rule 1.4:

> (1) The court must further the overriding objective by actively managing cases.
> (2) Active case management includes –
>
> ...
> (e) encouraging the parties to use an alternative dispute resolution procedure if the court considers that appropriate and facilitating the use of such procedure;
> (f) helping the parties to settle the whole or part of the case;
> ...
> (h) considering whether the likely benefits of taking a particular step justify the cost of taking it;
> ...

The court is also required to take any other step or make any other order for the purpose of managing the case and furthering the overriding objective, including hearing an early neutral evaluation with the aim of helping the parties settle the case (CPR rule 3.1(2)(m); see also **7.3.2**).

This is further backed up by the Chancery Guide (2016), para.18.18 and the specimen draft order as to FDR hearings.

Suggested case management directions in relation to the above for the purposes of your allocation questionnaire (AQ) might consist of the following:

1. The matter be listed for a directions appointment with a time estimate of one hour (at which the parties must attend at least one hour beforehand to use their best endeavours to reach agreement on all matters in issue between them or to narrow those issues) for the purpose of assessing the parties' positions and for discussion and negotiation, such appointment to be conducted on a without prejudice basis and in the event that the proceedings remain contested the District Judge conducting the hearing shall play no further part in the proceedings save conducting any further FDR appointment, making a consent order or listing the matter for a further case management conference or trial with consequential directions.
2. The claimant must, not less than seven days before the FDR appointment, file with the court a bundle (comprising no more than 250 pages of single side A4) for the FDR appointment which shall include as part of the preliminary documents:

    - agreed statement of issues;
    - position statements;
    - details of all offers;

- skeleton arguments (if appropriate and limited to no more than 10 pages).

3. At the conclusion of the FDR appointment, any documents filed under point 2 above, and any filed documents referring to them, must be returned to that party and not retained on the court file and the court will not retain a record of the hearing. No non-party will be entitled to obtain a transcript of the hearing.
4. The costs of and associated with the FDR hearing shall be costs in the case.

7.3.4.9 Variation of the court's timetable

If you do need to make an application to vary any procedural directions already given then the earlier the better and be prepared to set out fully the reasons for doing so.

Any application should be made prior to the deadline for compliance, even if the application is heard after the date for which the extension is sought, otherwise the application will be one for relief from sanctions (see **7.3.4.13**).

Rule 3.8(4) of the CPR provides that where a rule, practice direction or court order requires a party to do something within a specified time and specifies the consequences of failure to comply, the parties may, by prior written agreement, extend up to a maximum of 28 days the time for doing the act in question, provided that any hearing date is not put at risk as a result. Extensions beyond that, however, require court approval.

However, there are certain dates you can't vary without making an application:

- a CMC;
- a PTR;
- the return of a LQ;
- the trial or trial window;
- any step which is subject to a sanction.

7.3.4.10 Judgment in default

In Part 7 claims, failure to file an acknowledgment of service or defence within the requisite time period will necessitate an application for a default judgment in accordance with CPR Part 12.

However, the filing of an acknowledgment of service or a defence, albeit late, will be a bar to a subsequent application for a default judgment.

Once obtained, judgment may be entered either for a specified amount or, more usually, for an amount to be determined by the court.

The request must be made in the prescribed practice form (N225 or N227 depending upon the type of judgment sought) and the court must be satisfied that the defendant has been served and that they have failed to file an acknowledgment, a defence or an admission.

Upon entering judgment, the court will then go on to give directions and, if appropriate, allocate the matter to a track.

This procedure will not be of much help in joint names cases where the only issue is the quantification of the beneficial entitlement, but will be useful in sole name cases where, if judgment is obtained, it will mean that a beneficial interest on behalf of the claimant has been established through default, the only remaining matter for the court to determine being the extent of that interest.

7.3.4.11 Setting aside judgment in default

CPR Part 13 sets out the provisions with regard to an aggrieved party applying to have any default judgment set aside.

To be successful there has to be a real prospect of successfully defending the claim or some other good reason why the judgment should be set aside or varied, or why the defendant should be allowed to defend the claim.

The remedy is a discretionary one in which the court will apply the overriding objective and proportionality, having regard to the promptness of the application.

CPR rule 13.3(2) however, states that promptness of the application is just one of the factors the court must consider and therefore 'promptness' is not solely determinative of the issue, however, the longer the delay and the lack of adequate reasons given for it the more likely it is that weight will be given to that factor.

HOW 'PROMPT' IS 'PROMPT'?

In *Regency Rolls Ltd* v. *Carnall* [2000] EWCA Civ 379 30 days was held to be too long and in *Hart Investments Ltd* v. *Fidler* [2006] EWHC 2857 (TCC) a delay of 59 days was regarded as being 'at the outer edge of what could possibly be acceptable' (at [26]).

In my view anything more than 21 days is likely to raise judicial eyebrows.

However, promptness is to be measured not solely by reference to the length of delay but also by considering the reasons for any delay.

If the judgment is irregular, however (i.e. the claim was not served), the judgment must be set aside.

In essence, default judgments will be set aside where the injustice of preventing the adjudged party from presenting their defence outweighs the injustice to the claimant of allowing them to present their defence. In other words, one must conduct a 'balancing of prejudice' exercise.

Accordingly, the court's discretion to set aside a default judgment is a broad one which may be exercised if there is 'some other good reason' why a defendant should be allowed to defend the claim.

An application to set aside a default judgment pursuant to CPR rule 13.3 is also an application for relief against sanctions. It is therefore necessary to consider not only the elements of rule 13.3 but also the three-stage test on relief from sanctions set out in *Denton* v. *TH White Ltd* [2014] EWCA Civ 906 (*Gentry* v. *Miller* [2016] EWCA Civ 141; and see **7.3.4.13**).

In *TPE* v. *Franks* [2018] EWHC 1765 (QB) Knowles J underlined that on an application to set aside a default judgment the proper approach under CPR rule 13.3 was first to consider whether the applicant has shown that they have real prospects of a successful defence or some other good reason to set the judgment aside. If they do show this, the court's discretion is to be exercised in the light of all the circumstances and the overriding objective, taking the *Denton* factors into account.

7.3.4.12 Part 8 procedure

The appropriate claim form in respect of a Part 8 application is Form N208.

The claim form must state on it that Part 8 applies to the claim, the question which the claimant wants the court to decide, the remedy the claimant is seeking and the legal basis for it. It must also state the statutory provision the claim is being brought under, namely TOLATA 1996.

As with Form N1 the claim must be verified by a statement of truth.

As already outlined, the Part 8 procedure applies to decisions that are unlikely to involve a substantial dispute of fact and, except in those instances where beneficial entitlement is not in issue, will not normally be the correct procedure for claims that do involve a substantial dispute of fact.

Although CPR rule 64.2 says that Part 8 applies to claims for the court to determine any question arising in the execution of a trust, TOLATA 1996 claims are essentially declaratory claims as to whether or not a trust exists in the first place, and if so to what extent.

That said, *M* v. *B, A and S (by the OS)* [2006] 1 FLR 117 held that a substantial dispute of fact was not an automatic bar to the use of the Part 8 procedure. The more important question was whether the factual and legal issues were such that full pleadings would assist in the resolution of the dispute.

The Part 8 procedure is flexible, and while its main aim is to move quickly to a final hearing where it is unlikely that substantial disputes of fact will arise, it could be used where there were such substantial factual disputes.

Moreover, there is a spectrum of cases between Part 7 and Part 8 where a flexible approach could be taken so as to adapt directions to the individual needs of the proceedings, whether the claim remains a Part 8 claim or is required to continue under Part 7.

That being said, 'flexibility under Part 8 has its limits':

> Whenever a party is contemplating commencing proceedings under CPR Part 8 in respect of a claim which could be started under CPR Part 7, the following steps ought generally to be taken:
>
> (a) The proposed Defendant ought to be notified that the use of CPR Part 8 is being contemplated.
>
> (b) A brief explanation ought to be provided as why CPR Part 8 is considered to be more appropriate than under CPR Part 7 in the particular circumstances of the case.

(c) A draft of the precise issue or question which the Claimant is proposing to ask the Court to decide ought to be supplied to the Defendant for comment.
(d) Any agreed facts relevant to the issue or question ought to be identified.
(*Cathay Pacific Airlines Ltd* v. *Lufthansa Technik AG* [2019] EWHC 484 (Ch) at [42])

When the Part 8 procedure is used, the claim form, when served, need only be accompanied by an acknowledgment of service.

Unlike under the Part 7 procedure, the claimant must file the written evidence upon which they intend to rely at the same time as filing the claim form which must also be served upon the defendant at the same time.

Upon issue of the claim the court will provide the claimant with a notice of issue and the defendant with a response pack.

A defendant who wishes to respond to the claim need only file an acknowledgment of service supported by a statement of truth (Form N210) which must be done within 14 days of service of the claim form. The requirement therefore for filing a defence and reply does not apply, unlike under the Part 7 procedure.

The acknowledgment must state whether or not the defendant contests the claim and, if the defendant seeks a different remedy from that set out in the claim form itself, must set out what that remedy is.

Section D of Form N210 allows the defendant to object to the Part 8 procedure being used, for example if the claim involves a substantial dispute of fact.

As with the claimant, the defendant must also file and serve any written evidence upon which they intend to rely at the same time as filing the acknowledgment. It will usually be preferable to set out the witness statement in a separate document.

A defendant who fails to submit their written evidence when filing the acknowledgment of service cannot later rely upon such evidence unless the court gives permission.

The claimant has 14 days to file any evidence in reply, which period can be extended by up to 28 days from the service of the defendant's evidence by agreement.

On receipt of the acknowledgment, or after the date for its due submission is passed, the file will be placed before the District Judge who will either list the matter for a case management conference or give standard case management directions.

Under the Part 8 procedure, case management directions will be identical to those under the Part 7 procedure, although they will not normally include witness statements as they should already have been filed.

If it appears that the claim itself is disputed so as to make the Part 8 procedure inappropriate, the judge can direct that it proceeds under the Part 7 procedure at the same time as giving initial case management directions.

Other differences applying to the Part 8 procedure include that the claimant is not able to obtain judgment by request on an admission or judgment in default following the failure to file an acknowledgment of service. In the light of such failure, however, a defendant, while still being able to attend a hearing, cannot take any part in it unless the court grants them permission to do so.

The claim will also be treated as having been allocated automatically to the multi-track and therefore the allocation procedure set out in CPR Part 26 does not apply and neither does costs budgeting unless the court directs otherwise, which may well be likely in these types of cases.

In essence, therefore, the principal features that differentiate the Part 8 procedure from that of Part 7 are as follows:

- Evidence must be filed and served with the claim form.
- The defendant is not required to file and serve a defence but is required to file and serve their witness evidence at an earlier stage.
- Default judgment and judgment following admission are not available.
- The case is listed at the outset and allocated to the multi-track, and the provisions relating to directions questionnaires are dispensed with.

7.3.4.13 Relief from sanctions

The word 'sanction' has no definition in the CPR, although it might be thought to be (as set out in rule 3.1(3)(b)) '… the consequence of failure to comply with the order or a condition' (as adopted by Leggatt J in *Summit Navigation Ltd* v. *Generali Romania Asigurare Reasigurare SA* [2014] EWHC 398 (Comm)).

CPR rule 3.8(4) provides that where a rule, practice direction or court order requires a party to do something within a specified time and specifies the consequences of failure to comply, the parties may, by prior written agreement, extend up to a maximum of 28 days the time for doing the act in question, provided that any hearing date is not put at risk as a result.

In all other cases an application will be required to extend the date for compliance or, if the date has passed, for relief from sanctions with supporting evidence, the onus being on the party in default.

Note the distinction between applications for extensions of time made prospectively and those made retrospectively.

An in-time application should not be treated as if it were an application for relief from sanctions as an application for an extension of the time to take any particular step in litigation is not an application for relief from sanctions, provided that the applicant filed their application notice before the expiry of the permitted time period. This is the case even if the court deals with the application after the expiry of the relevant period.

Moreover, the court should not refuse reasonable in-time applications for extensions of time as long as they do not imperil the hearing dates or disrupt the proceedings.

Having reviewed all the relevant authorities Mr Alexander Nissen QC (sitting as a Deputy High Court Judge) in *Everwarm Ltd* v. *BN Rendering Ltd* [2019] EWHC 2078 (TCC), at [36] came to the following conclusions:

(a) An application for an extension of time allowed to take a particular step in litigation is not an application for relief from sanctions provided that the applicant files his application notice before the expiry of the permitted period …
(b) This is the case even if the court actually deals with the application after the expiry of the relevant period …
(c) Although there may be little practical difference between an application made just before the expiry of the permitted period and one made just after it had expired, the law has sound practical and policy reasons for distinguishing between the two …
(d) An in-time application for an extension of time is neither an application for relief from sanctions nor is it closely analogous to one …
(e) An 'unless' order is an order of last resort. There is a powerful public interest in ensuring that parties recognise the importance of complying with 'unless' orders …
(f) However, the power to extend time for compliance with a court order pursuant to Rule 3.1(2)(a) does not distinguish between routine court orders on the one hand and 'unless' orders on the other.
(g) Accordingly, when determining an in-time application for an extension of time for compliance with both routine court orders and 'unless' orders, the court applies the overriding objective.

Thus, get your application in before the expiry of the deadline; otherwise make your application promptly.

'Acting promptly' means acting with 'reasonable celerity' and without 'needless delay' (*Tinkler* v. *Elliott* [2012] EWCA Civ 1289 at [20] quoting from *Regency Rolls Ltd* v. *Carnall* [2000] EWCA Civil 379).

Note also PD23A, para.2.7:

> Every application should be made as soon as it becomes apparent that it is necessary or desirable to make it.

Under CPR rule 3.8 any party who is in default of a court order or rule must apply to the court for relief from sanctions supported by evidence.

The obligation to obtain such relief is thus on the defaulter if they wish to escape the consequences of any court-imposed sanction.

CPR rule 3.9 sets out the provisions as to relief from sanctions:

> (1) On an application for relief from any sanction imposed for a failure to comply with any rule, practice direction or court order, the court will consider all the circumstances of the case, so as to enable it to deal justly with the application including the need –
>
> (a) for litigation to be conducted efficiently and at proportionate cost; and
> (b) to enforce compliance with rules, practice directions and orders.
>
> …

The power to grant relief is a discretionary one.

Mitchell v. *News Group Newspapers Ltd* [2013] EWCA Civ 1537 established the following:

1. The starting point is that any sanction for which relief is sought has been properly imposed and complies with the overriding objective.

2. One must ask: what is the nature of the non-compliance? If it can properly be regarded as trivial the court will usually grant relief, provided that an application is made promptly.
3. If it is not trivial then the burden is on the defaulting party to persuade the court to grant relief. The court will want to consider why the default occurred. If there is a good reason for it, the court will be likely to decide that relief should be granted. Good reasons are likely to arise from circumstances outside the control of the party in default.
4. Merely overlooking a deadline, whether on account of overwork or otherwise, is unlikely to be a good reason. The fact that solicitors are busy will rarely be a good excuse.
5. An application for extension of time made before time has expired will be looked upon more favourably than applications for relief from sanctions made after the event.

Subsequently, the Court of Appeal in *Denton* v. *TH White Ltd* [2014] EWCA Civ 906 revisited the *Mitchell* guidance in light of a number of conflicting High Court decisions, and propounded a three-stage test:

1. For the first stage one has to identify and assess the seriousness or significance of the relevant failure or breach. Triviality is not part of this stage. There are clearly degrees of seriousness and significance. The assessment ought not to involve consideration of past unrelated failures, only the seriousness and significance of the very breach in respect of which relief from sanctions is sought. If a breach is not serious or significant, relief will usually be granted and there will be no need to spend much time on the second and third stages.

   At the first stage the court is concerned solely with the gravity of the breach and nothing else. Triviality is now replaced by 'neither serious nor significant'. A useful, though not exclusive, benchmark is whether the breach imperils a hearing date or otherwise disrupts the conduct of the litigation. The implication is, if it does not, the breach is neither serious nor significant.
2. At the second stage the court has to consider why the failure or default occurred.
3. The third stage requires the court to consider all the circumstances of the case so as to enable it to deal justly with the application. A serious breach for no reason does not automatically prevent relief. Factors (1)(a) and (b) in CPR rule 3.9 remain of particular importance and are to be given particular weight at the third stage but are not paramount or determinative.

If the effect of a breach is to prevent the efficient and proportionate conduct of litigation, that will weigh against relief being granted. However, other factors will also be relevant and will vary on a case-by-case basis.

As to the approach to this by the legal profession the following observations were made:

- It is wholly inappropriate for litigants or their lawyers to take advantage of mistakes made by opposing parties in the hope that relief from sanctions will be denied and that they will obtain a windfall, strike-out or other litigation advantage.
- In a case where (a) the failure can be seen to be neither serious nor significant, (b) a good reason is demonstrated, or (c) it is otherwise obvious that relief from sanctions is appropriate, parties should agree that relief from sanctions be granted without the need for further costs to be expended in satellite litigation.
- The parties should in any event be ready to agree limited but reasonable extensions of time up to 28 days as envisaged by CPR rule 3.8(4).
- It should be very much the exceptional case where a contested application for relief from sanctions is necessary. This is for two reasons: firstly, because compliance should become the norm, rather than the exception as it was in the past; and secondly, because the parties should work together to make sure that, in all but the most serious cases, satellite litigation is avoided even where a breach has occurred.

Furthermore, 'the court will be more ready in the future to penalise opportunism' because:

- The duty of care owed by a legal representative to their client takes account of the fact that litigants are required to help the court to further the overriding objective.
- Representatives should bear this important obligation to the court in mind when considering whether to advise their clients to adopt an unco-operative attitude in unreasonably refusing to agree extensions of time and in unreasonably opposing applications for relief from sanctions.
- It is as unacceptable for a party to try to take advantage of a minor inadvertent error, as it is for rules, orders and practice directions to be breached in the first place.
- Heavy costs sanctions should, therefore, be imposed on parties who behave unreasonably in refusing to agree extensions of time or unreasonably oppose applications for relief from sanctions.

Following on from this, *Freeborn* v. *Marcal (t/A Dan Marcal Architects)* [2017] EWHC 3046 (TCC) stated as follows:

> Parties need to consider carefully whether the alleged breach of the rules is, on analysis, any such thing and, even if it is, whether it is proportionate and appropriate to require or oppose an application for relief from sanctions in all the circumstances of the case. (at [16])

The following conclusions were reached:

- An order to pay the costs of the application under CPR rule 3.9 may not always be sufficient.

- The court can, in an appropriate case, also record in its order that the opposition to the relief application was unreasonable conduct to be taken into account under CPR rule 44.11 when costs are dealt with at the end of the case.
- If the offending party ultimately wins, the court may make a substantial reduction in its costs recovery on grounds of misconduct under CPR rule 44.11.
- If the offending party ultimately loses, then its misconduct may be a good reason to order it to pay indemnity costs.
- Such an order would free the winning party from the operation of CPR rule 3.18 in relation to its costs budget.

The following further guidelines were also offered:

- The court must consider the effect of the breach in every case.
- If the breach has prevented the court or the parties from conducting the litigation (or other litigation) efficiently and at proportionate cost, that will be a factor weighing in favour of refusing relief.
- The court must always bear in mind the need for compliance with rules, practice directions and orders, because the old lax culture of non-compliance is no longer tolerated.
- But it is always necessary to have regard to all the circumstances of the case. The factors that are relevant will vary from case to case.
- The promptness of the application will be a relevant circumstance to be weighed in the balance.
- Likewise, other past or current breaches may also be taken into account at stage 3.
- The approach to non-compliance:

> has changed not by transforming rules and rule compliance into trip wires. Nor has it changed it by turning the rules and rule compliance into the mistress rather than the handmaid of justice. If that were the case then we would have, quite impermissibly, rendered compliance an end in itself and one superior to doing justice in any case.
>
> (*Mitchell* at [38] quoting from the 18th implementation lecture on the Jackson reforms delivered on 22 March 2013 by the Master of the Rolls at [26])

The court indicated:

- the culture of compliance that the new rules are intended to promote requires that judges ensure that the directions they give are realistic and achievable;
- the court must have regard to the realities of litigation in making orders in the first place;
- the court and the parties need to be aware of the consequences of non-compliance when making or agreeing directions;
- 'unless' orders should be reserved for situations in which they are truly required: these are usually so as to enable the litigation to proceed efficiently and at proportionate cost.

In summary, a judge should approach the question of relief from sanctions in three stages:

1. Identify and assess the seriousness of the failure to comply.
2. Consider why the default occurred.
3. Evaluate all the circumstances of the case so as to enable the court to deal justly with the application, including the need for litigation to be conducted efficiently and the need to enforce compliance with rules, practice directions and orders.

In practice, practitioners can face three types of situation:

1. An in-time application to extend a deadline.
2. An application to extend a deadline made after the deadline where no express sanction has been imposed.
3. An application to extend the deadline made after the deadline where a sanction applies.

Denton applies to points 2 and 3 above, but not point 1.

Of course, as regards point 3 a party who fails to comply with an unless order is normally in breach of an original order or rule as well as the unless order, and this is also a consideration when it comes to the exercise of discretion:

> The court usually only makes an 'unless' order against a party which is already in breach.
>
> The unless order gives that party additional time for compliance with the original obligation and specifies an automatic sanction in default of compliance. It is not possible to look at an unless order in isolation.
>
> (*British Gas Trading Ltd* v. *Oak Cash & Carry Ltd* [2016] EWCA Civ 153 at [38])

A few examples may prove instructive.

EXAMPLES OF NON-COMPLIANCE

The fact that a party is not professionally represented cannot of itself be a reason for disapplying rules and orders (*Chadwick* v. *Burling* [2015] EWHC 1610 (Ch)).

An inability to instruct solicitors because of a shortage of funds is also not a good reason for a failure to comply with the rules, and a litigant who is awaiting a Legal Aid Agency decision is in essentially the same position as a litigant in person. A delay in obtaining legal aid is not a complete answer to a failure to comply with procedural requirements in relation to an appeal. It is merely one factor to be taken into account (*Kigen* v. *Secretary of State for the Home Department* [2015] EWCA Civ 1286).

However, in *Al Ahmed* v. *The Mayor and Burgesses of the London Borough of Tower Hamlets* [2020] EWCA Civ 51 it was said as follows:

> Where an applicant relies on the fact that he was unrepresented and was seeking legal aid as a reason for non-compliance, the circumstances will need to be examined with care,

> including scrutiny of the diligence with which he acted in seeking legal aid. And even if the court is satisfied as to good reason, that simply opens up a discretion ... (at [35])

In *The Varajah* v. *Riordan* [2015] UKSC 78 it was held that where a party is subject to a debarring order for failing to comply with an unless order and relief from sanctions was refused at a time when he was still in default, the mere fact that he belatedly complied with the unless order could not amount to a material change of circumstances entitling him to make a second application for relief from sanctions.

It is also important to note that where the court sends out notification that a fee is due (e.g. the hearing fee for the trial), the case will automatically be struck out without further order if that fee is not paid in time. There is, in addition, a deemed order as to costs where there is such strike-out as a result of non-payment of fees.

However, while non-payment of the trial fee is a serious matter it is at the bottom of the range of seriousness:

> Part of the purpose of the early payment of a trial fee is to enable the listing of cases for trial to proceed in an orderly way, in the interests of all court users. But as has been acknowledged in other cases, it is clearly far from the most serious of the breaches that litigants can commit.
>
> (*Badejo* v. *Cranston* [2019] EWHC 3343 (Ch) at [16])

PRACTICE POINTS

- Frontload case preparation before issuing to ensure compliance with standard directions on issue. Do not wait until the receipt of the directions order before taking steps to progress the case because everybody worth their salt knows what they are going to be.
- Advise clients and experts of their obligations to comply with orders and the potential sanctions.
- Record all attempts and steps taken to ensure compliance by way of a chronology.
- Diarise orders and make notes regarding any sanction appearing on the face of the order itself or contained within the CPR.
- When drafting suggested template orders build in potential reasonable slippage time with provision for the parties to agree to vary the timetable without order before any non-compliance occurs, provided the court timetable is not affected.

The key message is: if you need more time in which to take a procedural step ask the other side for consent for this, and if such consent is not forthcoming apply for an extension in time (applications within time are not applications for relief from sanctions). Conversely, the other side should respond positively and in a spirit of co-operation to reasonable requests for such an extension.

Furthermore, once you are aware that rules have not been complied with, immediate effort should be made to rectify the situation in order to try and head off further criticism from the court.

7.3.4.14 Strike-out and summary judgment

Sometimes, it might occur to you that the other party, on the evidence available, has not got a hope of succeeding with their claim or defence, and in those instances you can consider either an application to strike out the defence (or if acting for the defendant, the claim itself) (CPR rule 3.4(2)) or an application for summary judgment, or more commonly both (CPR Part 24) (e.g. in cases where there is an express declaration as to trust).

Practice Direction 3A, supplementing CPR rule 3.4, states as follows:

> **1.7** A party may believe he can show without a trial that an opponent's case has no real prospect of success on the facts, or that the case is bound to succeed or fail, as the case may be, because of a point of law (including the construction of a document). In such a case the party concerned may make an application under rule 3.4 or Part 24 (or both) as he thinks appropriate.

In *Three Rivers DC* v. *The Bank of England (No. 3)* [2003] 2 AC 1 Lord Hope said of the tests in rule 3.4 and Part 24:

> While the difference between the two tests is elusive, in many cases the practical effect will be the same. (at [92])

In *Moroney* v. *Anglo-European College of Chiropractice* [2009] EWCA Civ 1560, Ward LJ said:

> Although the Rules give the court two distinct powers which may be used to achieve summary disposal of the issues which do not need full investigation at the trial, there is this overlap of approach. In those circumstances, I do not see how the judge can be criticised for dealing with the case either on the 3.4 route or on the Part 24 route, and to have approached the case asking whether there is a realistic prospect of success. (at [25])

By way of contrast, a different view was expressed in the case of *Ministry of Defence* v. *AB* [2010] EWCA Civ 1317:

> In our view, this power [rule 3.4(2)] is intended to be exercised on examination of the pleading itself, not after examination of the evidence supporting it. It is open to the court to raise the issue of strikeout under this rule of its own motion. It should not be necessary and is not appropriate for evidence to be served in support of or opposition to an application to strike out under this rule. (at [71])

Here, the court took the view that rule 3.4 could be considered in isolation and did not necessarily need to be supplemented by Part 24, which allows for evidence in support.

Mr Andrew Sutcliffe QC, sitting as a Judge of the High Court in *St Clair* v. *King & Farrell* [2018] EWHC 682 (Ch), said that in appropriate circumstances the court has a discretion to treat an application under rule 3.4 as including an application for summary judgment under CPR Part 24:

> I was referred to the note at paragraph 3.4.6 in the 2017 White Book and to *S* v. *Gloucestershire County Council* [2000] 3 All ER 346 at pages 372c–373f, *Taylor* v. *Midland Bank Trust Co Ltd* [2002] WTLR 95 at pages 107C–108H and 113E–G, and *Moroney* v. *Anglo-European College of Chiropractice* [2009] EWCA Civ 1560. However, it is clear that in none of these cases was there any procedural unfairness to the claimants in proceeding in this way because they had had a full opportunity to meet the application for summary judgment. In other cases the court has refused to grant summary judgment in the absence of a formal application, particularly if the party is left in doubt that he is facing an application for summary judgment. In *Ministry of Defence* v. *AB and others* [2010] EWCA Civ 1317, the Court of Appeal indicated that it would have set aside a summary judgment made without formal notice (in fact it did not have to do so because, although the application was allowed to be made, it was dismissed) on the grounds that it was not appropriate on the facts of that case to place on the judge the decision as to whether or not to exercise the jurisdiction under CPR Part 24 of his own motion. (at [28])

However, it is best to make both applications explicit rather than implicit.

As with most applications within proceedings (including applications for relief from sanctions and variations to case management directions) the appropriate application form is N244. The procedure is set out in Part 23 for strike-out and Part 24 for summary judgment and is not dissimilar in format to the procedure under the Family Procedure Rules 2010, Part 18.

In any event, such applications should be made at the earliest possible opportunity and as soon as it becomes apparent that one is appropriate. Although such an application can be made at trial, this will only be allowed in unusual circumstances.

STRIKE-OUT

CPR rule 3.4(2) provides that the court may strike out a statement of case if it appears:

> (a) that the statement of case discloses no reasonable grounds for bringing or defending the claim;
> (b) that the statement of case is an abuse of the court's process or is otherwise likely to obstruct the just disposal of the proceedings; or
> (c) that there has been a failure to comply with a rule, practice direction or court order.

The practice direction supplementing rule 3.4 says that such applications should be made as soon as possible and before allocation, if possible.

The court can, exceptionally, also make such orders of its own initiative.

The striking out of a statement of case is one of the most powerful weapons in the court's case management armoury and should not be deployed unless it can be fully justified.

Ground 1: CPR rule 3.4(2)(a) This usually applies where on the face of it the case appears hopeless; however, if the court is in any doubt as to its merits it is likely to direct that further information and disclosure be provided first on an unless basis.

The pleadings themselves should comprise a precise statement of facts allowing one's opponent to know the case they have to meet, with issues of both fact and law fully identified.

If a claim or defence is not properly pleaded the court is likely to grant permission to amend, but with a strike-out provision upon subsequent non-compliance.

CPR PD3A, para.1.4 sets out some examples where the court may conclude that the statement of case discloses no reasonable grounds for bringing or defending the claim:

- Those which set out no facts indicating what the claim is about.
- Those which are incoherent and make no sense.
- Those which contain a coherent set of facts but those facts, even if true, do not disclose any legally recognisable claim against the defendant.

CPR PD3A, para.1.6 states that a defence may fall within CPR rule 3.4(2)(a) where:

- It consists of a bare denial or otherwise sets out no coherent statement of facts (CPR rule 16.5(2) provides that if the defendant denies an allegation they must state their reasons for doing so, and if they intend to put forward a different version of events from that given by the claimant they must state their own version).
- The facts it sets out, while coherent, would not – even if true – amount to a defence to the claim in law.

The onus is on the applicant to satisfy the court that there are no reasonable grounds for bringing or defending the claim.

A court will not simply strike out a claim or defence if the statement of case does present an arguable claim or defence but does so poorly.

The court will also not strike out a statement of case if it appears that the claim or defence is unlikely to succeed as the court must be satisfied that the claim is bound to fail.

If an issue can only be determined by oral evidence at trial then the court should not strike out the claim without first hearing that evidence. The court must avoid an inappropriate mini-trial without evidence.

Ground 2: CPR rule 3.4(2)(b) A statement of case may be struck out in whole or in part if it is an abuse of the court's process or is otherwise likely to obstruct the just disposal of the proceedings or – as CPR PD3A, para.1.5 states – is 'vexatious, scurrilous or obviously ill-founded'.

The word 'obstruct' means 'to impede to a high extent'.

Abuse of the court's process has been defined as 'using that process for a purpose or in a way significantly different from its ordinary and proper use' (*Attorney General* v. *Barker* [2000] 1 FLR 759, DC).

It has also been described as a duty of the court to:

> prevent misuse of its procedure in a way which … would nevertheless be manifestly unfair to a party to litigation before it, or would otherwise bring the administration of justice into disrepute.
>
> (*Hunter* v. *Chief Constable of West Midlands Police* [1982] AC 529 at [536])

In *Asturion Foundation* v. *Alibrahim* [2020] EWCA Civ 32 the court set out the approach to an application to strike out for an abuse of process.

In essence there is a two-stage test:

- Firstly, the court has to determine whether the claimant's conduct was an abuse of process.
- Secondly, if it was, the court has to exercise its discretion as to whether or not to strike out the claim.

It is at the second stage that the usual balancing exercise as between the parties, and in particular considerations of proportionality and fairness, becomes relevant (see *Cable* v. *Liverpool Victoria Insurance Co Ltd* [2020] EWCA Civ 1015).

An example of what may constitute an abuse of process is where there has been an excessive and inexcusable delay in proceeding with a claim or where the claimant issues proceedings without knowing the legal basis of the claim and containing few details as to its nature, or the claim could and should have been brought in previous proceedings.

Failure to comply with a pre-action protocol may also amount to an abuse of process (*Cable* v. *Liverpool Victoria Insurance Co Ltd* [2020] EWCA Civ 1015).

The crucial question is whether in all the circumstances a party is abusing or misusing the court's process, and the remedy should be proportionate to the abuse. The abuse must also be clearly established to the civil standard.

Mis-stating the claim for tactical reasons in paying the court fee is also an abuse of process (*Barnes: Bhatti* v. *Asghar* [2016] EWHC 1049 (QB); *Lewis* v. *Ward Hadaway* [2016] 4 WLR 6; *Dixon* v. *Radley House Partnership* [2016] EWHC 2511 (TCC); *Glenluce Fishing Company Ltd* v. *Watermota Ltd* [2016] EWHC 1807 (TCC); *Atha & Co Solicitors* v. *Liddle* [2018] EWHC 1751 (QB)).

However, these are conflicting High Court opinions and authoritative guidance is needed.

In *Livesey* v. *Vinters-Armstrongs Ltd* (4 October 2019), where there were a number of cases where the statement of value was understated and a lower issue fee was paid, HHJ Beech made an order that:

> unless the Claimant does … apply to amend the Claim Form to increase the statement of value and pays any increased court fee in accordance with that value (subject to any entitlement to apply for fee remission) then the Claim shall be limited to the amount stated in the statement of value, notwithstanding CPR 16.3(7).

Ground 3: CPR rule 3.4(2)(c) This could include a failure to comply with a time limit provided by the CPR or a court order, or that the claim or defence is non-compliant to a material degree with the rules.

The question to be posed is: is there a substantial risk that a fair trial is impossible because of inordinate and inexcusable delay, and do the interests of justice require it?

The court has discretion as to whether to strike out a statement of case in these circumstances but is likely to use an unless order in the first instance, as any sanction imposed must be appropriate and proportionate in the circumstances subsisting when the order is made. Even in these circumstances an unless order should not be made unless the court is satisfied that in all the circumstances such a sanction is appropriate.

In *Biguzzi* v. *Rank Leisure* [1999] 1 WLR 1926 the Court of Appeal held that while on occasions it may be appropriate to deal with non-compliance by striking out a statement of case, the court has at its disposal other methods of ensuring compliance. Courts should not abuse their case management powers by going to extremes by striking out claims for delay where a proportionate use of a more flexible power would be appropriate.

In *Asiansky Television plc* v. *Bayer Rosin* [2001] EWCA Civ 1792 Clarke LJ stated that:

> It is to my mind important that the Master or Judge exercising his discretion should consider alternative possibilities short of striking out. (at [49])

Faced with a strike-out application the court will consider all the circumstances of the case, and the overriding objective of dealing with cases justly will be a key element that the court will have to bear in mind. As mentioned above, the activation of a sanction in an unless order is a powerful weapon in a judge's case management armoury and should only be deployed where its consequences can be fully justified.

The other sanctions that are available to the court include the following:

- **An adverse costs order**

  The court may order that the defaulting party should pay the costs occasioned by the delay on an indemnity basis and summarily assess them.

  If the court is of the view that the fault lies with the solicitor and not the party, the court may make a wasted costs order such that the legal representative should pay the other party's wasted costs subject, of course, to the court giving the legal representative a reasonable opportunity to attend a hearing to give reasons why the court should not make such an order.

- **Interest**

  Interest arises from the date of service. If the defaulting party is the claimant the court may restrict the interest that is otherwise payable.

- **Unless orders**

  Unless orders are potent weapons in a litigant's armoury.

In reality, a court faced with a strike-out application is likely, at least initially, to make an unless order provided due warning is given and the remedy is proportionate to the alleged breach.

Such an order tends to read that in the event of default the claim 'will be treated as having been struck out'.

Such sanction will automatically have effect unless the defaulting party applies for and obtains relief from the sanction (CPR rules 3.8 and 3.9).

Any order made of the court's own initiative and without a hearing will need to have the provision as to the options to seek to have the order varied or set aside, as set out in CPR rules 3.3(5) and 23.10.

- **Conditional orders**

  To further the overriding objective an order may also be made subject to conditions, and specify the consequences of failing to comply with those conditions.

  The conditions must be clear and precise and capable of being complied with. The court is not obliged to impose an express sanction for failure to comply; however, it can do so at a later date, i.e. striking out all or part of a statement of case of a party who fails to comply.

  Any sanction imposed, of course, must be proportionate to the default and take into account not only the nature of the default and the conduct of the party in default but also whether a fair trial is still possible.

SUMMARY JUDGMENT

CPR rule 24.2 provides that the court may give summary judgment against a claimant or defendant if:

(a) it considers that –

  (i) that claimant has no real prospect of succeeding on the claim or issue; or
  (ii) that defendant has no real prospect of successfully defending the claim or issue; and

(b) there is no other compelling reason why the case or issue should be disposed of at a trial.

The rationale behind Part 24 is to allow the claimant or the defendant to obtain judgment at an early stage, thus avoiding the time and costs incurred in taking the matter to trial:

> It is important that a judge in appropriate cases should make use of the powers contained in Part 24. In doing so he or she gives effect to the overriding objectives contained in Part 1. It saves expense; it achieves expedition; it avoids the court's resources being used up on cases where this serves no purpose, and I would add, generally, that it is in the interests of justice. If a claimant has a case which is bound to fail, then it is in the claimant's interests to know as soon as possible that that is the position. Likewise, if a claim is bound to succeed, a claimant should know that as soon as possible.

(*Swain* v. *Hillman* [2001] 1 All ER 91)

There is a clear overlap between CPR rule 24.2 and rule 3.4: the court is allowed to strike out a statement of case or part of a statement of case if it appears that it discloses no 'reasonable grounds' for bringing or defending a claim (rule 3.4) and has 'no real prospect of succeeding' (rule 24.2).

'Real' means that the prospects of success must be realistic rather than fanciful. If the grounds are fanciful they are not likely to be reasonable.

In *Three Rivers DC* v. *Bank of England (No. 3)* [2001] 2 All ER 513 the following principles were spelled out for dealing with an application for summary judgment:

1. The court must consider whether the defendant has a 'realistic' rather than a 'fanciful' prospect of success, i.e. a defence that is more than merely arguable.
2. The court must not conduct a 'mini-trial'.
3. The court must take into account not only the evidence placed before it on application, but also the evidence that could reasonably be expected to be available at trial.
4. The court should hesitate about making a final decision without a trial where reasonable grounds exist for believing that a full investigation into the facts of the case would add to or alter the evidence available to a trial judge, and so affect the outcome of the case.

There are two limbs to the rule:

- Firstly, the applicant must show that the respondent has no real prospect of succeeding or successfully defending the claim.
- Secondly, that there is no other compelling reason why the case or issue should be disposed of at trial.

Limb 1: 'no real prospect of succeeding ... or successfully defending' The test is the same as that which has to be satisfied on an application to set aside judgment under CPR Part 13.

A judge can still summarily dispose of a claim or defence under this rule if it does not have a real or realistic (as opposed to a fanciful) prospect of success. But provided a claim has some chance of success, the court should not strike it out merely because it looks weak and unlikely to succeed. However, a claim which is really hopeless should not be allowed to continue.

The correct approach on an application for summary judgment is thus to consider whether the claimant or defendant has a realistic or more than merely arguable, as opposed to a fanciful, prospect of success.

The overall burden of proof rests on the applicant; however, 'It is incumbent on a party responding to an application for summary judgment to put forward sufficient evidence to satisfy the court that it has a real prospect of succeeding at trial' (*Korea* v. *Allianz* [2007] EWCA Civ 1066 at [14]).

In deciding whether to dispose of a claim or defence summarily, the court must not conduct a mini-trial of the issues or make findings on disputed matters of fact as these are best left for trial. Summary judgment is not the appropriate medium to conduct such an exercise, as that would usurp the function of the trial judge and lead to conclusions being reached without cross-examination and on documentation and submissions only:

> In my judgment the court should ... hesitate about making a final decision without a trial where, even though there is no obvious conflict of fact at the time of the application, reasonable grounds exist for believing that a fuller investigation into the facts of the case would add to or alter the evidence available to a trial judge and so affect the outcome of the case.
>
> (*Doncaster Pharmaceuticals Group Ltd* v. *The Bolton Pharmaceutical Co 100 Ltd* [2006] EWCA Civ 661 at [18])

To that extent the court must work on the assumption that the statements before the court are unlikely, at that stage, to contain the totality of the evidence and should consider the evidence reasonably to be expected to be available at trial. However, a judge should not simply allow a case to go forward on the basis that there is a possibility of some other evidence arising.

Limb 2: 'no other compelling reason ... [for] a trial' A respondent that has failed to establish that they have a real prospect of success may still prevent an order for summary judgment if they can show that there is a compelling reason for a trial, e.g. the case requires proper consideration at trial due to its complexity.

Furthermore, it is not within the purview of a court hearing a case on an application for summary judgment to determine complex questions of law and fact.

However, it is possible to give summary judgment on a short point of construction if the court is satisfied that it has before it all the evidence necessary for the proper determination of the question.

Bearing in mind the nature of these claims, however, it is often difficult to convince a judge that a claim, or indeed a defence, has no real prospect of success, as TOLATA 1996 claims often involve substantial disputes of fact which ultimately will have to be determined at trial, and therefore would be unsuitable for these kinds of applications.

An example of a case where this did occur, however, was that of *Sandhar* v. *Sandhar & Kang* [2008] EWCA Civ 238 where it was held that the claimant's assertion as to a beneficial interest in a property was fantastical and unsupported by any evidence.

A summary Helpful guidance has been provided by Lewison J in *Easyair Ltd (Trading as Openair)* v. *Opal Telecom Ltd* [2009] EWHC 339 (Ch), at [15]:

> The court must be careful before giving summary judgment on a claim. The correct approach on applications by defendants is, in my judgment, as follows:
>
> i. The court must consider whether the claimant has a 'realistic' as opposed to a 'fanciful' prospect of success: *Swain* v. *Hillman* [2001] 2 All ER 91;

ii. A 'realistic' claim is one that carries some degree of conviction. This means a claim that is more than merely arguable: *ED & F Man Liquid Products* v. *Patel* [2003] EWCA Civ 472 at (8);

iii. In reaching its conclusion the court must not conduct a 'mini-trial': *Swain* v. *Hillman*;

iv. This does not mean that the court must take at face value and without analysis everything that a claimant says in his statements before the court. In some cases it may be clear that there is no real substance in factual assertions made, particularly if contradicted by contemporaneous documents: *ED & F Man Liquid Products* v. *Patel* at (10);

v. However, on reaching its conclusion the court must take into account not only the evidence actually placed before it on the application for summary judgment but also the evidence that can reasonably be expected to be available at trial: *Royal Brompton Hospital NHS Trust* v. *Hammond (No. 5)* [2001] EWCA Civ 550;

vi. Although a case may turn out at trial not to be really complicated, it does not follow that it should be decided without the fuller investigation into the facts at trial than is possible or permissible on summary judgment...

vii. On the other hand it is not uncommon for an application under Part 24 to give rise to a short point of law or construction and, if the court is satisfied that it has before it all the evidence necessary for the proper determination of the question and that the parties have had an adequate opportunity to address it in argument, it should grasp the nettle and decide it...

Procedural matters While there is no general mandatory requirement for an applicant to serve evidence in support, if they do intend to rely on such evidence it must be included and identified in the application notice, and indeed it is advisable to do so (PD24, para.2(4)). (Note also the requirement of PD24, para.2(2), (3) and (5) regarding the application notice.)

In particular PD24, para.2(3) reads as follows:

(3) The application notice or the evidence contained or referred to in it or served with it must –

(a) identify concisely any point of law or provision in a document on which the applicant relies, and/or

(b) state that it is made because the applicant believes that on the evidence the respondent has no real prospect of succeeding on the claim or issue or (as the case may be) of successfully defending the claim or issue to which the application relates,

and in either case state that the applicant knows of no other reason why the disposal of the claim or issue should await trial.

7.3.4.15 Orders made in a party's absence (CPR rule 39.3)

CPR 39.3(5), which only applies to orders made in a party's absence, must be contrasted with CPR Part 13 (judgment in default – see **7.3.4.10**).

Rule 39.3 relates to orders made at a trial when a party fails to attend. What amounts to a 'trial' in this context was considered in *Pickard* v. *Roberts* [2016] EWHC 187 (Ch). Trials (as distinct from interim hearings) lead to orders carrying finality.

To have such an order set aside the requirements are:

1. the applicant must act promptly;
2. there must be a good reason for not attending the trial;
3. the applicant must have a reasonable prospect of success at trial.

Satisfaction of the first two conditions is fact-sensitive and it is not appropriate to apply a rigorous test.

If each of these three hurdles is surmounted the judgment will be set aside, save in a very exceptional case. The court no longer has a broad discretion whether to grant such an application: all three conditions have to be satisfied to enable it to set aside an order.

Like all other rules, CPR rule 39.3 is subject to the overriding objective.

In *Brazil* v. *Brazil* [2002] EWCA Civ 1135 Mummery LJ said this in relation to 'good reason':

> There has been some debate before us, as there was before the judge, about what is or is not capable of being a 'good reason.' In my opinion the search for a definition or description of 'good reason' or for a set of criteria differentiating between good and bad reasons is unnecessary. I agree with Hart J that, although the court must be satisfied that the reason is an honest or genuine one, that by itself is not sufficient to make a reason for non-attendance a 'good reason.' The court has to examine all the evidence relevant to the defendant's non-attendance; ascertain from the evidence what, as a matter of fact, was the true 'reason' for non-attendance; and, looking at the matter in the round, ask whether that reason is sufficient to entitle the applicant to invoke the discretion of the court to set aside the order. An over analytical approach to the issue is not appropriate, bearing in mind the duty of the court, when interpreting the rules and exercising any power given to it by the rules, to give effect to the overriding objective of enabling it to deal with cases justly.
>
> The perfectly ordinary English phrase 'good reason' as used in CPR 39.3(5) is a sufficiently clear expression of the standard of acceptability to be applied to enable a court to determine whether or not there is a good reason for non-attendance. (at [12])

In *Estate Acquisition and Development Ltd* v. *Wiltshire* [2006] EWCA Civ 533 the Court of Appeal followed what Mummery LJ had said in *Brazil* v. *Brazil*, Dyson LJ adding this:

> Moreover, [the rule] must be interpreted so as to comply with article 6 of the European Convention on Human Rights (right to a fair hearing). I refer to the judgment of Brooke LJ in *Goode* v. *Martin* [2001] EWCA Civ 1899, [2002] 1 WLR 1828 paragraph 35. In my view, it is necessary to have both article 6 and the overriding objective in mind when interpreting and applying the phrase 'good reason'. It should not be overlooked that the power to set aside an order made in the absence of the applicant may only be exercised where all three of the conditions stated in CPR 39.3(5) are satisfied. In addition to the need to show a good reason for not attending, the applicant must have acted promptly and that he has a reasonable prospect of success. If the phrase 'good reason' is interpreted too strictly against an applicant, there is a danger that the interpretation will not give effect to the overriding objective and not comply with article 6. (at [25])

Note also the guidelines set out in *Bank of Scotland* v. *Pereira* [2011] EWCA Civ 241:

> If the case is disposed of in the absence of a party, and the party (i) has not attended for good reasons, (ii) has an arguable case on the merits, and (iii) has applied to set aside promptly, it would require very unusual circumstances indeed before the court would not set aside the order. (at [25]) ... The strictness of this trio of hurdles is plain, but the rigour of the rule is modified by three factors. First, what constitutes promptness and what constitutes a good reason for not attending is, in each case, very fact-sensitive, and the court should, at least in many cases, not be very rigorous when considering the applicant's conduct; similarly, the court should not pre-judge the applicant's case, particularly where there is an issue of fact, when considering the third hurdle. Secondly, like all other rules, CPR 39.3 is subject to the overriding objective, and must be applied in that light. Thirdly, the fact that an application under CPR 39.3 to set aside an order fails does not prevent the applicant seeking permission to appeal the order. It is not very convenient, but an applicant may be well advised to issue both a CPR 39.3 application and an application for permission to appeal at the same time, or to get agreement from the other party for an extension of time for the application for permission to appeal. (at [26])
>
> ... if the defendant concludes that she cannot establish that she had a good reason for not attending the trial and/or that she made her CPR 39.3 application promptly, it would obviously be silly for her to make a CPR 39.3 application. In such a case, she can nonetheless seek to appeal against the trial judge's decision in the same way as any other defendant ... CPR 39.3 is, in that sense, merely an additional potential course given to a defendant who, with good reason, was unable to attend the trial. (at [38])

However, *Williams* v. *Hinton* [2011] EWCA Civ 1123 held that where a party is dissatisfied with a judgment at a hearing at which they failed to attend and their main principle of appeal is focused on the judge proceeding in their absence as opposed to adjourning the matter, then the proper route to challenge the judgment is by way of an application to set it aside under CPR 39.3(3) rather than appeal.

Either way, the test of good reason may well mean that whatever route is taken the end result will be the same.

Tinkler v. *Elliott* [2012] EWCA Civ 1289 held that the following propositions could be derived from the authorities:

1. promptness is a mandatory requirement;
2. it requires the applicant to act 'with all reasonable celerity in the circumstances';
3. only if the mandatory requirements are satisfied did the court have a discretion which, at that stage, is 'somewhat narrow'.

The element of discretion comes into play only after an applicant has satisfied the three positive requirements, including promptness. The court's approach at that stage is essentially evaluative rather than discretionary.

CPR rule 39.3 contemplates a trial in the absence of a party who has had notice of the trial and been served under the rules, or in respect of whom service has been dispensed with. It does not apply, however, to judgments irregularly obtained in the sense of being obtained without service of the claim form in accordance with the rules, for example, as in that case the court's discretion to set aside a judgment arises under CPR rule 3.10(b).

Notwithstanding this, it does not follow that a defendant is entitled to have the judgment set aside as of right or that the court's discretion can only be exercised one way. Inexcusable delay, for example when being made aware of the adverse judgment, would justify the court in not setting such judgment aside given the criteria as to promptness under the CPR.

The following principles can therefore be gleaned from the authorities:

1. All three conditions in rule 39.3(5) have to be satisfied before a judgment can be set aside.
2. If the conditions are satisfied the court can exercise its residual discretion to set aside.
3. Each condition has to be interpreted in accordance with the overriding objective and the ECHR, art.6.
4. 'Good reason' is fact-sensitive.
5. When conducting the good reason assessment, the court has to look at why a party did not attend.
6. In identifying the reason for not attending the court has to ask why a party was unaware.
7. A holistic approach has to be taken.
8. An appellate court can only interfere if the lower court had not had regard to the case law and the overriding objective.

(*Blake-Coulter* v. *Anne Alexander Hotels* [2016] EWHC 1457 (QB).)

Mohun-Smith v. *TBO Investments Ltd* [2016] EWCA Civ 403 held that the court should not generally adopt a too rigorous approach in its assessment of the evidence adduced in an application under CPR rule 39.3(3), particularly where the applicant has a reasonable prospect of success at trial.

The reason for this is that, unlike an application for adjournment of a forthcoming trial, if an application under rule 39.3(3) failed, the applicant would have had no opportunity to have an adjudication by the court on the merits.

That difference is important, and provides justification for generally adopting a more draconian approach to an application for an adjournment than to an application under rule 39.3(3) (see also *Solanki* v. *Intercity Telecom Ltd* [2018] EWCA Civ 101 and *SF* v. *Family Channel Ltd & Riaz* [2020] EWCA Civ 824).

Accordingly, in an application to set aside judgment under this provision, the court should not adopt too rigorous an approach to the question of whether good reason has been shown for the applicant's non-attendance. Rather, it should have regard to the need to give effect to the overriding objective of dealing with cases justly and to the applicant's right to a fair trial.

Gentry v. *Miller* [2016] EWCA Civ 141 held that the tests in *Denton* (see **7.3.4.13**) should be applied not only to applications to set aside default judgments under CPR rule 13.3, but also to applications to set aside judgments or orders made when a party has failed to attend under CPR rule 39.3.

Moreover, CPR rule 39.3(3)–(5) provides for a specific procedural remedy with its own self-contained code of applicable principles, albeit subject to a consideration of rule 3.9 (which reflects the overriding objective) and the '*Denton* principles'.

In dealing with either application, therefore, it is necessary to consider the express requirements of the respective rules before going on to apply the *Denton* tests.

The case of *F* v. *Family Channel Ltd* [2020] EWCA Civ 824 raised an important point of principle, namely the interplay between an unsuccessful application to adjourn a trial under CPR rule 3.1(2)(b) and a subsequent application under CPR rule 39.3 to set aside a judgment against a non-attending party.

The conclusions of the court were as follows:

- Firstly, an application under CPR rule 39.3(3) is not an appeal of any sort (or, for that matter, an application to vary the previous decision not to adjourn and/or proceed in the absence of a party). It can be pursued instead of, or in appropriate circumstances alongside, an appeal.
- Secondly, CPR rule 39.3(3)–(5) provides for a specific procedural remedy with its own self-contained code of applicable principles – albeit subject, on the question of ultimate discretion, to a consideration of CPR rule 3.9 which reflects the overriding objective and the *Denton* principles.
- Thirdly, there is a material distinction between an application for adjournment of a trial and an application to set aside a judgment under CPR rule 39.3(3), the latter justifying a less 'draconian' approach.

The approach to the question of whether or not there is a good reason for non-attendance is different and more generous to the applicant under CPR rule 39.3(3) than it is on an application to adjourn:

> For these reasons, the hearing of an application under CPR Part 39.3(3) involves a separate exercise of discretion which is unfettered by any previous exercise of discretion on an adjournment application. (at [49])
>
> ... There is no principle of consistency or judicial comity which requires the judge hearing the application under CPR Part 39.3(3) to follow the trial judge ... It is open to the judge hearing the application under CPR Part 39.3(3) to reach a different decision on the same facts. (at [51])

FAILURE TO ATTEND AN APPLICATION HEARING

So far we have been looking at the situation where a litigant has failed to attend the trial.

What amounts to a 'trial' was considered in *Pickard* v. *Roberts* [2016] EWHC 187 (Ch). Trials, as distinct from interim and application hearings, lead to orders carrying finality.

What of the situation where a litigant fails to attend an application hearing?

The court may choose to re-list the application on its own initiative (CPR rule 23.11(2)); however, this power is to be used sparingly bearing in mind the need to conserve the court's resources and allot no more than an appropriate share of them to a claim (CPR rule 1.1(2)(e)).

In considering whether to re-list under rule 23.11(2) the court can take account of the factors set out in CPR rule 39.3(5) (*Morgan* v. *Dooner* [2019] EWHC 679 (Comm)).

7.3.4.16 Part 36 offers of settlement

Part 36 has a self-contained, carefully structured and highly prescriptive set of rules dealing with formal offers to settle proceedings which have specific consequences in relation to costs in those cases where the offer is not accepted and the offeree fails to do better after a trial.

In cases where an offer has not been made in accordance with these rules it will not have the consequences as to cost protection and the judge has a broad overriding discretion in dealing with costs within the framework provided by CPR Part 44.

In seeking to settle the proceedings, therefore, although the parties are not bound to make use of the mechanism provided by Part 36, if they wish to take advantage of the particular consequences for costs and other matters that flow from making a Part 36 offer in relation to which the court's discretion is much more confined than under Part 44, they must follow its requirements.

CPR rule 36.5(1) provides that an offer made in accordance with that part must:

(a) be in writing;
(b) make clear that it is made pursuant to Part 36;
(c) specify a period of not less than 21 days within which the defendant will be liable for the claimant's costs in accordance with rule 36.13 or 36.20 if the offer is accepted;
(d) state whether it relates to the whole of the claim or to part of it or to an issue that arises in it and if so to which part or issue; and
(e) state whether it takes into account any counterclaim.

An offer that does not comply with these requirements cannot constitute a Part 36 offer, and must be dealt with as part of the court's general discretion as to costs under CPR Part 44.

A Part 36 offer can be made at any time, including before the commencement of proceedings. So the sooner the better!

If a Part 36 offer is accepted the claim is stayed, and the claimant will be entitled to recover the costs of the proceedings up to the date on which notice of acceptance was served on the offeror.

CPR rule 36.14(6) also provides that a Part 36 offer in relation to an offer to pay a lump sum must be paid within 14 days of its acceptance unless the parties agree otherwise. Failure to do so enables the claimant to enter judgment for the unpaid sum.

EFFECTS OF A PART 36 OFFER

If the claimant fails to obtain a judgment more advantageous than the defendant's offer the defendant will be entitled to:

- costs; and
- interest on those costs from the date on which the offer expired.

If the judgment against the defendant is at least as advantageous to the claimant as the claimant's offer then the claimant will be entitled to:

- interest on the judgment;
- costs on an indemnity basis;
- interest on those costs; and
- an additional premium, being 10 per cent of the amount awarded on the first £500,000 and 5 per cent on the amount in excess of that (up to a limit of £1 million).

Note the differential provisions as between claimant and defendant as to 'more advantageous' and 'at least as advantageous'.

In relation to a money claim 'more advantageous' and 'at least as advantageous' mean in money terms and 'more' means by any amount, however small.

In other words, for the costs consequences of Part 36 to follow the defendant has to obtain judgment for an amount more than their offer, while the claimant only has to equal or beat their own offer.

In both the above circumstances interest can be awarded at a rate not exceeding 10 per cent above base rate.

As can be seen, particularly for the claimant, there is a large incentive to make a Part 36 offer.

Furthermore, there is no stigma or moral disapproval implied by obtaining an indemnity costs order and such an order should generally be made once the conditions are satisfied.

These provisions automatically follow unless it is 'unjust' for them to do so. In determining this the court must take into account all the circumstances of the case. Departure from the normal consequences of the costs regime under Part 36 must be the exception, not the rule.

As eloquently provided for in the case of *Rolf* v. *De Guerin* [2011] EWCA Civ 78:

> The Part 36 mechanism provides a formal, regulated, procedure for a party, including a claimant, to express a willingness to accept something less than total success in his open position in the litigation. If the offer is not accepted and the offeror does better in the final result than his offer, he is entitled, unless the court considers it would be unjust, to costs on an indemnity basis from the expiry of the 'relevant period' (i.e. a basic three weeks, unless the offer extends it) plus interest at an enhanced rate up to 10 per cent above base rate. Therefore there are advantages to a party in pitching his offer realistically, and there are potential disadvantages to an offeree in declining the offer ... The three weeks is given to protect the offeree, who has that period to make up his mind... (at [34])

Pursuant to CPR rule 36.17(5), in determining whether it is unjust to apply the provisions of Part 36 in relation to the automatic costs consequences, the court must take into account all the circumstances of the case including:

(a) the terms of any Part 36 offer;
(b) the stage in the proceedings when any Part 36 offer was made, including in particular how long before the trial started the offer was made;
(c) the information available to the parties at the time when the Part 36 offer was made;
(d) the conduct of the parties with regard to the giving of or refusal to give information for the purposes of enabling the offer to be made or evaluated; and
(e) whether the offer was a genuine attempt to settle the proceedings.

As to the proper approach to the injustice test in rule 36.17(5)(a)–(e), courts should apply the 'injustice' test separately for each factor, and then go on to consider, in the round, the overall effect of applying all five.

An example of the above in practice was the case of *Walsh* v. *Singh* [2010] EWHC 1167 (Ch) in which the issue of conduct justified departure from the normal costs consequences which normally flow from the Part 36 offer.

The judgment also emphasises the width of judicial discretion in respect of costs, and delivers an important message that:

> A well-judged Part 36 offer does not give the offerer licence to conduct the trial thereafter in whatever way the offerer thinks fit without fear of costs reprisals, where appropriate. (at [25])

In relation to the issue of whether an offer made is a genuine attempt to settle the proceedings, the questions that need to be posed are:

- Is the offer a legitimate Part 36 offer?
- If so, is it genuinely intended to settle the question of liability?
- Would it be unjust to award costs that reflect some or all of the incentives outlined in Part 36?

WITHDRAWING A PART 36 OFFER

Provided an offer has not been accepted and the 21-day period in which it is open for acceptance has expired, withdrawal of such an offer must be made by service of a written notice. No specific form of written notice is required. An offeror just has to serve something in writing which states in terms that its offer is withdrawn.

Once the offer is withdrawn, the costs consequences of Part 36 do not apply. Notwithstanding this, there is still the overall discretion provided by CPR Part 44 as the court can still consider withdrawn offers when assessing costs/conduct issues.

A Part 36 offer, however, remains valid until withdrawn even if it has been unequivocally rejected.

Thus, rejection of an offer does not mean that it ceases to be available for later acceptance; the making of a counter offer also does not mean that the first offer ceases to be available for acceptance; furthermore, the making of a further offer by a party does not mean that an earlier offer by that party ceases to be available for acceptance.

Accordingly, several different offers may be available for acceptance at the same time. Thus, if in doubt, withdraw!

ACCEPTANCE OF A PART 36 OFFER

Where a Part 36 offer is accepted within the relevant period the claimant will be entitled to the costs of the proceedings up to the date on which notice of acceptance was served on the offeror.

Where a Part 36 offer is accepted after expiry of the relevant period, if the parties do not agree liability, the claimant will be entitled to the costs of the proceedings up to the date on which the relevant period expired, and the offeree will be liable for the offeror's costs for the period from the date of expiry of the relevant period to the date of acceptance unless the court orders otherwise.

KEY POINTS

1. The requirements of CPR Part 36 must be strictly complied with; however, if offers are not made in the requisite format and do not comply, the court is not prevented from considering such offers when exercising its discretion as to costs under Part 44.
2. Once made, and provided it is not accepted, a Part 36 offer can only be withdrawn or altered prior to the expiry of the 21-day period with permission of the court. Upon expiry of the 21-day period, permission is not so required unless the offer has been accepted.
3. An offer can be accepted at any time even after the period for acceptance has expired without needing the permission of the court.
4. Where a Part 36 offer is made less than 21 days before the start of the trial and is accepted, the court's permission is not required even if the parties cannot agree costs.
5. Claimants who not only beat their offer but also equal their offer will be entitled to receive the Part 36 benefits.
6. Any offer will be treated as inclusive of interest up until the end of the time for acceptance.

7.3.4.17 General provisions as to costs

The costs consequences of Parts 7 and 8 claims are governed by the general rules as to costs set out in CPR Part 44. In essence the normal rule, unlike with the Family Procedure Rules 2010 (FPR), SI 2010/2955, is that costs follow the event.

However, the court can make a different order and CPR rule 44.2 gives the court a general discretion as to costs, which is to be exercised having regard to all the circumstances of the case, including the matters set out in CPR rule 44.2(4) and (5):

> (4) In deciding what order (if any) to make about costs, the court will have regard to all the circumstances, including –
>
> (a) the conduct of all the parties;
> (b) whether a party has succeeded on part of its case, even if that party has not been wholly successful; and

(c) any admissible offer to settle made by a party which is drawn to the court's attention, and which is not an offer to which costs consequences under Part 36 apply.

(5) The conduct of the parties includes –

(a) conduct before, as well as during, the proceedings and in particular the extent to which the parties followed the Practice Direction (Pre-Action Conduct) or any relevant pre-action protocol;
(b) whether it was reasonable for a party to raise, pursue or contest a particular allegation or issue;
(c) the manner in which a party has pursued or defended its case or a particular allegation or issue; and
(d) whether a claimant who has succeeded in its claim, in whole or in part, exaggerated its claim.

In *Johnsey* v. *The Secretary of State for the Environment* [2001] EWCA Civ 535 Chadwick LJ set out the principles to be applied to the determination of costs:

1. Costs cannot be recovered except under an order of the court.
2. Whether to make a costs order and, if so, what order to make is at the discretion of the trial judge.
3. The starting point for the exercise of discretion is that costs should follow the event.
4. The judge may make different orders for costs in relation to discrete issues. In particular, the judge should consider doing so where a party has been successful on one issue but unsuccessful on another, and in that event may make an order for costs against the party who has been generally successful in the litigation.
5. The judge may deprive a party of costs on an issue on which that party has been successful if satisfied that the party acted unreasonably in relation to that issue.
6. An appellate court should not interfere with the judge's exercise of discretion merely because it takes the view that it would have exercised the discretion differently.

Thus, costs are now more issues-based and a claimant will recover costs in accordance with the proportion of success:

> The court generally approaches the matter by asking itself three questions: first, who has won; secondly, has the winning party lost on an issue which is suitably circumscribed so as to deprive that party of the costs of that issue; and thirdly, are the circumstances (as it is sometimes put) suitably exceptional to justify the making of a costs order on that issue against the party that has won overall.
>
> (*Hospira UK Ltd* v. *Novartis AG* [2013] EWHC 886 (Pat) at [2])

As to issue-based costs orders, the principle which has guided the court in applying its discretion as to costs where a party has succeeded overall but lost on one or more issues has been considered in many cases, and was summarised in *Pigot* v. *Environmental Agency* [2020] EWHC 1444 (Ch) as follows:

- The fact that a party was not successful on every issue did not, alone, justify an issue-based costs order or make it appropriate to deprive the party of their costs.
- An issue-based costs order might be appropriate if raising a discrete or distinct issue had caused additional costs to be incurred or where the overall costs were materially increased by the unreasonable raising of one or more issues on which the successful party failed.
- If a discrete issue causing additional costs to be incurred was reasonably raised, the overall successful party was likely to be deprived of its costs on that issue. If the issue was unreasonably raised, the overall successful party was likely to be ordered to pay the costs incurred by the overall unsuccessful party on that issue. An issue might be treated as unreasonably raised if it was hopeless and should never have been pursued.
- Where an issue-based costs order was appropriate, the court should attempt to reflect it by ordering payment of a proportion of the receiving party's costs, if that was practicable.
- An issue-based costs order should reflect the extent to which the costs were increased by the raising of the issue; costs which would have been incurred even if the issue had not been raised should still be paid by the overall unsuccessful party.
- Before making an issue-based costs order, it was important to stand back and ask whether, applying the principles in CPR rule 44.2, it was the right result in all the circumstances of the case and reflected the overall justice of the case.

Overall a broad scope approach must be adopted which takes into account all the facts of the case and the conduct of the parties.

In cases which conclude in one day the court will generally conduct a summary assessment of those costs as opposed to a detailed assessment (CPR PD44, para.9.2).

In such circumstances (as with applications generally when seeking costs), you should ensure that a costs schedule is prepared (N260) and served on the other side in advance of the hearing (see, however, *MacDonald* v. *Taree Holdings* (2000) TLR 28.12.2000, ChD in cases of non-compliance).

What approach should be taken on the issue of costs following a compromise outside the Part 36 regime?

Effectively, there are two positions:

- Firstly, in such a situation the court's approach could be one that looked to securing justice between the parties without incurring unnecessary court time and additional costs, i.e., to apply the overriding objective.

  If it is obvious which party would have succeeded on the substantive issue that party ought to be awarded costs.

  If it is not obvious, then it will depend on the circumstances and the court may wish to look at the substantive issue to determine the question of costs. However, in the absence of a good reason no order as to costs will be the usual approach to take.

- Secondly, the court could take the approach that if costs are not compromised then the action itself is not compromised and must therefore continue.

(See *Conversant Wireless Licensing SARL* v. *Huawei Technologies Co Ltd* [2018] EWHC 2549 (Ch).)

ASSESSING COSTS

The two ways of assessing costs are set out in CPR rule 44.3, namely the standard and the indemnity basis.

For assessment of costs on the standard basis, CPR rule 44.3(2) provides as follows:

> Where the amount of costs is to be assessed on the standard basis, the court will –
>
> (a) only allow costs which are proportionate to the matters in issue. Costs which are disproportionate in amount may be disallowed or reduced even if they were reasonably or necessarily incurred; and
>
> (b) resolve any doubt which it may have as to whether costs were reasonably and proportionately incurred or were reasonable and proportionate in amount in favour of the paying party.

Accordingly, the court on the standard basis will only allow proportionate costs and may disallow or reduce any costs incurred even if they are reasonably and necessarily incurred if they are themselves not proportionate.

Thus, a successful claimant or defendant will have their recoverable costs reduced if they are disproportionate, even if they were reasonably or necessarily incurred.

Proportionality means, therefore, that the parties should assess matters at the outset and plan in advance the necessary work, the time and the appropriate resources needed, and the probable overall costs.

CPR rule 44.3(5) sets out the broad principle on proportionality and the five factors underpinning it:

> (5) Costs incurred are proportionate if they bear a reasonable relationship to –
>
> (a) the sums in issue in the proceedings;
> (b) the value of any non-monetary relief in issue in the proceedings;
> (c) the complexity of the litigation;
> (d) any additional work generated by the conduct of the paying party; and
> (e) any wider factors involved in the proceedings, such as reputation or public importance.

CPR rule 44.4 provides as follows:

> (1) The court will have regard to all the circumstances in deciding whether costs were –
>
> (a) if it is assessing costs on the standard basis –
>
> (i) proportionately and reasonably incurred; or

(ii) proportionate and reasonable in amount, or

(b) if it is assessing costs on the indemnity basis –

(i) unreasonably incurred; or
(ii) unreasonable in amount.

And CPR rule 44.3(3) states:

> (3) Where the amount of costs is to be assessed on the indemnity basis, the court will resolve any doubt which it may have as to whether costs were reasonably incurred or were reasonable in amount in favour of the receiving party.

As can be seen, an award of costs on the indemnity basis entitles the successful party to:

- recover all of their reasonable costs, removing the issue of proportionality from the eventual equation; and
- the benefit of the doubt as to whether costs have been reasonably incurred.

The practical effect of costs on an indemnity basis, therefore, is that the successful party is likely to recover more of their actual costs than would be recovered under the standard basis, although on both bases costs unreasonably incurred or unreasonable in amount will not be allowed.

An award for indemnity costs also disapplies CPR rule 3.18 and the receiving party is therefore not constrained by any costs budget.

For indemnity costs to be awarded there needs to be some conduct or circumstance taking the case out of the norm, whereby that party's conduct could properly be categorised as either deliberate misconduct, or conduct which was unreasonable to a serious degree, justifying the court's censure.

When assessing the reasonableness of the conduct of the paying party to see whether it is outside the norm, the court has to avoid an assessment based on hindsight.

An order for indemnity costs should not be made simply because the paying party has been found to be wrong or their evidence rejected in preference to that of the receiving party:

> conduct, albeit falling short of misconduct deserving of moral condemnation, can be so unreasonable as to justify an order for indemnity costs ... such conduct would need to be unreasonable to a high degree; unreasonable in this context certainly does not mean merely wrong or misguided in hindsight ... It is of its nature penal rather than exhortatory.
> (*Excelsior Commercial & Industrial Holdings Ltd* v. *Salisbury Hamer Aspden & Johnson (Costs)* [2002] EWCA Civ 879 at [30] quoting from *Kiam* v. *MGN Ltd (No.2)* [2002] 2 All ER 242)

The fact that the claim or defence has been brought on a factual premise which is fundamentally false – and which the claimant or defendant knew to be false – will be sufficient to take the case out of the norm.

For a seminal analysis of the principles determining an award for indemnity costs see *Three Rivers DC* v. *Bank of England* [2006] EWHC 816 (Comm):

(1) The court should have regard to all the circumstances of the case and the discretion to award indemnity costs is extremely wide.
(2) The critical requirement before an indemnity order can be made in the successful party's favour is that there must be some conduct or some circumstance which takes the case out of the norm.
(3) Insofar as the conduct of the unsuccessful party is relied on as a ground for ordering indemnity costs, the test is not conduct attracting moral condemnation, which is an *a fortiori* ground, but rather unreasonableness.
(4) The court can and should have regard to the conduct of an unsuccessful party during the proceedings, both before and during the trial, as well as whether it was reasonable for the party to raise and pursue particular allegations and the manner in which they pursued their case and their allegations.
(5) Where a claim or defence is speculative, weak, opportunistic or thin, a party who chooses to pursue it is taking a high risk and can expect to pay indemnity costs if it fails.
(6) *A fortiori*, where the claim or defence includes allegations of dishonesty, let alone allegations of conduct, and those allegations are pursued aggressively *inter alia* by hostile cross examination.
(7) Where the unsuccessful allegations are the subject of extensive publicity, especially where it has been courted by the unsuccessful party, that is a further ground.
(8) The following circumstances take a case out of the norm and justify an order for indemnity costs, particularly when taken in combination with the fact that a party has discontinued only at a very late stage in proceedings:

    (a) Where the party advances and aggressively pursues serious and wide-ranging allegations of dishonesty or impropriety over an extended period of time;
    (b) Where the party advances and aggressively pursues such allegations, despite the lack of any foundation in the documentary evidence for those allegations, and maintains the allegations, without apology, to the bitter end;
    (c) Where the party actively seeks to court publicity for its serious allegations both before and during the trial in the international, national and local media;
    (d) Where the party, by its conduct, turns a case into an unprecedented factual enquiry by the pursuit of an unjustified case;
    (e) Where the party pursues a claim which is, to put it most charitably, thin and, in some respects, far-fetched;
    (f) Where the party pursues a claim which is irreconcilable with the contemporaneous documents;
    (g) Where a party commences and pursues large-scale and expensive litigation in circumstances calculated to exert commercial pressure on the other, and during the course of the trial of the action, that party

> resorts to advancing a constantly changing case in order to justify the allegations which it has made, only then to suffer a resounding defeat.

When deciding the amount of costs CPR rule 44.4 provides as follows:

> (3) The court will also have regard to –
>
> (a) the conduct of all the parties, including in particular –
>
> (i) conduct before, as well as during, the proceedings; and
> (ii) the efforts made, if any, before and during the proceedings in order to try to resolve the dispute;
>
> (b) the amount or value of any money or property involved;
> (c) the importance of the matter to all the parties;
> (d) the particular complexity of the matter or the difficulty or novelty of the questions raised;
> (e) the skill, effort, specialised knowledge and responsibility involved;
> (f) the time spent on the case;
> (g) the place where and the circumstances in which work or any part of it was done; and
> (h) the receiving party's last approved or agreed budget.
>
> (Rule 35.4(4) gives the court power to limit the amount that a party may recover with regard to the fees and expenses of an expert.)

CPR rule 44.11 sets out the court's powers in relation to misconduct: the court may either disallow some or all of a party's costs or order them to pay the costs incurred by the other party due to such misconduct.

There is a two-stage test:

- Stage 1: the court has to determine whether the relevant threshold criteria had been met (namely whether there had been improper or unreasonable behaviour).
- Stage 2: the court has to determine whether it would be unjust to impose the sanction. This is a discretionary exercise.

As to what amounts to 'unreasonable and improper conduct', guidance can be gleaned from authorities concerning wasted costs orders.

In *Ridehalgh* v. *Horsefield* [1994] Ch 205 'improper' conduct was said to cover:

> conduct which would ordinarily be held to justify disbarment, striking off, suspension from practice or other serious professional penalty. (at [232])

In *Lahey* v. *Pirelli Tyres Ltd* [2007] EWCA Civ 91 the court indicated that 'unreasonable' was to be narrowly construed, and, in *Gempride Ltd* v. *Bamrah* [2018] EWCA Civ 1367, 'unreasonable and improper conduct' was interpreted as conduct which the consensus of professional opinion would regard as improper:

> Whilst 'unreasonable' and 'improper' conduct are not self-contained concepts, 'unreasonable' is essentially conduct which permits of no reasonable explanation, whilst

> 'improper' has the hallmark of conduct which the consensus of professional opinion would regard as improper. (at [26])

ADR AND DUTY TO NEGOTIATE

There is no general presumption that a successful party will be penalised in costs if they fail to participate in ADR, particularly if their case is very strong; however, an unreasonable refusal to mediate may well lend itself to penalisation, albeit the onus will always be on the loser to show why costs should not follow the event even if the winner did refuse mediation:

> The question whether a party has acted unreasonably in refusing ADR must be determined having regard to all the circumstances of the particular case … in many cases no single factor will be decisive.
>
> (*Halsey* v. *Milton Keynes* [2004] 1 WLR 3002 at [3009])

The court is also entitled to take an unreasonable refusal into account even when it occurs before the start of formal proceedings, particularly given the ethos of the pre-action protocol.

In determining the issue in relation to this the following factors will need to be considered:

- nature of the case;
- merits of the case;
- failure of other methods of settlement;
- cost of mediating;
- prospects of success at mediation.

For an example of a TOLATA 1996 case where costs did not follow the event see *Hannan* v. *Maxton* [2010] 1 FLR 27 (due primarily to the rejection of a reasonable offer of ADR).

Even if ADR only works in part, it is still likely to narrow the issues and save costs, as well as the court's time and resources:

> experience shows that it is often in those cases where the facts are most hotly disputed that ADR can be useful, because it focuses attention of the parties on the commercial reality of the litigation and the costs involved, rather than on the very uncertain question of which of them will ultimately be believed by the judge on the bare factual dispute.
>
> (*Hannan* v. *Maxton* [2010] 1 FLR 27)

In *DSN* v. *Blackpool Football Club Ltd* [2020] EWHC 670 (QB) at [28] it was said as follows:

> No defence, however strong, by itself justifies a failure to engage in any kind of alternative dispute resolution … Settlement allows solutions which are potentially limitless in their ingenuity and flexibility, and they do not necessarily require any admission of liability, or even a payment of money.

> Even if they do involve payment of money, the amount may compare favourably (if the settlement is timely) with the irrecoverable costs, in money terms alone, of an action that has been successfully fought.
>
> The costs of an action will not always be limited to financial costs. [...] A trial is likely to require a significant expenditure of time, including management time, and may take a heavy toll on witnesses even for successful parties, which a settlement could spare them.

This decision is consistent with previous ADR authorities, in particular *PGF* v. *OMFS* [2013] EWCA Civ 1288 and *Thakkar* v. *Patel* [2017] EWCA Civ 117, which make clear that it is not enough for a party to decline to engage with ADR simply because they believe that they have a strong defence or claim.

Thus, a refusal to mediate could have serious costs implications for the party concerned. Clients should therefore be advised to engage in mediation and warned of the potential consequences should they refuse, even in circumstances where they believe that they have a watertight case.

If a client refuses to mediate a reasonable Part 36 settlement offer should be put to the other side, as a refusal to accept such a settlement offer could mitigate the potential cost consequences of failing to engage in mediation.

Furthermore, always be prepared to set out in correspondence your justification as to why you feel that mediation is inappropriate and pay heed to the advice in *The Jackson ADR Handbook*, 2nd edition (OUP, 2016, para.11:56):

> A party who is faced with a request to engage in ADR, but who believes that they have reasonable grounds for refusing to participate in an ADR process at that stage of the proceedings should consider the following practical steps to avoid a sanction:
>
> - Do not ignore an offer to engage in ADR. Failure to respond is likely to be treated as an outright refusal.
> - Respond promptly, in writing, giving clear and full reasons why ADR is not appropriate at this stage of the dispute or proceedings. The reasons... should be justified... The response should be contained in an open letter or in a letter marked 'without prejudice except as to costs'.
> - If lack of evidence or information is an obstacle... this must be canvassed with the other party... in... correspondence, and consideration should be given to whether that evidence or information can be obtained during the ADR process or in advance of [it].
> - Letters replying to requests to engage in ADR should be written with care. A party may have good reason to refuse ADR at that point in time, but the correspondence should not be written in such a way that closes off exploration of ADR processes at a later date. An outright refusal to use ADR at any time is more likely to be construed as unreasonable.

7.3.4.18 Conduct of the trial: evidential requirements

Remember, evidence is only admissible if it is relevant to the issues between the parties.

CPR rule 32.2(3) provides that the court may give directions in relation to factual evidence:

- identifying or limiting the issues to which such factual evidence may be directed;
- identifying which witnesses may be called;
- limiting the length or format of witness statements.

CPR PD32, para.27.2 provides that all documents contained in bundles which have been agreed for use at a hearing are admissible as evidence as to their contents unless:

> (1) the court orders otherwise; or
> (2) a party gives written notice of objection to the admissibility of particular documents.

Note that under CPR rule 32.19 a party is deemed to admit the authenticity of a document disclosed under CPR Part 31 unless they serve notice that they wish for the document to be proved at trial. Time limits for service apply.

Evidence at trial is proved by oral evidence and CPR rule 32.1 provides as follows:

> (1) The court may control the evidence by giving directions as to –
>
> (a) the issues on which it requires evidence;
> (b) the nature of the evidence which it requires to decide those issues; and
> (c) the way in which the evidence is to be placed before the court.
>
> (2) The court may use its power under this rule to exclude evidence that would otherwise be admissible.
> (3) The court may limit cross-examination.

Where a witness is called to give oral evidence their witness statement will stand as their evidence in chief unless the court orders otherwise.

If the witness statement is not served within the time specified by the court then the witness may not be called to give oral evidence unless the court gives permission.

A witness giving oral evidence at trial may, with the permission of the court, amplify their witness statement and give evidence in relation to new matters which have arisen since the witness statement was served on the other party.

However, the court will only give such permission if it considers that there is good reason not to confine the evidence of the witness to the contents of their witness statement.

It can, therefore, be seen from the above that it is vital that witness statements are filed and served and that they contain the witness's full evidence on the issues.

As to the preparation for the trial generally, as in the family jurisdiction note the words of warning in *Network Rail Infrastructure Ltd, R* v. *The Secretary of State for the Environment, Food and Rural Affairs* [2017] EWHC 2259 (Admin) at [11]–[12]:

> Prolix or diffuse 'grounds' and skeletons, along with excessively long bundles, impede the efficient handling of business in the Planning Court and are therefore contrary to the

rationale for its establishment. Where the fault lies at the door of a claimant, other parties may incur increased costs in having to deal with such a welter of material before they can respond to the Court in a hopefully more incisive manner. Whichever party is at fault, such practices are likely to result in more time needing to be spent by the judge in pre-reading material so as to penetrate or decode the arguments being presented, the hearing may take longer, and the time needed to prepare a judgment may become extended. Consequently, a disproportionate amount of the Court's finite resources may have to be given to a case prepared in this way and diverted from other litigants waiting for their matters to be dealt with. Such practices do not comply with the overriding objective and the duties of the parties (CPR 1.1 to 1.3). They are unacceptable.

The Court has wide case management powers to deal with such problems (see for example CPR 3.1). For example, it may consider refusing to accept excessively long skeletons or bundles, or skeletons without proper cross-referencing. It may direct the production of a core bundle or limit the length of a skeleton, so that the arguments are set out incisively and without 'forensic chaff'. It is the responsibility of the parties to help the Court to understand in an efficient manner those issues which truly need to be decided and the precise points upon which each such issue turns. The principles in the CPR for dealing with the costs of litigation provide further tools by which the Court may deal with the inappropriate conduct of litigation, so that a party who incurs costs in that manner has to bear them.

7.3.4.19 Discontinuance of a claim

CPR rule 38.2 provides:

(1) A claimant may discontinue all or part of a claim at any time.

Rule 38.3 provides that:

(1) To discontinue a claim or part of a claim, a claimant must –

(a) file a notice of discontinuance; and
(b) serve a copy of it on every other party to the proceedings.

A very important function of the notice of discontinuance is to clearly describe what the claimant is seeking to do. Defendants need to know precisely what is being discontinued, and the parties and the costs judge have to be able to work out the costs consequences.

The general rule is that a claimant who has been granted an order discontinuing their action is liable for the defendant's costs up to the date when notice of the discontinuance is served, the burden being on the claimant to show that a different order is appropriate.

The fact that a claimant's decision to discontinue a claim is motivated by practical, pragmatic or financial reasons as opposed to a lack of confidence in the merits of the case itself will not on its own assist them in avoiding the normal presumption as to costs. Thus, before commencing what can often be a costly claim a thorough costs risk/benefits analysis will need to be undertaken and the client fully advised.

In most cases, to show good reason the claimant would need to show a change of circumstances since the claim had been made, and even then such change of circumstances would be simply the beginning of the enquiry, not the end of it. Moreover, such change would itself need to be connected to the conduct of the defendants themselves.

CHAPTER 8

Transfer of tenancies

8.1 INTRODUCTION

The relevant legislation dealing with the transfer of tenancies is the Family Law Act (FLA) 1996, Part IV.

Under that Act, various 'relevant' tenancies including secured (council house) and assured (housing association) tenancies can be transferred from one tenant to another; this does not, however, include assured shorthold tenancies (private landlords) which lack security of tenure. In essence, only 'social landlords' are covered.

FLA 1996, Sched.7 gives the court (but not lay justices) the power to transfer tenancies on the separation of cohabitants.

Cohabitants are defined by s.62 of the Act as:

> two persons who are neither married to each other nor civil partners of each other but are living together as if they were a married couple or civil partners.

The specific power as to transfer of tenancies is provided for by FLA 1996, Sched.7, paras.3 and 4, as follows:

> 3
>
> (1) This paragraph applies if one cohabitant is entitled, either in his own right or jointly with the other cohabitant, to occupy a dwelling house by virtue of a relevant tenancy.
>
> (2) If the cohabitants cease to cohabit, the court may make a Part II order.
>
> 4 The court shall not make a Part II order unless the dwelling house is or was –
>
> ...
>
> (b) in the case of cohabitants, a home in which they cohabited.

For the purposes of Sched.7 to the Act a cohabitant also includes a former cohabitant and it is worth noting that there is no statutory time limitation under FLA 1996 within which such an application may be made by a former cohabitant.

An order for a transfer of tenancy is known as a 'Part II order': in other words, an order made under FLA 1996, Sched.7, Part II.

Accordingly, if one cohabitant is entitled, either in their own right or jointly with another cohabitant, to occupy a dwelling house by virtue of a relevant tenancy, upon them ceasing to reside together the court may make an order transferring the tenancy to one or other party.

However, such an order cannot be made unless the property concerned was a home in which the cohabitants lived together as husband and wife or in an equivalent relationship if as a same-sex couple.

8.2 APPLICABLE PRINCIPLES

FLA 1996, Sched.7, Part 1, para.5 sets out the matters to which the court shall have regard when deciding what order to make.

In essence, these are:

> ... all the circumstances of the case including –
>
> (a) the circumstances in which the tenancy was granted to either or both of the ... cohabitants or, as the case requires, the circumstances in which either or both of them became tenant under the tenancy;
>
> (b) the matters mentioned in section 33(6)(a), (b) and (c) and, where the parties are cohabitants and only one of them is entitled to occupy the dwelling house by virtue of the relevant tenancy, the further matters mentioned in section 36(6)(e), (f), (g) and (h); and
>
> (c) the suitability of the parties as tenants.

As can be seen, the catch-all 'all the circumstances of the case' gives the court a wide discretion and para.5(a) highlights the relevance of which party is the tenant and how it was that they became the tenant.

Other relevant considerations will include:

- the housing needs and housing resources of each of the parties and of any relevant child;
- the financial resources of the parties; and
- the likely effect of any order or any decision by the court not to exercise its powers on the health, safety and wellbeing of the parties and of any relevant child.

(See FLA 1996, s.33(6)(a), (b) and (c).)

'Relevant child' is defined as any child who is living with or might reasonably be expected to live with either party or any other child whose interests the court considers relevant. It therefore includes children who are not necessarily the biological children of the parties.

Specifically in relation to cohabitants, the court must also consider:

- the nature of the parties' relationship and in particular the level of commitment involved in it;
- the length of time during which they have cohabited;

- whether there are or have been any children who are children of both parties or for whom both parties have or have had parental responsibility; and
- the length of time that has elapsed since the parties ceased to live together.

(See FLA 1996, s.36(6)(e), (f), (g) and (h).)

As previously highlighted, although there is no prescribed time limit in which a former cohabitant can make an application to the court, the lapse of time since cohabitation last took place will still be considered by the court in the exercise of its discretion.

Of particular note is the requirement that the court must also have regard to the suitability of the parties as tenants.

As any application concerning a transfer of tenancy will need to be served upon the landlord, any subsequent issue raised by the landlord as an objection to the transfer because of, for example, rent arrears and/or anti-social behaviour may well be relevant when considering a transfer of tenancy. Thus, when serving such notice it may well be worth posing a specific question to check whether there are any such issues.

That said, however, the court still has the power to transfer a tenancy notwithstanding any objection from the landlord (see *Newlon Housing Trust* v. *Alsulainen* [1997] 1 WLR 914).

Once an order is made, for secure tenancies and assured tenancies, it is the order itself which effects the transfer and no further documentation (such as an assignment or a transfer) will be required to give formal effect to it.

FLA 1996, Sched.7, Part III contains supplementary provisions relating to orders which may be made in addition to an order for the transfer of a tenancy. The most notable of these relates to an order for a lump sum payment in return for the transfer.

In deciding whether to exercise such supplementary powers, and if so in what manner, the court is directed to have regard to all the circumstances, in particular:

- the financial loss that would otherwise be suffered by the transferor as a result of the order;
- the financial needs and financial resources of the parties; and
- the financial obligations which the parties have, or are likely to have, in the foreseeable future, including financial obligations to each other and to any relevant child.

Again, the discretion is a wide one.

Payment of such a sum can be made by instalments or even deferred; however, such a direction will only be given if it appears to the court that immediate payment of the sum required by the order would cause the transferee financial hardship, such hardship being greater than the hardship that would be caused to the transferor if the direction were given (a balance of hardship test).

A further supplementary provision which might be made is in respect of the liabilities and obligations in relation to the property.

By virtue of Sched.7, para.11 the court may direct that both parties be jointly and severally liable to discharge and perform any obligation or liability in respect of the property.

When such a direction is made, the court may also direct that either party shall be liable to indemnify the other in whole or in part against any payment made or expenses incurred by the other in discharging or performing any such liability or obligation.

8.3 PROCEDURE

The appropriate rules for governing applications for a transfer of tenancy can be found in FPR rules 8.29–8.34. The Part 19 procedure applies.

The application is made on Form D50B with a supporting statement verified by a statement of truth.

Once the application is issued, the court provides the applicant with a notice of proceedings endorsed with the return date and will also proceed to serve both the respondent and landlord, informing the latter of their right to make representations either in writing or by way of attendance at the hearing.

The application, statement and notice of proceedings will need to be served upon the respondent; the landlord need only be served with the application and notice of proceedings but does not need to be served with the statement.

If the applicant elects to effect service they must file a certificate of service before the first hearing.

If the landlord so requests the court will direct that they be made a party to the proceedings.

If the respondent wishes to contest the application they must, within the time limit for filing the acknowledgment of service (14 days), file and serve a statement in response. Failure to do so will mean that although the respondent may attend the hearing of the application they may play no part in it unless the court gives them permission.

Upon the respondent filing and serving their written evidence the applicant may also file and serve a statement in response.

If the order is unopposed, a final order can be made on the occasion of the initial hearing.

If the order is contested, the court will set the matter down for a hearing with additional orders such as disclosure, the supply of further and better particulars and a statement in response if one has not already been filed by the respondent.

8.4 EFFECT OF SERVICE OF A NOTICE TO QUIT

Service of a notice to quit by one joint tenant will have the effect of determining the tenancy, unless the tenancy agreement provides otherwise, even if given without the agreement of the other tenant (*Hammersmith & Fulham LBC* v. *Monk* [1992] 1 AC 478 and *Harrow LBC* v. *Johnstone* [1997] 1 FLR 887).

This is a prospective problem which is difficult to surmount. One suggestion would be to contact the other party's solicitors seeking an undertaking that the other party will not determine the tenancy in such manner. However, the mere fact of such notice could prove a tempting invitation to do the opposite!

In default of such an assurance, one may have to consider obtaining an injunction pursuant to the Family Law Act 1996 (FPR rules 8.34 and 20.4).

However, such possibility might now be considered a violation of the European Convention on Human Rights (ECHR), art.8.

Reference may be had to the opposing decisions of *McCann* v. *UK* [2008] Fam Law 729 and *London Borough of Wandsworth* v. *Dixon* [2009] EWHC 27 (Admin). *Dixon* may be distinguished from *McCann* in that in that case the service of the notice to quit was a voluntary and unprompted act by the tenant, whereas in *McCann* it had been served at the instigation of the local authority.

Notwithstanding the above decisions, however, in *Wilson* v. *London Borough of Harrow* [2010] EWHC 1574 (QB) the court held that unless the terms of a tenancy agreement provide otherwise, a notice to quit given by one joint tenant is effective to determine a periodic tenancy.

Where this occurs, the other joint tenant's right to occupy the premises as a tenant ceases and the landlord therefore obtains an unqualified right to possession. Such a rule was held to be compatible with the ECHR, art.8.

However, this decision was subsequently thrown into doubt by the case of *Manchester CC* v. *Pinnock* [2010] UKSC 45 which held that one must always ask 'whether the eviction is a proportionate means of achieving a legitimate aim' (at [52]) following possession proceedings in such circumstances.

In a further development in *Sims* v. *Dacorum BC* [2013] EWCA Civ 12, the Court of Appeal held that the rule in *Hammersmith and Fulham LBC* v. *Monk* [1992] 1 AC 478 – that at common law a periodic joint residential tenancy was terminated automatically if one joint tenant unilaterally served a notice to quit on the landlord – was not incompatible with the other joint tenant's rights under the ECHR, art.8 and Protocol 1, art.1 and the Human Rights Act 1998. It follows, therefore, that a party has no right to remain in a local authority property as a sole tenant after the other tenant, who was a joint tenant, has left the property and given notice quitting the joint tenancy.

This decision was upheld in the Supreme Court in *Sims* v. *Dacorum BC* [2014] UKSC 63.

While on the face of it, depriving one of two joint tenants of their tenancy purely as a result of notice served by the other joint tenant seems unfair, nevertheless, there is logic behind it.

If the tenant who wanted to leave could not terminate the tenancy they would be forced to remain a tenant against their will and jointly and severally liable for the rent, in comparison to the alternative scenario whereby the landlord would be landed with one tenant instead of two, which would give them less security.

CHAPTER 9

Applications under the Children Act 1989, Sched.1, s.15

9.1 INTRODUCTION

The Children Act 1989, Sched.1, para.1(2) enables the court to make financial provision in respect of children irrespective of whether or not the parents of the child or children concerned are married to one another:

- Paragraph 1 details the orders that can be made against parents.
- Paragraph 2 details the orders that can be made if the child is over 18.
- Paragraph 3 details the duration of the orders.
- Paragraph 4 details the matters that the court has to take into account.

Although there is no definition of 'parent' in the Children Act 1989, in *T* v. *B (Parental Responsibility: Financial Provision)* [2010] 2 FLR 1966 it was held that for the purposes of Sched.1 the term should be strictly interpreted to include only a legal and biological parent and not 'social or psychological' parents (see also *Morgan* v. *Hill* [2007] 1 FLR 1480).

Thus, the Act only relates to the biological or adopted children of both parties.

For the purposes of the Act a 'child' is defined as a person under the age of 18 (s.105(1)). The Act also contains provisions for making orders in respect of adult children over the age of 18. However, the provisions are not without difficulty.

In the circumstances set out in the Schedule the application must be made either by the 'child' themselves, and can only relate to periodical payments and lump sum orders, or by their parents, provided they do so before the subject child attains the age of 18.

In light of this, it may be contended that Sched.1 does not allow a parent to seek periodical payments on behalf of a child, in any circumstances, if the application is made after the child has turned 18.

In *DN* v. *UD (Sch. 1 Children Act: Capital Provision)* [2020] EWHC 627 (Fam) the question was left open as to whether such a restriction could possibly lead to a potential declaration of incompatibility pursuant to the Human Rights Act 1998, s.4.

Note also Sched.1, para.2(3) which provides that:

> An application may not be made under this paragraph by any person if, immediately before he attained the age of 16, a periodical payments order was in force with respect to him.

The reference to 'any person' is, it is submitted, confusing. However, this should be read alongside the further reference to 'he' and 'him' so as to refer to the adult child concerned as opposed to anyone else, for example a parent on their behalf.

Furthermore, either the applicant must also be in full-time education or there must be some 'special circumstances' justifying the making of the order (see **9.3.1**).

Accordingly, an adult child whose parents are not living with each other in the same household, and in respect of whom there was no periodical payments order in force before they reached the age of 16, can apply for periodical payments or a lump sum order themselves if either they are receiving further education or training or there are special circumstances.

However, if such an order was in force, this option is not open to them unless one of their parents makes an application on their behalf and does so before they attain the age of 18.

The reason for this is because there is provision for variation under the Matrimonial Causes Act 1973, s.31 for children of formerly married parents, or in the alternative, application can be made by the formerly unmarried parent.

Furthermore, the effect of Sched.1, para.3, which permits the court to backdate a periodical payments order to the date of the application and to extend it beyond the child's 18th birthday – thus supporting the construction that an order for periodical payments can be made *after* the child reaches 18 provided that the application is made prior to their 18th birthday – also supports the contention that the court also retains the jurisdiction to make other species of orders under Sched.1, para.1.

For further academic exploration of these issues see the article: 'Illegitimate claims? Schedule 1 claims for periodical payments by parents of adult children' [2019] Fam Law 505.

That said, absent special or exceptional circumstances, capital orders which provide a benefit beyond minority or the cessation of tertiary education should not be made. What amounts to special or exceptional circumstances has to be construed restrictively.

DN v. *UD (Sch. 1 Children Act: Capital Provision)* [2020] EWHC 627 (Fam) is the first reported example of long-term capital provision being made for a child which extended into independent adulthood.

Mr Justice Williams made the unprecedented decision to award capital sums to the two youngest children to purchase their own properties outright in the future, holding that, although the power to make outright capital transfers exists, it should only be deployed in limited circumstances and where the court identifies some continuing dependency. However, dependency connotes some form of vulnerability or need continuing into adulthood which can in certain circumstances be remedied by way of capital provision:

> The net effect of all of the authorities is clear. Absent special or exceptional circumstances, capital orders which provide a benefit beyond minority or the cessation of tertiary education should not be made. It is equally clear that what can amount to special or exceptional circumstances is restricted. Matters relating to changing societal attitudes, the wealth of a parent, or the like will not suffice. Disability creating an ongoing need for support might. The absence of a parent playing any supporting role for their child might.
>
> The appellate courts have recently eschewed glosses upon statutory language. In this case the identification of exceptional or special circumstances warranting the making of outright capital orders for the benefit of children does not seem to me to amount to a gloss but rather is an application of the statutory powers based on principles which emerge from case law. The power to make outright capital transfers exists but will only be deployed in limited circumstances and where the evidence justifies it. It seems to me that what one is focusing on is the child and whether there is something about this child or this child's situation in particular vis-à-vis that parent that creates a situation which exceptionally (i.e. as an exception to the usual rule) generates a need for the child to be provided with capital which will be of benefit to them as an adult possibly for many years. (at [85])

In summary, the following orders are available under the Children Act 1989, Sched.1, para.1(2):

- lump sum;
- periodical payments (including secured periodical payments);
- settlement of property;
- transfer of property.

Let us look at each of these in turn.

9.2 LUMP SUM ORDERS

It is important to note that there is no bar to multiple applications for lump sum orders (see para.1(5)(a)) unlike under the matrimonial jurisdiction.

The reason for this is that throughout their lives, children's needs for financial provision by way of capital need continuous review as circumstances change, whether by way of commencement of school, transition to secondary school, or driving lessons and the acquisition of a car or other circumstances requiring an injection of capital.

Also of note is the fact that, unlike under the matrimonial jurisdiction, the court can also order interim lump sums to be payable, there being no prohibition within the Children Act 1989.

Of course, it may be argued that there is no express jurisdiction enabling the court to do so, as Sched.1, para.9 sets out the interim orders which the court can make but makes no reference within it to interim lump sums:

> (1) Where an application is made under paragraph 1 or 2 the court may, at any time before it disposes of the application, make an interim order –
>
> (a) requiring either or both parents to make such periodical payments, at such times and for such term as the court thinks fit; and
>
> (b) giving any direction which the court thinks fit.

However, Sched.1, para.1(2)(c) provides that the orders the court may make include:

> An order requiring either or both parents of a child –
>
> (i) to pay to the applicant for the benefit of the child; or
> (ii) to pay to the child himself,
>
> such lump sum as may be so specified.

Paragraph 1(3) provides that: 'The powers conferred by this paragraph may be exercised at any time.'

CF v. *KM (Financial Provision for Child: Costs of Legal Proceedings)* [2010] EWHC 1754 (Fam) held that parliament would not have intended to restrict the court's jurisdiction to make a lump sum order only on the final determination of all aspects of a claim under Sched.1, since this would run counter to the underlying purpose of the Schedule to enable the court, in the exercise of a judicial discretion, to provide fair and appropriate financial support for the benefit of a child, from time to time.

Thus, there is an interesting argument that one could issue an application for an interim lump sum order under the Children Act 1989, s.15 (Sched.1) (*Re G (Maintenance Pending Suit* [2006] EWHC 1834 (Fam); *CF* v. *KM (Financial Provision for Child: Costs of Legal Proceedings)* [2010] EWHC 1754 (Fam)) and seek to consolidate this so that it is heard within the financial order proceedings, much as was the case with *Miller-Smith* v. *Miller-Smith* [2010] 1 FLR 1402 in relation to an application under TOLATA 1996.

The overall proper approach to applications for lump sum orders is to consider reasonable needs with a mindful eye on the comparative lifestyle enjoyed by the other parent.

The court is given specific power under Sched.1, para.5 to order a lump sum to be paid to meet the liabilities or expenses incurred in connection with the birth of a child or in maintaining the child and reasonably incurred before the making of the order. Thus, past expenditure as well as future expenditure is covered.

In the case of *J* v. *C (Child: Financial Provision)* [1999] 1 FLR 152, however, excluded from the allowable items on the mother's list of past expenditure were disposable nappies, baby cleansing materials and baby food on the basis that these were day-to-day living expenses that should have been met by income provision, and that to order a sum for their repayment would run counter to the principle enumerated in *Phillips* v. *Peace* (see below).

A lump sum order can also be made to enable the discharge of debts:

> … the debts exist. They need to be provided for. If they are not provided for, that will jeopardize [the child's] welfare.
>
> (*H* v. *M* (unreported))

However, the court will be reluctant to reimburse a mother who has been guilty of unreasonable or reckless expenditure.

Note the 'rolling/trade in' solution provided in the case of *PG* v. *TW (No.2) (Child: Financial Provision)* [2014] 1 FLR 923 which had the advantage of eliminating the recurrent negotiation required and the possibility of a further lump sum application in the future in cases of ongoing necessary car replacement during the dependency of the child.

Unlike with a property transfer/settlement order, a lump sum payment is not designed to revert to the payor (see **9.4**). Such payments are intended either to reimburse a past expenditure or to provide for a current or future need.

Any capital sum, however, intended to provide for a child's housing needs by way of a capital settlement *will* revert to the payor when the child concerned attains the age of 18 or completes tertiary education.

Therefore, such expenditure must be 'one-off' in nature and likely to depreciate over time, as otherwise it might be contended that such provision should be classified as a settlement of property order that perhaps ought to be subject to a settlement returnable to the settlor at the end of the child's financial dependency.

In the case of *H* v. *C* [2009] EWHC 1527 (Fam) it was considered that the question of whether a lump sum to fund home improvements was a settlement of property was not amenable to precise scientific analysis but called for a broad-brush approach.

In that case the judge compared funding for an extension to provide additional accommodation which would be likely to have a permanent effect on the value of the house to funding for a new kitchen which would be unlikely to have a material impact upon its value.

Note in that case the definition was important as there had already been one settlement of property order and therefore any further settlement order would not be permissible (para.1(5)(b)).

A lump sum order can also be made payable by instalments; however, although the size of the lump sum itself cannot be varied, the size or frequency of the instalment payments can be.

One cannot, however, use a lump sum order payable by instalments as a 'backdoor order' to obtaining periodical payments in contravention of the Child Support Act (CSA) 1991, s.8(3):

> The undoubted power which I have to make a lump sum award should not be exercised in such a way as to provide for the regular support of the child, which would ordinarily have been provided by an order for periodical payments. I hold that in a case to which the Child Support Act 1991, and in particular section 8(1) applies, then in exercising its remaining jurisdiction under Schedule 1 to the Children Act 1989, here to order a lump sum, a court should do so only in order to meet the need of a child in respect of a particular item of capital expenditure.
>
> (*Phillips* v. *Peace* [1996] 2 FLR 230)

> the court should not use its power to order lump sums to get round the prohibition on providing for recurrent income needs which is implicit in the provisions of the Child Support Act.
>
> (*J* v. *C (Child: Financial Provision)* [1999] 1 FLR 152)
> (see also *Dickson* v. *Rennie* [2014] EWHC 4306 (Fam))

In so far as future capital provision – more particularly housing – is concerned:

> The starting point for the judge should be to decide, at least generically, the home that the respondent must provide for the child. The value, the size and location of the home all bear upon the reasonable capital cost of furnishing and equipping it as well as upon future income needs, directly in the case of outgoings but also indirectly in the case of external expenditure such as travel, education, and perhaps even holidays. The home will ordinarily be transiently required during the child's minority or until further order. The appropriate legal mechanism is therefore a settlement of property order. Since the respondent is entitled to the reversion, which in certain circumstances may fall in before the child's majority, the respondent must have some rights to veto an unsuitable investment ... the choice of home introduces some useful boundaries.
>
> Once that decision has been taken the amount of the lump sum should be easier to judge. For the choice of home introduces some useful boundaries. In most cases the lump sum meets the cost of furnishing and equipping the home and the cost of the family car.
>
> (*Re P (Child: Financial Provision)* [2003] 2 FLR 865)

To summarise the position, the court will need to decide the child's reasonable needs in respect of their home in terms of size, location and value and which must bear 'some sort of relationship to the father's current resources and ... present standard of living' and thereafter what further capital provision there needs to be made in addition to that, i.e. provision of a lump sum other than for housing (car, white goods and refurbishment of the home) (*N* v. *D* [2008] Fam Law 627).

Thus, the starting point in any capital award will be the home to be provided, the reasonable capital cost of furnishing and equipping the same, the cost of a car, the budget to maintain the home – including school fees and holidays – and an allowance for the caring parent.

The resources of the applicant themselves, of course, will be relevant to what order the court should make.

Of particular interest is that the court also has jurisdiction to entertain an application for a lump sum for the provision of housing even where there has been a clean break in divorce proceedings; however, the circumstances have to be exceptional (*MB* v. *KB* [2007] EWHC 789 (Fam); *PK* v. *BC (Financial Remedies: Schedule 1)* [2012] EWHC 1382 (Fam)).

The court even has jurisdiction to make an order for capital provision for the benefit of a child against a resident parent in favour of a non-resident parent (e.g. to maintain and provide a home for the purposes of contact), but such an order again would be unusual and is a jurisdiction that will only be exercised rarely (*Re S (Child: Financial Provision)* [2005] 2 FLR 94; *N* v. *C (Financial Provision: Schedule 1 Claims Dismissed)*, 14 January 2013).

9.3 PERIODICAL PAYMENTS

Subject to the jurisdiction of the Child Maintenance Service (CSA 1991, s.8(3)) the court can make orders for periodical payments (including interim orders) provided:

- a maximum assessment is in place (CSA 1991, s.8(6)) – 'A topping-up order' (high-earners);
- a written agreement is in place pursuant to CSA 1991, s.8(5);
- the child falls out of the jurisdiction of CSA 1991 due to their age, habitual residence, educational status (educational costs: CSA 1991, s.8(7)) and state of health (disability costs: CSA 1991, s.8(8)).

That said, even if the Child Maintenance Service does not have jurisdiction in the particular circumstances of the case, the appropriate rate of a maintenance calculation/assessment which would have applied if it had, can be informative in considering the level of periodical payments as the appropriate starting point (*E* v. *C (Child Maintenance)* [1996] 1 FLR 472; *GW* v. *RW* [2003] EWHC 611 (Fam); *SW* v. *RC* [2008] EWHC 73 (Fam); *Re M-M (Sch. 1 Provision)* [2014] EWCA Civ 276; *Re TW & TM* [2015] EWHC 3054 (Fam); *CB* v. *KB* [2019] EWFC 78).

However, any order made cannot be extended beyond a child's 17th birthday unless it is considered right to do so in the circumstances of the case, and in any event cannot be extended beyond their 18th birthday unless the child concerned is or will be receiving instruction at an educational establishment or undergoing training for a trade, profession or vocation, whether or not in gainful employment, or there are special circumstances justifying the making of an order beyond the child's 18th birthday (Children Act 1989, Sched.1, para.3(1) and (2)).

As was said in *J* v. *C* [1999] 1 FLR 152:

> Children are entitled to provision during their dependency and for their education, but they are not entitled to a settlement beyond that, unless there are exceptional circumstances such as a disability, however rich their parents may be.

Moreover, as was said in the unusual case of *FS* v. *RS and JS* [2020] EWFC 63 which concerned an application by a 41-year-old man for continued financial support from his parents:

> conventional wisdom and practice would suggest that these provisions were never intended to be used and cannot be used to fund the education of a perpetual student. (at [142])

In any event, by virtue of Sched.1 to the Children Act 1989, para.2, headed 'Orders for financial relief for persons over eighteen', he was barred by para.2(4) which states that no order is to be made 'at a time when the parents of the applicant are living with each other in the same household'.

Nor could the applicant rely on the court's inherent jurisdiction as:

- Such a claim lay far outside the accepted parameters of the branch of the inherent jurisdiction relied on by the applicant.
- It was a fundamental principle that the inherent jurisdiction could not be used to compel an unwilling third party to provide money or services.
- Exercise of the inherent jurisdiction was ousted by any relevant statutory scheme. The Children Act 1989 provided a comprehensive statutory scheme dealing with the circumstances in which a child, including an adult child, could make a financial claim against a living parent. The 1989 Act explicitly prohibited the claim the applicant sought to pursue.

Arguments pertaining to the ECHR were also rejected.

As for an extension to cover continuing education generally, one cannot argue that students themselves should be self-sufficient (see *B* v. *B (Adult Student: Liability to Support)* [1998] 1 FLR 373).

However, in making such application one must have regard to the possible impact of the award on the student maintenance loan system, as such an award is likely to be classified as income which would have the effect of reducing entitlements that otherwise might exist (*R* v. *Sheffield City Council, ex p. Parker* [1993] 2 FLR 907).

One possible way of mitigating this potential problem is to perhaps make a split order as in *G* v. *G (Periodical Payments: Jurisdiction to Vary)* [1997] 1 FLR 368, providing an income stream to the parent providing the home and a separate one to the child from which they can meet their educational costs.

An order could also possibly cover a gap year or postgraduate education, although provision for the latter would be unusual (*Re N* [2009] 1 FLR 1442).

One could also possibly build into a periodical payments order the costs of future upgrading of the home as this might properly be considered as general costs of maintenance and, therefore, quite proper and prudent for the recipient to be able to carry forward an amount from one year to the next in order to save sufficiently for future refurbishment costs (*H* v. *C* [2009] EWHC 1527 (Fam)).

Also of interest is the observation by Hale J in *J* v. *C* (see above), which mirrors case law in matrimonial proceedings, that in order to place responsibility for financial provision on the appropriate parent as opposed to the state:

> Where resources allow, the family obligation should be respected in such a way as to reduce, or even eliminate, the need for children to be supported by public funds.

An order for periodical payments, once made, can be varied or discharged and can also be backdated to the date of the application.

Once made, any periodical payments order will also cease to have effect if the parties should subsequently live together for a period in excess of six months.

9.3.1 Special circumstances

Clearly, special circumstances will cover 'some physical or other handicap' (disability costs: CSA 1991, s.8(8)):

> There is indisputably jurisdiction in the Children Act to extend indefinitely a periodical payments order for the benefit of someone over the age of 19. It is part of the philosophy of the Children Act that a young person … with a total dependence on others for the rest of his life should look for continuing financial support from his parents for whatever period may be necessary.
>
> (*C* v. *F (Disabled Child: Maintenance Orders)* [1998] 2 FLR 1)

See also *DN* v. *UD (Sch. 1 Children Act: Capital Provision)* [2020] EWHC 627 (Fam) referred to above at **9.1** in relation to capital awards.

9.4 PROPERTY TRANSFER AND SETTLEMENT ORDERS

Clearly, a child's need for a carer enables account to be taken of the caring parent's needs for accommodation.

Such an order is for the benefit of the child even though the child has no legal or beneficial interest in the property transferred (*K* v. *K (Minors: Property Transfer)* [1992] 2 FLR 220).

It is also worth noting the comments of Thorpe LJ in *Re S* [2006] EWCA Civ 479 as to there being a recognised need to avoid 'creating an excessive disparity between' the mother's and father's respective homes.

In relation to the mechanics of property transfer and settlement orders, as the provision to be made is for the child during their minority, any property which is to be transferred for the benefit of a child will revert to the transferor when the child reaches the age of 18 or ceases full-time education, whichever occurs first, unless any of the circumstances set out in Sched.1, paras.2, 3 and 6 apply:

> … Children are entitled to provision during their dependency and for their education, but they are not entitled to a settlement beyond that, unless there are exceptional circumstances such as a disability …
>
> (*J* v. *C* [1999] 1 FLR 152)

In *PG* v. *TW (No. 2) (Child: Financial Provision)* [2014] 1 FLR 923, however, the court directed that such term should be until the child was 21 or until the completion of a first degree, whichever was the later, with permission to apply, so as to avoid future unnecessary extension applications.

This, of course, is in stark contrast to the provision for outright property adjustment orders in matrimonial proceedings and therefore only offers transient security for the caring parent during the child's minority and potentially delayed poverty for the carer.

Furthermore, only one substantive order can be made for a settlement or transfer of property (see para.1(5)(b) and *Phillips* v. *Peace* [2005] 2 FLR 1212).

This is particularly important to bear in mind in cases of an agreement for a property transfer or settlement, as a failure to convert any such written agreement into an order will not prevent an applicant from returning to court in the future to seek another property transfer or settlement order, opening matters up to a potential negligence claim. Thus, any such agreement should be converted into an order to prevent this from happening.

The definition of property also includes a tenancy, and therefore the court has power under Sched.1 to transfer a secure or assured tenancy outright into the sole name of the parent with care which mirrors the power under the Family Law Act 1996, Part IV. Thus, applicants have a choice of remedies.

Although there is no provision under the Children Act 1989 for the court to award compensation for such transfer as there is under the Family Law Act 1996, Part IV, most cohabitants will seek a transfer of tenancy order pursuant to the provisions of the Family Law Act 1996, s.53 and Sched.7 due to the fact that under the Family Law Act 1996 there is no reversion to the settlor upon the attainment of majority by the children as there is under the Children Act 1989, Sched.1.

The seminal case of *J* v. *C (Child: Financial Provision)* [1999] 1 FLR 152 is notable for the following salient points:

- While the child reaching the age of 21 or completing full-time education would mean the reversion of any settled property on to the father, the cohabitation or the marriage of the mother would not so result, as the marriage/cohabitation would not affect the child's need for their mother to care for them.
- No further maintenance funding was ordered to fund the upkeep of the property because it was in the father's interest voluntarily to maintain the property which would in any event revert to him in due course.

However, that latter point should be treated with caution as a cynic might say that the temptation would be to leave the costs of upkeep to the occupant and only expend money on essential repairs in the run-up to its subsequent reversion.

Following on from such an order (be it a property transfer/settlement or a lump sum to acquire such property) it is usual to draw up a trust deed dealing with both occupation and reversion to the settlor.

The terms of such trust deed need to be carefully considered to include but not be limited to the following matters:

- the choice and location of the property and how this choice is to be made (including whether the settlor has a right of veto);
- a mechanism for a definition of the type of property to be purchased;
- how the purchase costs are to be dealt with;
- who the trustees will be;
- whether there should be any provision for an alternative replacement property to be purchased during the currency of the trust;
- the terms of occupation;
- provision for a change of circumstances, e.g. does it trigger a sale if the mother remarries or cohabits (which cannot be compelled under the statutory provisions and should normally be resisted by the occupier) or the child moves to live with the father;
- who will pay for external and internal repairs and decoration;

- the provision for any charges of the trustees;
- who will pay any service charge and ground rent;
- provision with respect to any mortgage payment;
- tax consequences;
- whether the occupier should provide an account of expenditure (see **9.7**);
- should there be provision for a buyout clause; and
- a mechanism for a subsequent change of trustees.

As for the power to vary property settlement orders once made see *Re C (A Child) (Schedule 1 Children Act Variation)* [2018] All ER (D) 32.

Also note the provision in FPR rule 9.11(1) which specifically empowers the court to direct that where the application is for a variation of settlement the court *must*, unless it is satisfied that the proposed variation does not adversely affect the rights or interests of the child concerned, direct that the child be separately represented. If it is not so satisfied, the court *must* direct that the child be separately represented.

In so far as any other financial remedy is concerned, the court *may* direct that the child be separately represented.

Curiously, the rule only refers to 'representation' and makes no reference to 'joinder'. This is particularly relevant in so far as applications under the Children Act 1989, Sched.1 are concerned in light of the sentiments expressed in *Walker* v. *Jeffries*; *Re S (A Child)* [2006] EWCA Civ 479 and *Morgan* v. *Hill* [2007] 1 FLR 1480 (see **9.10**).

9.5 PRINCIPLES TO BE APPLIED

The matters to which the court must have regard when dealing with a Sched.1 application are contained within the Children Act 1989, Sched.1, para.4(1) and broadly speaking, are not dissimilar from the matters to be considered when the court is exercising its discretion pursuant to the Matrimonial Causes Act 1973, s.25(3).

The exercise of the Sched.1 jurisdiction is thus highly discretionary.

The court will look at all the circumstances of the case and, in the case of a variation or discharge of an existing order, any change in any of the matters to which the court was required to have regard when making the order in the first place. Thus, there has to be some justification for departing from the original order.

In particular, the court must have regard to the following:

- The parties' present or foreseeable future likely financial position, which includes income, earning capacity, property and other financial resources.
- The parties' present or foreseeable future likely needs, obligations and responsibilities.
- The financial needs of the child.

- The income, earning capacity (if any), property and other financial resources of the child.
- Any physical or mental disability of the child.
- The manner in which the child was being, or was expected to be, educated and trained.

It may be contended that the 'millionaire's defence', which is now defunct in matrimonial cases, can still be used in Sched.1 applications such that the respondent only needs to give a broad picture of their financial position as:

> It is ... important not to seek to compensate for the absence of a father as a primary carer, by providing the child and the mother with an over lavish, artificial or indulgent lifestyle ...
>
> (*H* v. *M* (unreported))

However, in *PG* v. *TW (No. 2) (Child: Financial Provision)* [2014] 1 FLR 923 this was questioned on the basis that Sched.1 requires information to be provided as to a party's assets, liabilities, income and expenditure (Form E1) and regard also has to be had to any disparity between the respective parties' standard of living.

Even so, this does not enable the court to disregard the overriding objective of enabling the court to deal with cases justly having regard to welfare issues involved.

In circumstances of significant wealth the judicial exercise involved in determining a Sched.1 application would be unlikely to call for a detailed examination of financial resources.

In *Re A (A Child)* [2014] EWCA Civ 1577 it was held that a broad indication of the non-residential parent's wealth is all the 'essential information' that is needed, as its extent will inform the reasonableness of the budgetary claims as well as the ability to pay them.

A balance therefore has to be struck between, on the one hand, providing an accurate outline of a party's financial affairs, and on the other, being circumspect in terms of the detail required so that, at a certain level of disclosed financial wealth, a detailed further enquiry may be disproportionate and irrelevant to the issues as to the provision of a house for the child's period of dependency given that this, in essence, is no more than an enforced property investment for the settlor who will, in due course, reap the benefits of that investment.

In a case where the millionaire's defence is taken, the court has to take a view as to what is reasonable in the particular circumstances.

As case law has developed a number of discrete principles have emerged which are worth exploring.

9.5.1 Standard of living

The first principle which bears consideration is that the child who is the subject of the application is entitled to be brought up in circumstances which bear some sort of resemblance to the father's current resources and the father's present standard of living:

> In a case ... where the lifestyle of the parties is a factor which does seem to me to impact to an extent on the outcome, standard of living is clearly amongst the totality of the circumstances which the Court is to hold in view, even though it does not find a place in the schedule checklist. In some cases ... the standard of living enjoyed ... during lengthy pre-separation cohabitation ... could ... promote the standard of living so long enjoyed by the child to the position of an important, if not the dominant, feature of the case.
>
> (*F* v. *G* [2004] EWHC 1848 (Fam))

However, the court has to equally guard against unreasonable claims being made on the child's behalf with the disguised element of providing for the applicant's benefit rather than for the child, as the provision must be for the child and not for the parent with care (e.g. spousal support through the back door).

The tension, therefore, is between seeking to achieve that the child has a standard of living bearing:

> some sort of relationship with the father's current resources and standard of living yet that the mother is not in the process provided for just the same as if she and the father had undertaken the commitment of marriage.
>
> (*Re P (Child: Financial Provision)* [2003] 2 FLR 865)

Essentially, the court has to consider the reasonableness of the amount claimed for the child's benefit and, having determined what is reasonable, consider whether it is reasonable for the father to pay that amount.

The exercise is highly discretionary and involves an essentially broad-brush assessment.

9.5.2 Carer's allowance

In fixing any award for financial provision for the benefit of the child a child's need for a carer enables account to be taken of the caring parent's financial needs as well.

Accordingly, the amount of maintenance for the child can include an allowance for the carer (carer's allowance).

However:

> ... The court ... must guard against unreasonable claims made on a child's behalf but with the disguised element of providing for the mother's benefit rather than for the child. That said, it is also well established that a child's needs for a carer enables account to be taken of the caring parent's financial needs.
>
> (*N* v. *D* [2008] 1 FLR 1629)

In *N* v. *C* [2013] EWHC 399 (Fam), for example, a mother's application for financial relief under the Children Act 1989, Sched.1 was dismissed as the claim was, in reality, a disguised claim for the benefit of the mother as opposed to for the child.

In *FG* v. *MBW* [2011] EWHC 1729 (Fam) a carer's allowance was included, reflective of the primary carer's commitment, responsibility and often sacrifice:

> ... the welfare of the child is a constant influence on the exercise of the broad judicial discretion conferred by the statute and that the award for the benefit of the child can include an allowance for the primary carer which recognises the commitment, responsibility and often the sacrifice of that carer. (at [136])

However, in determining that amount, the benefits that the mother was entitled to and the impact of her obtaining paid employment were also taken into account.

The court also considered it appropriate to look at the standard of living during the relationship, the expectations of the parties during it for any child they may have and the father's present and expected standard of living for himself and all his children.

PG v. *TW (No.2) (Child: Financial Provision)* [2014] 1 FLR 923, however, favoured a more broadly based (and not sub-divided) order for maintenance that was not bedevilled by categorisation and more simply reflected the reasonable needs of both mother and child, which it has to be said seems a more realistic approach.

In *Re A (A Child)* [2014] EWCA Civ 1577 it was held that the court should not dispense with any budget and sanction an award supportive of a lavish lifestyle devoid of context to the child's circumstances.

The court is responsible for ensuring appropriate financial support for the child and should confine the carer's allowance within the award to its legitimate purpose. The nature of the child's home environment provides the obvious baseline from which to consider commensurate levels of maintenance.

Furthermore, a literal or purposive interpretation of Sched.1 permits neither the concept of sharing or compensation for the benefit of the child, nor – by the back door – financial provision and compensation for the carer beyond the element attributable to the care of the child.

Courts should 'guard... against giving the mother a former wife's entitlement on [the child's] coat tails' (at [30] quoting from the judgment below of Bodey J)

9.5.3 Step-siblings

Financial provision itself does not generally become unreasonable just because others may incidentally benefit from it, e.g. step-siblings.

However, in the case of *Morgan* v. *Hill* [2006] EWCA Civ 1602 Thorpe LJ indicated that in such circumstances there ought to be separate applications against each of the fathers, either consolidated or heard consecutively.

In practical terms this is unlikely as it may be that one father is impecunious or of modest means when compared to the subject respondent to the application. It also rather flies in the face of encouraging negotiated settlements.

Respondent fathers faced with such circumstances will therefore need to argue, and indeed prove, that the claim is inflated because of the additional child or children.

9.5.4 New relationship

What of any new relationship that the caring parent may enter into?

> Marriage of the mother or a settled period of cohabitation may justify a reconsideration of the father's contribution in the light of the new circumstances, but, in my judgement, there is nothing automatic in this – the needs of the child continue.
>
> (*H* v. *M* (unreported))

9.5.5 Summary

The following principles, therefore, can be derived from case law:

1. The financial needs of the child include the need to be cared for by a parent who is in a position both financially and generally to provide that care.
2. The parent with care should be able to live and bring up the child in circumstances that have some relationship to the other parent's resources and way of life.
3. The parent with care should have control of a budget that reflects their position and that of the other parent, both social and financial. The object of the budget should be to provide them with sufficient funds to discharge their parental responsibilities without financial anxiety.

   > [The Carer] should not be burdened with unnecessary financial anxiety or have to resort to parsimony when the other parent chooses to live lavishly.
   >
   > (*Re P (Child: Financial Provision)* [2003] 2 FLR 865)

   The object, however, is not to meet the carer's aspirations which fall outside their reasonable needs as the child's carer, nor to provide them with surplus funds to save or invest.

   > There can be no slack to enable the recipient to fund a pension or an endowment policy or otherwise to put money away for a rainy day.
   >
   > (*Re P (Child: Financial Provision)* [2003] 2 FLR 865; see also *H* v. *M* (unreported))

   But note the possible provision for future property refurbishment as outlined previously.
4. The assessment of what falls within a carer's reasonable budgetary needs and what falls outside is not something that can be done with arithmetical

precision. In fixing the appropriate sum the court will undertake a broad common sense assessment.

5. The term 'for the benefit of the child' should be given a wide construction and includes welfare as well as financial benefits. All that the court can do is to seek to strike an appropriate balance. Thus, the court must look at whether or not the particular expenditure is for the benefit of the child in the widest sense of the word, and it matters not if the expenditure itself benefits the carer as long as the child also derives benefit from it.

9.6 MATRIMONIAL CAUSES ACT 1973, S.25 VERSUS SCHED.1, PARA.4(1)

It is interesting to compare the Children Act 1989, Sched.1 statutory checklist with that pursuant to the Matrimonial Causes Act (MCA) 1973, s.25(2).

Although the child's welfare is not specifically mentioned as being the court's first or paramount consideration it is clearly relevant as a 'constant influence', bearing in mind that any order made has to be for the benefit of the child and the overall result achieved by orders under Sched.1 should be fair, just and reasonable in all the circumstances.

In *Re P (Child: Financial Provision)* [2003] EWCA Civ 837 it was held that the welfare of the child, while a minor, although not paramount was:

> naturally a very relevant consideration as one of ... all the circumstances ... of the case. (at [76])

> I would only wish to amplify by saying that welfare must be not just one of the relevant circumstances but in the generality of cases, a constant influence on the discretionary outcome. I say that because the purpose of the statutory exercise is to ensure for the child of parents who have never married and who have become alienated and combative, support and also protection against adult irresponsibility and selfishness, at least insofar as money and property can achieve those ends. (at [44])

> ... in cases under the Children Act 1989 the welfare of the child concerned, even if neither the paramount nor the first consideration must be one of the relevant circumstances to be taken into account when assessing whether and how to order provision.
>
> (at [38], quoting *J* v. *C* [1999] 1 FLR 152)

In addition to the welfare of the child, conspicuous by their absence are factors relating to the age of each parent, the duration of their relationship, the standard of living enjoyed by each parent during their relationship, any physical or mental disability of either parent, any contribution made or likely to be made by the parent to the welfare of the family, and conduct.

Considerations as to the length and nature of the parents' relationship and whether or not the child was planned are generally of little if any relevance, since the child's needs and dependency are the same irrespective:

> … The length of relationship is not in itself significant under Schedule 1 for two reasons: the child has his or her needs in any event (however long the parents were together) and also Schedule 1 makes no reference to consideration of the length of the relationship.
>
> (*N* v. *D* [2008] 1 FLR 1629)

> People who have children should support them, whether or not those were wanted children. As a general proposition children should not suffer because their parents are irresponsible or uncaring towards them.
>
> (*J* v. *C* [1999] 1 FLR 152)

> In the exercise of a Judge's discretion no great significance should be attached to the issue of whether a pregnancy was planned or otherwise. There was nothing in the private law to distinguish between wanted and unwanted children.
>
> (*Re P (Child: Financial Provision)* [2003] 2 FLR 865)

> Children should not suffer (financially) just because their parents have, for whatever reason, not been married to one another.

> Parents are responsible for their children throughout their dependency. The fact that such riches as they have come after the breakup of a relationship cannot affect that.
>
> (*J* v. *C* [1999] 1 FLR 152)

> Neither of these parties seems sufficiently to have considered or expected that a sexual relationship would lead to the birth of a child. However, that is a known consequence. If a child arrives, then parenthood brings with it significant financial and other responsibilities. Both these parties have to make a continuing contribution in that regard for the good of their son. Both will suffer financially because the new circumstances will mean that they do not have the freedom and the financial flexibility that they once had. But that is a consequence of their own actions. As adults, they have to bear responsibility for such.
>
> (*DE* v. *AB* [2011] EWHC 3792 (Fam) at [46])

Note also the observations in *A* v. *A (A Minor: Financial Provision)* [1994] 1 FLR 657 where it was stated:

> conduct, or more accurately, misconduct, which is not a specific factor in the paragraph 4 checklist as it is in the Matrimonial Causes Act, section 25, checklist, is therefore material only as a hazard light which will flash through my journey down the rest of paragraph 4.

And of course, standard of living is itself seen as a benchmark for any subsequent award.

Accordingly, the missing elements of the s.25 checklist will form aspects of 'all the circumstances of the case' but their impact will be limited in considering the needs of the child in light of the individual factual matrix of the case.

9.7 KEEPING AN ACCOUNT

Should the child's carer have to keep an account of the monies they are spending for the benefit of the child? *Re P (Child)* [2003] EWCA Civ 837 indicated yes in the particular circumstances of that case.

However, my favoured approach is set out in *Re C (Financial Provision)* [2007] 2 FLR 13:

> I would consider it almost always unhelpful and counterproductive to encourage a father to ask that the mother keep such accounts of her expenditure. The intrusion into the life of the mother and child would be likely to fuel resentments, which would already be present because of the litigation. That in turn would probably have an adverse effect on contact arrangements and other areas, such as schooling, in which the parents may need to co-operate with each other in the best interests of the child.

This was further backed up in the case of *H* v. *C* [2009] EWHC 1527 (Fam) where the judge held that it would not be appropriate to require the mother to provide detailed accounts of her expenditure.

Nevertheless, if there is an argument that the award has been inflated due to a combination of a carer's allowance in which there is cohabitation or remarriage and there are in addition non-subject children (step-siblings), this may justify such an approach being taken.

9.8 LITIGATION FUNDING

There have been cases where an award has been sought (be it for maintenance or for lump sum provision (including interim provision) where the court had no jurisdiction to award maintenance) so as to provide 'litigation funding' for extraneous proceedings, not just proceedings within Sched.1 itself.

To that extent the criteria established for this in *Currey* v. *Currey (No. 2)* [2006] EWCA Civ 1338 will inform the decision-making of the court.

In essence, the applicant must demonstrate that they cannot reasonably procure legal advice and representation by any other means.

Such an application, however, will need to be treated with some degree of caution as the success of such an application will turn upon whether or not it is considered to be manifestly for the benefit of the child, although that term will be given a wide construction.

See *W* v. *J (Child: Variation of Financial Provision)* [2004] 2 FLR 300; *Re S (Child: Financial Provision)* [2005] 2 FLR 94; *MT* v. *T* [2007] 2 FLR 925; *Currey* v. *Currey (No. 2)* [2006] EWCA Civ 1338; *G* v. *G* [2009] EWHC 2080 (Fam).

> care needs to be taken to see that the monies are not being spent to satisfy the Applicant's taste for litigation. But that is a matter relating to exercise of discretion rather than jurisdiction … the proper construction of Schedule 1 is that it includes the ability of the Court to order by way of interim payment, a payment towards costs. To my mind it

> certainly can be for the benefit of children in cases under Schedule 1 to ensure that they are properly represented and have an appropriate equality of arms with the Respondent to those proceedings.
>
> (*M* v. *T* [2006] EWHC 2494 (Fam))

The case of *R* v. *F (Schedule 1: Child Maintenance: Mother's Costs of Contact Proceedings)* [2011] 2 FLR 991 confirmed that an order to meet a party's prospective, as well as retrospective, costs of litigation must be seen as being 'for the benefit of the child'.

The applicant must not have access to public funding nor any other source of funds which could reasonably be used to pay their costs. The respondent must also be able to reasonably afford to pay the sums sought. Furthermore, the court must also consider broadly the reasonableness and merit of the stance taken in the related proceedings for which funding is sought.

In the case of *MT* v. *T* [2007] 2 FLR 925, the interim payment, including the upfront payment of legal costs, was categorised as relating to the payment of periodical payments.

Again, in the case of *G* v. *G* [2009] EWHC 2080 (Fam) it was held that there was jurisdiction to include an allowance for legal costs in an order for interim periodical payments under Sched.1, para.9 if the court considered it appropriate to do so for the benefit of the children.

The overarching consideration is whether it could be demonstrated that the recipient could not reasonably procure legal advice and representation at a level of expertise apt to the proceedings to enable proper representation.

Reference must also be made to the case of *CF* v. *KM* [2010] EWHC 1754 (Fam) where provision for legal costs was met by a lump sum order on an interim basis as opposed to a periodical payments order, as there was no jurisdiction under Sched.1 to make such provision by way of interim periodical payments.

In summary, the following factors will be taken into account in determining whether to make such an award:

- the availability of public funding;
- the availability of other assets or resources;
- a party's borrowing ability;
- the willingness of the solicitors to enter into a 'Sears Tooth' agreement;
- whether such an order would be unfair to the paying party;
- whether there is a realistic prospect of a substantive award being made against the respondent at the final hearing;
- the prospects of recoupment from the award made in favour of the applicant.

See also *Rubin* v. *Rubin* [2014] EWHC 611 (Fam), *BC* v. *DE* [2016] EWHC 1806 (Fam) and *LKH* v. *TQA AL Z* [2018] EWHC 1214 (Fam) in the context of legal services payment orders within matrimonial claims (MCA 1973, s.22ZA), which in essence codifies the principles set out in *Currey* v. *Currey (No. 2)* [2006] EWCA Civ 1338.

Accordingly, there is no reason why the principles set out in those cases should not also apply to those under Sched.1.

9.9 ALTERATION OF MAINTENANCE AGREEMENTS

The Children Act 1989, Sched.1, para.10(3) deals with the relatively little known provision of alteration of maintenance agreements.

Where there is an existing maintenance agreement relating to a child and the court is satisfied either:

> (a) that, by reason of a change in the circumstances in the light of which any financial arrangements contained in the agreement were made (including a change foreseen by the parties when making the agreement), the agreement should be altered so as to make different financial arrangements; or
>
> (b) that the agreement does not contain proper financial arrangements with respect to the child;
>
> then that court may by order make such alterations in the agreement by varying or revoking any financial arrangements contained in it as may appear to it to be just having regard to all the circumstances.

A very useful power when considered in the light of, for example, separation deeds for not only unmarried but married couples as well.

9.10 PROCEDURE

A Sched.1 financial provision claim is 'family business', assigned to the Family Court (Matrimonial and Family Proceedings Act 1984, s.32 and the Senior Courts Act 1981, s.61 and Sched.1, para.3(e)).

Applications under Sched.1 are thus governed by the FPR, as under rule 2.3 the definition of financial remedy proceedings includes an order under Sched.1, and FPR rule 9.10(1)(a) confirms that a parent may apply for a financial remedy in respect of a child.

Accordingly, the Part 3 provisions – including the Pre-application Protocol for Mediation Information and Assessment – will apply as well as the pre-action protocol to Part 9.

The procedure governing the making of such applications is contained in FPR Part 9, Chapter 5 and follows the same procedure as with applications for a financial order made within divorce proceedings, albeit with a fast track procedure (FPR rules 9.18–9.20).

We thus have Forms A1 and E1 – and the first directions appointment (FDA), FDR and final hearing.

On issue of an application for an order, the court will fix a hearing date not less than six weeks and not more than 10 weeks after the date of filing of the application, and at the same time send a notice of hearing to both parties and a copy of the application to the respondent unless the applicant elects to effect service themselves.

Form E1 must be filed and exchanged not more than 21 days after the date of issue of the application.

Note also the requirement for the filing of open proposals and an estimate as to costs.

FPR rule 9.20 sets out those matters that must be dealt with by the first hearing.

At the FDA the court will timetable the proceedings and give directions for the filing of evidence and further documentation. The court can also at the first hearing treat it as an FDR.

On the occasion of the first hearing the court may be able to determine the application, although it is more than likely that the court will direct further evidence and documentation, set a date for further directions or interim hearing and FDR, or list the matter for a final hearing.

Under FPR rule 9.18A the parties may apply to change the procedure to the standard 'Chapter 4' procedure (see the examples given in PD9A, para.1.2). In that eventuality the application must state that such a direction is sought and the reasons why.

Under FPR rule 9.18A(5), the court will determine whether the Chapter 4 or Chapter 5 procedure should be used 'without notice to the parties and before the first hearing', and the parties will be notified of its determination and any necessary consequential directions.

Presumably either party will be able to apply to set aside that determination in accordance with FPR rule 4.3(5) if they so wish.

Although there is no equivalent to MCA 1973, s.37 to prevent an avoidance of disposition as to capital or property, injunctive relief may be sought to preserve a property which is the subject matter of the application and a freezing order obtained in an appropriate case (FPR Part 20).

In that case the following provisions will apply:

- The applicant has a good arguable case.
- There is a real risk that assets will be disposed of unless restrained and any judgment will remain unsatisfied.
- It is just and convenient to make the order in all the circumstances.

(See *Shipman* v. *Shipman* [1991] 1 FLR 250.)

Finally, in the current climate as to hearing the voice of the child, one must also consider the questions as to whether the children themselves should be separately represented within such claims.

The answer is probably not unless the case is exceptional. Examples where this might be appropriate are cases where the parent with care is striving to harm the other parent by extracting the maximum investment fund from them and cases where the other party is striving to conceal the extent of their true fortune:

> In exceptional cases consideration should be given to separate representation of the child. Even in cases where there is no financial impediment to separate representation special circumstances would need to be demonstrated. I think of cases in which a major task for the judge is discerning what are the child's objective needs and what may be the mother's subjective targets for herself as much as for the child.
>
> (*Morgan* v. *Hill* [2007] 1 FLR 1480)

> It is easy to see how ... the real crux of the case can be lost to view unless there is some advocate there to constantly urge the needs and interests of the child. For that, in the end, is what the award is largely designed to satisfy.
>
> (*Walker* v. *Jeffries*; *Re S (A Child)* [2006] EWCA Civ 479 at [17])

This is now specifically provided for in FPR rule 9.11.

9.11 COSTS

In so far as costs themselves are concerned these are regulated by FPR Part 28; however, the 'no order as to costs' principle set out in FPR rule 28.3(5) does not apply to Sched.1 proceedings (FPR PD28A, para.4.2(b)(i)) which instead are governed by CPR rules 44, 45.8, 46 and 47 (excluding rules 44.2(2), (3), 44.10(2) and (3)).

Furthermore, there is no prohibition on the court having regard to Calderbank offers.

In this respect regard must be had to the sentiments expressed in *KS* v. *ND (Schedule 1: Appeal: Costs)* [2013] EWHC 464 (Fam) wherein it was held that it was doubtful whether the principle of costs *prima facie* following the event should apply in Children Act 1989, Sched.1 proceedings and that the court instead should start with a 'clean sheet' as in *Baker* v. *Rowe* [2010] 1 FLR 761.

9.12 COMBINED APPLICATIONS UNDER SCHED.1 AND THE TRUSTS OF LAND AND APPOINTMENT OF TRUSTEES ACT 1996

Often one finds that there will be the need to hear an application for a declaration of beneficial interest alongside a requisite property order under the Children Act 1989, Sched.1 to preserve or settle such interest for the benefit of any child or children.

If there is already an application in existence pursuant to TOLATA 1996 and a subsequent application is issued under Sched.1, it will be preferable for the applications to be heard together (but not consolidated) (see *W* v. *W (Joinder of Trusts of Land Act and Children Act Applications)* [2004] 2 FLR 321).

In such a case, where there is no dispute as to the parties' respective beneficial interests, the Sched.1 application should be given lead status as this confers upon the court a much more extensive power by way of adjustive orders as opposed to merely declaratory orders between co-owners.

In cases where there is such a dispute, the dispute as to the extent of the parties' beneficial interests must be adjudicated upon first, thereafter applying the Sched.1 criteria to any decision as to the transfer of such interest or deferral of sale.

However, now that we have a single County Court and a single Family Court it must be remembered that the County Court has no jurisdiction to hear family cases and the Family Court has no jurisdiction to hear civil cases. Furthermore, there is no mechanism whereby one case can be transferred to the other court.

Accordingly, one must issue both applications at the same time and request them to be listed together before a judge who sits in both the Family Court and the County Court.

The following steps and directions are therefore recommended:

1. Issue at a court exercising Family Court and County Court jurisdiction.
2. Ensure the claims are heard together (but not consolidated).
3. Lead status should normally be ascribed to the TOLATA 1996 claim, save where there is no issue over beneficial ownership.
4. Consider whether the Sched.1 application is to proceed under FPR Part 9, Chapter 4 (Standard Procedure) or Chapter 5 (Fast Track Procedure) providing – in addition to the usual family disclosure – standard disclosure by list (unless another, less onerous, method of disclosure is warranted).
5. Consider whether costs budgeting is required.
6. List towards a FDR/ENE hearing.
7. Clarify whether the trial/final hearing (or any part of it) is to be in open court or in private.
8. Clarify, by reference to which application is lead, whether the applicable rules in preparing for a hearing (including the court bundle) are civil or family (noting the restrictions as to FPR PD27A – see for example the consequences of breach as set out in *Seagrove* v. *Sullivan* [2014] EWHC 4110 (Fam)).

Note that CPR PD32, para.27.4A provides that if a trial is to take place in the Family Division, bundles must be prepared in accordance with FPR PD27A.

A word of warning: do not ask the court to adjudicate on a TOLATA 1996 application only and then subsequently issue a Sched.1 application as a means of appeal or attack against a decision made under the latter, as the court will expect you to bring all claims relating to the same subject matter at one and the same time (see *Henderson* v. *Henderson* (1843) 3 Hare 100, 67 ER 313).

Furthermore, the Senior Courts Act 1981, s.49(2) provides that every court:

> ... shall so exercise its jurisdiction in every cause or matter before it as to secure that, as far as possible, all matters in dispute between the parties are completely and finally determined, and all multiplicity of legal proceedings with respect to any of those matters is avoided.

However, in recent times this has now been tempered.

Michael Wilson & Partners Ltd v. *Sinclair* [2017] EWCA Civ 3 held that the power to strike out a claim for abuse of process is founded on two interests: the private interest of a party not to be vexed twice for the same reason, and the public interest of the state in not having issues repeatedly litigated.

Both interests or either of them may be engaged and to determine whether proceedings are abusive the court must engage in a close 'merits-based' analysis of the facts. The crucial question is whether in all the circumstances a party is abusing or misusing the court's process.

The earlier decision of *Johnson* v. *Gore Wood & Co* [2002] 2 AC 1 also referred to the need for:

> a broad, merits-based judgment which takes account of the public and private interests involved and also takes account of all the facts of the case, focusing attention on the crucial question whether, in all the circumstances, a party is misusing or abusing the process of the court... (at [31])

See also *Walbrook Trustees (Jersey) Ltd* v. *Fattal* [2009] EWCA Civ 297 at [3]:

> In essence, the court must make a 'broad merits-based judgment' as to whether there is an abuse of process. It is not enough to show that the claim could have been brought in the earlier proceedings.

CHAPTER 10

Personal property

10.1 CHATTELS

Disputes over chattels are usually wholly disproportionate to the financial value of the claim at stake, and time and time again the courts have indicated a clear expectation that such matters should be resolved without recourse to litigation:

> It is extremely difficult to determine the ownership of property bought by parties who are living together and it is really for them to sort out, if possible, for themselves. It is very unfortunate that the Court should be called upon to perform that function for them.
>
> (*Windeler* v. *Whitehall* [1990] FCR 268)

> ... sorting out the ownership of chattels bought by parties who have been living together is something that the parties should be expected to achieve by agreement by themselves without the necessity of a court hearing.
>
> (*Hammond* v. *Mitchell* [1991] 1 WLR 1127 at [1138])

As a general rule of thumb, items owned by either party before the relationship began, or bought by one party from their own resources during the relationship, will remain the property of that party unless it can be shown that a gift of that item was made to the other or that there was a common intention for the property to be owned by them both jointly, whether in equal or other shares.

Gifts from one to the other will remain the property of the donee.

Unlike with real property where a declaration of beneficial interest must be in writing, personal property can be subject to an oral express declaration of trust (*Paul* v. *Constance* [1977] 1 WLR 527; *Rowe* v. *Prance* [1999] 2 FLR 787).

The mere fact that furniture, for example, is intended for joint use does not make it joint property. The basis for division will be determined by trust principles, whether it be by resulting trust, constructive trust or express trust.

Where goods are purchased on credit terms, contributions by way of payment of the deposit and the instalments will clearly be relevant.

The case of *Richards* v. *Dove* [1974] 1 All ER 888 sets out certain principles as follows:

1. As it is extremely difficult to define ownership by reference to disputed evidence on who paid most of the hire purchase instalments on particular terms, a broad approach is justifiable.
2. Merely paying one or two instalments on a particular item may not entitle the payer to a share.
3. It is unrealistic to suppose that substantial or regular contributions were not intended by the parties to be reflected in some corresponding beneficial interest.

In determining the issue itself the court will often take a broad-brush approach, particularly when dealing with items of insubstantial value.

Indeed, in relation to determining the size of any beneficial interest, in the absence of any conclusive evidence to the contrary, the court will often resort to the maxim 'equality is equity':

> While no one suggests that English law recognises or should develop a doctrine of community of property regarding the household goods of those who settle for an unmarried union, the parties must expect the court in ordinary cases to adopt a robust allegience to the maxim that 'equality is equity'...
>
> (*Hammond* v. *Mitchell* [1991] 1 WLR 1127 at [1138])

Thus, the clear message is to avoid court in relation to disputes pertaining to chattels unless they are of substantial value, and if you do bring proceedings be prepared for a robust decision as to their determination given the overriding objective as to dealing with matters in ways which are proportionate to the nature, importance and complexity of the issues and allotting to the case an appropriate share of the court's resources, while taking into account the need to allot resources to other cases.

10.2 BANK ACCOUNTS

In *Whitlock* v. *Moree* [2017] UKPC 44 the following points were made:

> There is no reason why property which is, slightly misleadingly, described as money in a bank account should be subject to any different principles when the court is called upon to resolve a dispute about its beneficial ownership. (at [26])

Thus, where parties have a joint account, there is a presumption that funds held within it and intended to be used as a common pool will be held in equal shares. This presumption, of course, can be rebutted by evidence showing a contrary intention, either express or implied:

> if ... the account opening document contains an express assignment by each account holder to the two of them jointly of any money separately owned by that account holder, it does indeed constitute a document of transfer, even in the strict sense. (at [27])

> … where two or more holders of a joint account all sign an account opening document (or separately sign identical documents) which, on their true construction, declare or set out their respective beneficial interests in the property constituted by the account (loosely, the money in the account), then those are the beneficial interests of the account holders, pending any subsequent variation of them by agreement or otherwise, and an examination of the subjective intentions of the account holders, or of those of them who place money in the joint account, is neither relevant nor permissible. Still less is recourse to the doctrine of presumed resulting trusts permissible, because the potential beneficial owners have declared what are their beneficial interests by signed writing. (at [29])

A joint holding of a bank account may be severed in the same way as a joint beneficial interest in land.

It will, of course, be necessary to take action as soon as the breakdown of the relationship occurs in order to ensure that the funds in the joint account are not removed unilaterally. Once the bank is alerted the account will generally be frozen so that neither party may withdraw funds without the consent of the other.

When undertaking this course of action it will be important to ensure that procedures are in place in respect of the setting up of a new account in the sole control of that party and the transfer of relevant direct debits and standing orders to that account.

10.3 PROCEDURE

If litigation cannot be avoided, then the appropriate procedure is to invite the court to decide the ownership of disputed chattels by way of a declaration as to the beneficial interest pursuant to FPR Part 19.

If the amount in dispute is less than £350,000 (the County Court limit) then, by virtue of the County Courts Act 1984, s.23 and the County Court Jurisdiction Order 2014, SI 2014/503, proceedings will be commenced in the Family Court by way of application notice (FP1).

CHAPTER 11

Effects of an engagement

11.1 INTRODUCTION

The status of a couple as to whether or not they are engaged does pose the possibility of additional claims over and above the ones already discussed, subject to proving, of course, that there has in fact been 'an engagement'.

Let us examine these additional claims in turn.

11.2 MARRIED WOMEN'S PROPERTY ACT 1882

First and foremost there is the Married Women's Property Act 1882, more particularly s.17 which reads as follows:

> In any question between husband and wife as to the title to or possession of property, either party may apply by summons or otherwise in a summary way to the High Court or the family court ... and the court may, on such an application ... make such order with respect to the property as it thinks fit.

The Law Reform (Miscellaneous Provisions) Act 1970, s.2(2) extended the provisions of the Married Women's Property Act 1882 to cover engaged couples whose engagement had been terminated prior to marriage.

On an application under s.17, the Matrimonial Causes (Property and Maintenance) Act 1958, s.7(7) gives the court the power to order a sale of the property. However, such application must also deal with the title or possession of the property, not merely whether it should be sold or not.

Section 17 thus provides for declaratory relief following an analysis of trust principles; there is no power to vary a party's established rights to the property concerned by way of property adjustment, although the court does have power to enforce those rights by way of a sale.

Under the Married Women's Property Act 1882, therefore, while the court has power to resolve disputes over the title to or possession of property, it cannot adjust the parties' interests in it.

For the purposes of the Act 'property' has a wide construction and incorporates property other than land (Matrimonial Causes (Property and Maintenance) Act 1958, s.8).

One advantage of such a wide construction is that it can also apply to foreign property, unlike that under TOLATA 1996 (see *Razelos* v. *Razelos* [1969] 3 All ER 929).

The court also has power under s.7 to make an order against property which is no longer in the possession of or the control of the other party, and order that party to pay to the other the value of their interest in such property that has been disposed of or transferred.

However, while s.17 provides a wider definition of property, its powers are more restrictive; for example there is no discretionary power to delay or postpone a sale, unlike that under TOLATA 1996.

Section 17 will most often be utilised in resolving disputes concerning the ownership of household chattels by way of a claim for declaration or enquiry as to the beneficial interests supported by evidence.

Any claim under the Married Women's Property Act 1882 must be made within three years of the date of the termination of the engagement.

11.2.1 Procedure

Application is made to the Family Court and the procedure is set out in FPR rules 8.12–8.17. The application notice (Form D50B) together with evidence in support and verified by a statement of truth should be made to the district in which the parties reside.

Any application in relation to real property must state whether the title to the land is registered or unregistered and, if registered, provide the title number. Details of any mortgage must also be set out and the mortgagee served.

A draft of the order sought must be attached to the application notice.

If the application is contested, the respondent will be required to file evidence in response setting out the basis for the opposition and the relief sought.

At the final hearing the court may make an order declaring the parties' beneficial interest and may order the sale of that property to realise that interest.

Where the court goes on to make an order for sale under the Married Women's Property Act 1882, s.17, FPR rule 9.24 applies as to the power to order a party to deliver up possession.

11.3 MATRIMONIAL PROCEEDINGS AND PROPERTY ACT 1970

One further statute worthy of mention is the Matrimonial Proceedings and Property Act 1970.

Section 37 provides as follows:

> It is hereby declared that where a husband or wife contributes in money or money's worth to the improvement of real or personal property in which or in the proceeds of sale of which either or both of them has or have a beneficial interest, the husband or wife so contributing shall, if the contribution is of a substantial nature and subject to any agreement between them to the contrary, express or implied, be treated as having then acquired by virtue of his or her contribution a share or an enlarged share, as the case may be, in that beneficial interest of such an extent as may have been then agreed, or in default of such agreement, as it may seem in all the circumstances just to any court before which the question of the existence or extent of the beneficial interest of the husband or wife arises (whether in proceedings between them or in any other proceedings).

Section 37 has been extended by the Law Reform (Miscellaneous Provisions) Act 1970, s.2 to cover engaged couples, thus providing that the law relating to property disputes between married couples applies equally to engaged couples.

In essence, s.37 provides that a substantial contribution in money or money's worth to the improvement of property in which either or both parties have a vested interest can serve to acquire a share that did not previously exist, or enlarge a share that does exist without any express or inferred common intention, subject to any agreement between the parties to the contrary.

Thus, a substantial contribution by one of the parties will effectively mean that they will be treated in law as having acquired or enlarged a beneficial interest in that property, whether it be real or personal property.

Under the Matrimonial Proceedings and Property Act 1970, if an application is successful the applicant is treated as acquiring a share or increasing an existing share by reference to their contribution: in other words, a statutory presumption akin to a resulting trust.

For an application under s.37 to be successful the contribution must be substantial and the court must find that the contribution was made on the basis of founding an interest in the property as opposed to there being an express agreement to the contrary (e.g. the contribution was purely gratuitous).

This section is particularly useful in cases where no beneficial interest in the property can be proved by constructive or resulting trust, but where a significant contribution has been made and it would be unjust to allow this to go uncompensated.

Although the procedure is not formally covered in the FPR, it is suggested that procedurally the same approach is adopted when pursuing a claim under the Married Women's Property Act 1882.

Note that in the case of *Dibble* v. *Pfluger* [2010] EWCA Civ 1005 everyone involved in it had overlooked the parties' engagement and the consequential application of the Law Reform (Miscellaneous Provisions) Act 1970, s.2 and the Matrimonial Proceedings and Property Act 1970, s.37.

11.4 ENGAGEMENT RINGS

Finally, perhaps specific mention ought to be made of disputes concerning the ownership of engagement rings.

The Law Reform (Miscellaneous Provisions) Act 1970, s.3(2) provides that a gift of an engagement ring is presumed to be an absolute gift.

This presumption, however, can be rebutted by evidence to show that the gift was expressly or by implication conditional upon the marriage itself actually taking place, which in my experience is not a common occurrence.

CHAPTER 12

Cohabitation/living together agreements

12.1 ADVISING THE CLIENT

As seen at the outset, there is a clear duty upon a solicitor acting for prospective purchasers of a property to provide advice about the legal implications of their joint ownership.

The experienced and conscientious solicitor will also, wishing not only to provide a holistic service to their client but also not to miss an opportunity to cross-sell, provide advice as to the desirability of entering into a cohabitation agreement.

In doing so they will also need to advise one or both parties to consider obtaining independent legal advice, as in attempting to act for them both there will almost certainly arise a potential conflict of interest.

12.2 AN ENFORCEABLE AGREEMENT

The case of *Sutton* v. *Mishcon de Reya and Gawor & Co* [2004] 1 FLR 837 has established that as long as the parties can establish an intention to create legal relations and that there is no express or implied provision for payment of sexual relations, and the agreement complies with the necessary requirements for a valid contract, the agreement subsequently entered into may be valid and enforceable.

A properly executed cohabitation agreement will seek to regulate the property and financial arrangements of the parties concerned.

If enforcement ever becomes an issue, those wishing to rely upon a cohabitation agreement will need to resort to the law of contract. Thus, even if a cohabitation agreement is valid, it could possibly face enforcement problems should it fail to comply with the essential requirements of contract law.

To be enforceable as a contract, the following have to be established:

1. **An intention to create legal relations.** There must be a genuine meeting of minds and therefore an offer and an acceptance of that offer. Clearly, the fact that there is a written agreement between the parties goes some way to establishing this and will cover such aspects as to whether or not the parties

were invited or indeed took up the offer of seeking independent legal advice, and whether or not the agreement itself was supported by full and frank disclosure.

2. **Consideration.** An agreement in the form of a deed means that formal consideration will not be necessary.
3. **Uncertainty.** The terms of the agreement must be sufficiently precise. If the terms of any contract are uncertain or vague, so as to be incapable of being enforced, this may jeopardise the agreement as a whole.

   In drawing up the agreement, therefore, one should ensure that there is no scope for uncertainty in the interpretation of its terms and for added safety a severance clause should always be included.
4. **Duress or coercion; inequality of bargaining power.** Although there is no presumption of undue influence as between cohabiting couples, there is clearly a potential for one party to expose the other to such, and therefore it is important that both parties are separately advised and represented, or at least that that facility is offered to them and that there is full and frank disclosure of their respective financial positions.
5. **Ousting of the court's jurisdiction.** There should be no provision in the agreement itself purporting to oust the jurisdiction of the court as this would be void. Neither must the terms be illegal or contrary to public policy.

   As a general rule, therefore, any cohabitation agreement should be confined to matters of property and money.
6. The formal requirements imposed by the Law of Property (Miscellaneous Provisions) Act 1989, s.2 (if applicable) must also be satisfied.

   This provides that a contract for the sale or other disposition of an interest in land must be made in writing and incorporate all the terms agreed in one document. However, this will not affect the creation or operation of a resulting, implied or constructive trust (s.2(5)).

12.3 SPECIFIC ISSUES TO CONSIDER

Moreover, specific and detailed instructions should be taken on the following:

- Is the property going to be held in one person's sole name or in joint names?
- If in joint names, should this be as beneficial joint tenants or tenants in common in equal or unequal shares? These terms will need to be explained in simple language.
- What, if any, contributions will each party make to the purchase?
- If the purchase is with the aid of a mortgage, what are the arrangements for repayment, and payment of the outgoings and maintenance of the property?
- Will any third parties, e.g. parents or grandparents, be making any financial contributions and on what basis?
- How will any repair, renovation and improvement costs be dealt with?

- What will happen if the relationship breaks down and one partner moves out before the property is sold?
- Who will pay the mortgage and other outgoings before the sale?
- What will happen to the property if one party dies?
- What arrangements will be made to enable one party to 'buy out' the other's share?
- How will the property be valued, how will the valuer be chosen and how long should the remaining party be given to raise the necessary funds?
- What is intended to happen if the client, or their partner, have children and one stops working to look after them and can no longer contribute financially?
- All clients purchasing a property with a cohabitant should also be formally advised to agree and execute a declaration of trust.
- That declaration of trust should in particular include:
  - how a payment by one party of a capital sum towards the reduction of the mortgage should be dealt with;
  - who will be responsible for mortgage payments in the event that one party cannot meet their obligations and whether or not this will adjust the parties' equitable interests; and
  - details of any third party interests and how they are to be dealt with when the property is sold.

CHAPTER 13

Call for reform

13.1 LAW COMMISSION REPORT

The need for reform has been spelt out in the Law Commission report *Cohabitation: The Financial Consequences of Relationship Breakdown* dated 31 July 2007 (Law Com No. 307):

> Cohabitation is ... already a significant social practice. It is growing, and continued growth is forecast ... if it is accepted that the current law is inadequate and gives rise to unwelcome consequences, the fact that these consequences potentially affect a significant and increasing proportion of the population is highly relevant. The issues ... are therefore not issues that will go away. We urge Government to take the necessary steps to provide this increasing significant section of society with legal remedies capable of dealing fairly with the financial consequences should they separate ... We are ... firmly of the view that reform is required.

The report recommended giving courts more power to make orders regarding the sharing of property, savings and pensions where one partner has made a significant contribution that has left them financially disadvantaged and where a couple have been together for a certain time or have had children together.

Such a scheme was introduced in Scotland by virtue of the Family Law (Scotland) Act 2006, ss.25–29.

Reference should also be had to the comments made by Lady Hale in *Gow* v. *Grant* [2012] UKSC 29 as to the pressing need for reform in this area. When referring to the Law Commission's report she said this:

> There is some reason to think that a family law remedy such as that proposed by the Law Commission would be less costly and more productive of settlements, as well as achieving fairer results, than the present law. (at [47])

Regrettably nothing has come of this despite persistent campaigning, notably by the organisation Resolution.

Neither has the Cohabitation Bill (a private member's bill introduced in 2008/09) or the Cohabitation Rights Bill (a private member's bill which has been introduced and re-introduced at various times from 2013 to 2017) seen the light of day.

It is fair to assume, therefore, that reform in this area is some way off.

APPENDIX A

Checklist

1. Is cohabitation accepted?

   If not, consider a fact-finding hearing (not necessary in cases of express declarations of trust).

2. Is there an express declaration of trust? (note the position as to pre- and post-1 April 1998 transfers).

   If so, is there an argument for rescission, rectification or proprietary estoppel?

   Is there a potential negligence claim against the conveyancer?

3. If no express declaration of trust:
   (a) Is the property in joint names? (If so, unless investment property, query relevance of resulting trust doctrine.) Sole question is did the parties intend their shares to be other than equal?
   (b) Is the property in a party's sole name? (If so, consider resulting trust or constructive trust doctrines to show, in the latter case, an intention to share notwithstanding the fact that the property is in one person's name only and, if established, the extent of that share.)
4. When arguing constructive trust are there express discussions as to an intention to share the beneficial interest and its extent? (Finding of fact.)
5. If no express discussions, can such intention be inferred from the parties' conduct?
6. Is there a potential argument for an alteration of such shares by way of an ambulatory constructive trust?
7. If there is a finding of an intention to share (or an alteration in such shares) but the court is unable to ascertain the consequential shares by virtue of express discussions or inferred from the parties' conduct, then and only then is it permissible to impute an intention as to the size of the shares, having regard to the concept of fairness and the whole course of dealing between the parties.
8. Is there scope for adjustment of those shares through equitable accounting?
9. Are there children? (Consider an application for a transfer/settlement of property order under the Children Act 1989.)
10. Were the parties ever engaged? (Consider an application under the Matrimonial Proceedings and Property Act 1970, s.37.)

APPENDIX B

Costs management case planner

Phase	Includes	Does NOT include
1. Pre-action	• Pre-Action Protocol correspondence • Investigating the merits of the claim and advising client • Considering ADR, advising on settlement and Part 36 offers • All other steps taken and advice given pre-action	• Any work already incurred in relation to any other phase of the budget
2. Issue/pleadings	• Preparation of claim form • Issue and service of proceedings • Preparation of particulars of claim, defence, reply, including taking instructions, instructing counsel and any necessary investigation • Considering opposing statements of case and advising client • Part 18 requests (request and answer) • Any conferences with counsel primarily relating to statements of case	• Amendments to statements of case (see below)

Phase	Includes	Does NOT include
3. CMC	• Completion of AQs • Arranging a CMC • Preparation of costs budget for first CMC and reviewing opponent's budget • Correspondence with opponents to agree directions and budgets, where possible • Preparation for, and attendance at, the CMC • Finalising the order	• Subsequent CMCs
4. Disclosure	• Obtaining documents from client and advising on disclosure obligations • Reviewing documents for disclosure, preparing disclosure report or questionnaire response and list • Inspection • Reviewing opponent's list and documents, undertaking any appropriate investigations • Correspondence between parties about the scope of disclosure and queries arising • Consulting counsel, so far as appropriate, in relation to disclosure	• Applications for specific disclosure • Applications and requests for third party disclosure
5. Witnesses	• Identifying witnesses • Obtaining statements • Preparing witness summaries • Consulting counsel, so far as appropriate, about witness statements • Reviewing opponent's statements and undertaking any appropriate investigations • Applications for witness summaries	• Arranging for witnesses to attend trial (include in trial preparation)

Phase	Includes	Does NOT include
6. Experts	• Identifying and engaging suitable expert(s) • Reviewing draft and approving report(s) • Dealing with follow-up questions of experts • Considering opposing experts' reports • Meetings of experts (preparing agenda, etc.)	• Obtaining permission to adduce expert evidence (include in CMC or as separate application) • Arranging for experts to attend trial (include in trial preparation)
7. PTR	• Bundle • Preparation of updated costs budgets and reviewing opponent's budget • Preparing and agreeing chronology, case summary and dramatis personae (if ordered and not already prepared earlier in case) • Completing and filing pre-trial checklists • Correspondence with opponents to agree directions and costs budgets, if possible • Attendance at the PTR	• Assembling and/or copying the bundle (this is not fee earners' work)
8. Trial preparation	• Trial bundles • Witness summonses, and arranging for witnesses to attend trial • Any final factual investigations • Supplemental disclosure and statements (if required) • Agreeing brief fee • Any pre-trial conferences and advice from counsel • Pre-trial liaison with witnesses	• Assembling and/or copying the trial bundle (this is not fee earners' work) • Counsel's brief fee and any refreshers

Phase	Includes	Does NOT include
9. Trial	• Solicitors' attendance at trial • All conferences and other activity outside court hours during the trial • Attendance on witnesses during the trial • Counsel's brief fee and any refreshers • Dealing with draft judgment and related applications	• Preparation for trial • Agreeing brief fee
10. Settlement	• Settlement negotiations, including Part 36 and other offers and advising the client • Drafting settlement agreement or Tomlin order • Advice to the client on settlement (excluding advice included in the pre-action phase)	• Mediation (should be included as a contingency)

Index